"Ann Edminster has been a major force behind the green residential construction movement for years. Through her architectural design, by her contributions to the development of green standards, and with her participation in such organizations as the US Green Building Council, Ann has made an indelible impact on the nation's march towards producing zero-energy homes. Now, with the publication of this fine book, Ann will spread the word to a much wider audience – one that will benefit immensely."

– Steve Winter, FAIA, Steven Winter Associates,
and Past Chairman, US Green Building Council

"Ann Edminster facilitated the integrated design process to help us achieve a zero-energy home, and I don't know how we would have done it without her expertise. Ann is the Mother Lode of residential green building, and in this book she has leveraged her vast network of expert contacts and her gift for distilling and clarifying technical information to produce the authoritative resource for anyone – homeowners, architects, contractors, and public policy-makers alike – who wants to develop, or encourage the development of, zero-energy homes. In addition to her green expertise, she is an architect with a beautiful aesthetic, and so seamlessly marries green building with high design and functionality for any lifestyle."

– Linda Yates, eco-activist, and Paul Holland, Partner, Foundation Capital

"Few books are as vital in their time as this one. It's not about the latest green thing – it's about the '*right*' thing. And the time is now."

– Mark Piepkorn, Associate Editor, BuildingGreen, LLC

"Net-zero energy is the watchword of the day, but little has been published about how to get there. *Energy Free* is the first cogent guidance document for everyone from the motivated home-owner to the affordable housing developer wanting to build homes that produce as much, or more, energy than they consume each year. Seasoned green building consultant and writer Ann Edminster has produced a clear, articulate, and much-needed resource."

– David Eisenberg, Executive Director,
Development Center for Appropriate Technology

ENERGY FREE
Homes for a Small Planet

A comprehensive guide to the
design, construction, and economics of
net-zero energy homes

by Ann V. Edminster

Green Building Press is committed to preserving ancient forests and natural resources. We elected to print *Energy Free* on 30% postconsumer recycled paper, processed chlorine-free. As a result, we have saved:

34 Trees (40' tall and 6-8" diameter)
11 Million BTUs of Total Energy
3,213 Pounds of Greenhouse Gases
15,475 Gallons of Wastewater
940 Pounds of Solid Waste

Green Building Press made this paper choice because our printer, Thomson-Shore, Inc., is a member of Green Press Initiative, a nonprofit program dedicated to supporting authors, publishers, and suppliers in their efforts to reduce their use of fiber obtained from endangered forests.

For more information, visit www.greenpressinitiative.org

Environmental impact estimates were made using the Environmental Defense Paper Calculator. For more information visit: www.edf.org/papercalculator

First Edition

Published by Green Building Press, PO Box 6397, San Rafael, CA 94903
www.greenbuildingpress.com
SAN 256-6559

Manufactured in the USA.
Printed on recycled paper.

Illustrations by Karen Chan unless noted otherwise.
Cover photo of Sullivan home by Catherine Wanek.

Edited by Jessie Lawson.
Designed by Debra Turner.

Library of Congress Cataloging-in-Publication Data
Ann Edminster

Energy Free; Homes for a Small Planet
ISBN: 978-0-9764911-3-2
1. Zero Energy Homes 2. Green Building 3. Architecture and Energy Efficiency

Dedication

This book is dedicated to my son, Quinn,
with whom I spent far less time than I would have liked
during his eleventh glorious summer and fall,
and who accepted my preoccupation with great grace.
I hope in years to come he finds my labor a worthy trade
for those hours I spent at my desk instead of with him.

✳

Acknowledgments

This book is a reflection of the work of many, many contributors – both people and organizations who have pioneered in the field of home energy performance, and individuals who have specifically assisted me with this manuscript. Those in the former group are too numerous to list, yet no less worthy of recognition. To all of them I extend my profound thanks and admiration for their dedication and foresight.

To those in the latter group I also offer my immense gratitude, and advance apologies to anyone I may have omitted inadvertently from the litany of thanks that follows –

- To my life and business partner, Hal Bohner, for his unwavering support, his countless hours of research and energy modeling, and his uncomplaining assumption of more than his fair share of parental and household duties;

- To the friends whose immediate enthusiasm for this book provided fuel sufficient to turn it from a stray thought into a solid commitment – Hal, Bruce and Sarah King, Peter Yost, Dana and Dave Charron, Mark Piepkorn;

- To my sister, Jessie Lawson, whose many talents include being a superb editor, and who was willing to perform this task for me despite having retired from such mundane pursuits in order to be a full-time artist;

- To Karen Chan, who applied her considerable knowledge of passive building design and her graphic talents to produce the wonderful drawings for this book;

- To the colleagues and friends who have provided guidance, information, and materials for inclusion in this book, notwithstanding all the other demands on their time – Peter Yost, Alex Wilson, and Nadav Malin, Building Green, LLC; Bruce Coldham, Andrew Webster, and Tom Hartman, Coldham & Hartman Architects; Ren Anderson, NREL; Chris Calwell, Ecos Consulting; Lisa Gartland; Heather Larson; Ted Bardacke, Global Green; Dan Chiras; George Loisos, Loisos + Ubbelohde; Gary Klein, Affiliated International Management; Dan Smith and Dietmar Lorenz, Daniel Smith & Associates; Dan Dempsey; Peter Rumsey and John Weale, Rumsey Engineers; Nancy Malone, Siegel & Strain Architects; Greg VanMechelen, VanMechelen Architects; Pete Shoemaker and Bill Burke, PG&E; Dariush Arasteh, LBNL; Graham Irwin, Zero Impact Architecture; Betsy Pettit and Kohta Ueno, Building Science Corporation; Mary Davidge; Mike Keesee, SMUD; Danny Parker and Phil Fairey, FSEC; Duncan Prahl, IBACOS; Rich Green, Rich Green Ink; Andrew Culver, iLiv; John Fulford; Larry Weingarten; Will Lichtig; Bill Reed; and Doug Brookman.

- To the numerous clients, colleagues, and organizations whose research, analysis, design efforts, and products are reflected in these pages and in our case studies – notably Linda Yates and Paul Holland, David and Stephania Kaneda, Naomi Porat, and Prakash and Bala Chandran;

- To my stalwart co-workers, Jenny Levinson and Mary Pat Dempsey, whose labors have kept my business firmly on course and my sanity intact during the months when my attention was largely focused elsewhere, and who stepped in to help with the finishing touches;

- To Debra Turner, who developed and executed the clear and lovely book design, and remained unfazed by all the changes in schedule and content along the way;

- To the myriad who generously provided contacts, comments, and stray bits of information that have contributed immeasurably to the whole;

And last, but certainly not least:

- To Serious Materials, whose sponsorship funded extensive energy modeling, the value of which to Serious was entirely uncertain at the time.

I knew before I began what an exceptional community I belong to. Even so, I have been awed by your collective generosity. Without all of you, named and unnamed, this would be a very incomplete document, and I am forever in your debt.

Notwithstanding the magnitude of others' contributions, I claim all errors, omissions, and lack of clarity as my own.

– Ann Edminster

Table of Contents

LIST OF FIGURES

ACRONYMS & ABBREVIATIONS

This list includes only those acronyms and abbreviations that relate specifically to the building industry. Refer to a dictionary or Wikipedia for other terms that may be unfamiliar.

ABAA	Air Barrier Association of America
AC	air conditioning or alternating current
ACCA	Air Conditioning Contractors of America
ACEEE	American Council for an Energy-Efficient Economy
ACH	air changes per hour
ACH_{50}	air changes per hour at 50 Pascals pressure
ACHNAT	natural air changes per hour
AFUE	annual fuel utilization efficiency (for furnaces and boilers)
AL	air leakage (windows)
ASHRAE	American Society of Heating, Refrigerating and Air-conditioning Engineers
AWEA	American Wind Energy Association
BIBS	blow-in-batt system
BIPV	building-integrated photovoltaics
Btu	British thermal unit(s)
CABEC	California Association of Building Energy Consultants
CAE	combined annual efficiency (for combination water and space heaters)
CDC	Centers for Disease Control
CDD	cooling degree days
CEA	Certified Energy Analyst
CEDIA	Custom Electronics Design and Installation Association
CEE	Consortium for Energy Efficiency
CEPE	Certified Energy Plans Examiner
CFL	compact fluorescent light
CFM	cubic feet per minute
CMHC	Canada Mortgage and Housing Corporation
COP	coefficient of performance (for heat pumps)
CPU	central processing unit
DC	direct current
DHW	domestic hot water
DOE	US Department of Energy
EBN	*Environmental Building News*
EEBA	Energy & Environmental Building Association
EER	energy efficiency ratio (for heat pumps)
EF	energy factor (for water heaters and dishwashers)
ELA	effective leakage area (for buildings)
EPA	US Environmental Protection Agency
EPS	expanded polystyrene

GHG	greenhouse gases
gpf	gallons per flush
gpm	gallons per minute
GSHP	ground-source heat pump
HDD	heating degree days
HERS	Home Energy Rating System
HSPF	heating seasonal performance factor (for heat pumps)
HVAC	heating, ventilation, and air-conditioning
IBACOS	Integrated Building and Construction Solutions
ICF	insulating concrete form
IDA	International Dark-Sky Association
kW	kilowatt
kWh	kilowatt-hour
LED	light-emitting diode (lighting)
LEED	Leadership in Energy and Environmental Design
Low-E	low-emissivity (glass, windows)
M&V	measurement and verification
MEF	modified energy factor (for clothes washers)
MEP	mechanical-electrical-plumbing (consultant)
MMBtu	million Btu
NACH	natural air changes per hour
NESEA	Northeast Sustainable Energy Association
NFRC	National Fenestration Rating Council
NREL	National Renewable Energy Laboratory
NZE	net-zero energy
NZEH	net-zero energy home
OOO	ongoing ownership and operating (costs)
OSB	oriented-strand-board
Pa	Pascals
PBB	polybrominated biphenyl
PBDE	polybrominated diphenyl ether
PEX	cross-linked polyethylene (piping or tubing)
PG&E	Pacific Gas & Electric Company
PIER	Public Interest Energy Research (State of California program)
PPA	power purchase agreement
PV	photovoltaics
QII	Quality Insulation Installation
quad	quadrillion Btu
R, R-value	thermal resistance; inverse of U
REC	renewable energy credit
RFP	request for proposals
RFQ	request for qualifications
RoHS	Restriction of Hazardous Substances (EU directive)
SEER	seasonal energy efficiency ratio (for heat pumps)

SHGC	solar heat gain coefficient (for windows)
SLA	specific leakage area (for buildings)
SMUD	Sacramento Municipal Utility District
TDV	time-dependent valuation
TVIS	visible transmittance
U, U-value, U-factor	inverse of R; thermal conductance
UAS	utility allowance schedules
UL	Underwriters Laboratories
URL	universal record locator (website address)
USGBC	US Green Building Council
VMT	vehicle miles traveled
VOCs	volatile organic compounds
VT	visible transmittance
W	Watt
WEEE	Waste Electrical and Electronic Equipment (EU directive)
WF	water factor (for clothes washers)
WFA	window-to-floor area (ratio)
XPS	extruded polystyrene
ZEB	zero energy building
ZEH	zero energy home

Foreword

If you are with me on this page, I think four things are true:

- You love the written word.
- You always seek insight.
- You cherish the Earth and the amazing way it works.
- You also read – in addition to forewords – the prefaces of books.

These are four things I love about the author, Ann Edminster, as well. Ann writes because she feels compelled to and because she loves to. As you read this book, you will feel both the urgency and the beauty of her words – clean, concise lines that cut to the core of the matter.

Ann writes with insight, and in my view, insight is what distinguishes mere information from knowledge, particularly practical knowledge. Ann writes from experience with energy-free homes, both her own and those of her clients. One of her strengths as an author is her readiness to distinguish between her own expertise and that of others; you will see this in the quotes, "guest" content, and references that round out her book.

In *Energy Free*, you will see Ann's passion for understanding buildings and the ways they can lighten the load they, and we, place on our Earth. Although Ann has written *Energy Free* as a technical guide, she also is on a mission. Ann writes to right the way we design, build, and run our homes.

Some forewords tell you a lot about the content of the book; this one does not need to, because Ann has treated her preface the way she treats everything she does – thoroughly, comprehensively, logically. Although I honestly do not know this, I would bet that Ann wrote the preface as her own sort of double-check, making sure she has given you full value on all aspects of *Energy Free* homes. Ann leaves blessed few loose ends or stones unturned in her work; *Energy Free* is certainly no exception.

So this foreword will conclude with a short story about Ann, giving you (that special reader who actually reads forewords) extra insight into Ann's character and how it sets the tone for all the work that she does.

Several years ago, Ann and I started work together on a number of projects based in California, meaning lots of time away from my home and family in Vermont. Without the slightest hesitation, Ann opened up her heart and home on my every visit, weaving me into both the personal and the professional fabric of her life. Did this make us better suited to the systems-thinking and integration our projects required? Do people who trust and enjoy each other's company make for a stronger professional team?

I think so. I think this same combined personal and professional commitment shines through in her new book, *Energy Free.* I hope you enjoy reading it as much as I know she enjoyed creating it.

– Peter Yost
Building Green, LLC

Preface

The Quest for Zero

Energy Free was inspired by my realization that the interest in zero energy homes (ZEH) was gaining momentum. What had been a background murmur in my green building community just a few years earlier had quickly turned into an audible conversation and was well on its way to becoming a clamor: piano to forte virtually overnight. In October 2007, the California Public Utilities Commission adopted four "big, bold" energy efficiency strategies, one of which mandates that all new residential construction in California will be net-zero energy by 2020; funding to implement that mandate was approved in September 2009.

And yet no synthesis had appeared, no book on zero energy homes in either the popular or the professional press. As a perpetual student, I wanted such a book and wanted to be able to provide it to my clients and colleagues, increasing numbers of whom are seeking the pinnacle of "green" achievement: the home that provides for all its own energy needs.

When I initially conceived of this book, I simply thought of it as *The Zero Energy Home*. Then, propelled by the publisher's catalog deadline, I had to decide upon a real title, long before the book was actually written. Thus ensued a lively conversation among my family and friends, including my publishers – Bruce and Sarah King of Green Building Press – and my frequent collaborator Peter Yost.

"Zero" is so nowhere, we all felt, connoting the absence of everything, not the achievement of something – in this case something notable, commendable, worth celebrating. "Zero" was, in short, a woefully inadequate term.

Furthermore, zero is a precise point on the number line, nearly as elusive as the statistical average family of 2.74 individuals. The homes I expected to write about would array themselves on both the plus and the minus sides of zero, some falling somewhat short and others surpassing the goal. The real point isn't hitting the zero mark; it's achieving freedom from the tyranny of oil addiction. Yes, it's about freedom. Now we were onto something – hence the genesis of the title and the central aim of the endeavors chronicled here.

The Body of Knowledge

For more than a decade, pioneering individuals and organizations, both public and private, have been working toward the goal of net-zero energy use in buildings. This dedicated corps includes the following institutions: US Department of Energy / National Renewable Energy Laboratory; Building Science Consortium / Building America Program; Florida Solar Energy Center; Sacramento Municipal Utility District; The Passive House Institute of the US; the State of California; and Affordable Comfort Inc.'s Thousand Home Challenge. This book is both a tribute to the creative and committed ZEH pioneers and an attempt to capture the critical lessons they are learning.

A list of projects and source documents from this roughly decade-long history is presented in Appendix B. You will also find case studies my associates and I have compiled on **GreenBuildingAdvisor.com.** (See Appendix D for more information.) I encourage you to review these projects, particularly those in climates or settings most similar to your own. Their common features are the starting points of what will become rules of thumb for climate-appropriate ZEH design.

The posted case studies are a work in progress. I apologize to anyone who may be disappointed not to find his or her project listed; your contributions are no less significant for my failure to note them. If you would like to add a project to the case study library, please contact me via my website, **www.designavenues.net.**

What Types of Homes Does *Energy Free* Cover?

In doing research, I discovered that much has been written about retrofitting existing homes, almost all of it targeted at single-family homeowners. Some books included projects suitable for renters or apartment-dwellers, but I found nothing covering the range of homes that I felt needed to be addressed and the circumstances unique to each. These are:

- Single-family homes, new and existing, urban and rural;
- Multi-family homes, new and existing, primarily urban.

Although I use the terms "home" and "homes" throughout the book in a general way, intending to connote neither single-family nor multifamily residences in particular, I have attempted, where appropriate, to distinguish between the two. I expect there are instances in which I have failed to make adequate distinctions, in which case I encourage you to submit your comments to me at my website.

Who Is *Energy Free* for?

I have written this book with two audiences in mind:

- Design professionals (architects, builders, engineers, interior designers, and others) who may be personally motivated to create zero-energy home designs, or whose clients are asking for ZEH projects;

- Owners and developers who want their home-building projects to achieve net-zero energy.

I have tried to provide sufficient technical information for those who require it, while not overwhelming readers who, preferring to delegate the more technical side to others, simply need a coherent road map. In many cases, more in-depth information is provided in appendices or in reference documents written by others, which are referred to in chapter endnotes and listed in Appendix A.

What *Energy Free* Is and Is Not

Energy Free summarizes and synthesizes (and opines upon) the findings from a wide variety of institutions and individuals who have been grappling with the net-zero energy challenge for many years. It is intended to serve as a guidebook, saving you time by distilling the experience and wisdom of the trailblazers. It explains what a net-zero energy home is and offers strategies and priorities to help you develop *your own plan*.

It is not a design manual – you will not find detailed instruction on passive solar design, for example. You will, however, find a discussion of the role of passive solar design in achieving net-zero energy.

I provide the following types of information to aid you in your design process:

- "mindset" guidance – e.g., definitions and priorities

- process-oriented advice – what steps you should take, and in what order

- decision-making and analysis tools

- overviews of relevant technologies

- empirical data from case studies

- resources for further research

▶ **NZE and green building:** Green building encompasses a broad agenda that includes energy-efficiency and resource conservation; NZE home design and construction fall within the green building realm. This book touches upon, but does not address comprehensively, many other green building concerns, including water use, material selection, indoor environmental quality, landscape design, and community design. Appendix A lists a number of excellent green building resources.

How is *Energy Free* Organized?

Chapter 1. What's it all about?

The chapter presents the reasons for designing net-zero energy homes, the various definitions of net-zero and their implications for design, and the scope of activities to be included within the target for net-zero.

Chapter 2. Net-zero home economics

The chapter includes a discussion of whether net-zero projects cost more than conventional buildings, and presents cost and payback findings from research to date. It also discusses who pays for the ZEH "upgrades," and what incentives and motivations exist for taking on this ambitious goal. The relative cost-efficiency of various options is also addressed.

Chapter 3. Integrated design

The chapter makes the case for undertaking an integrated design process and provides an overview of the principal steps, from setting goals to facilitating integration throughout the process.

Chapter 4. Minimize the energy your building needs

The chapter covers four broad strategies for minimizing your building's energy needs: employing basic principles of efficient design, minimizing enclosure-driven loads, minimizing loads associated with comfort systems (heating and cooling), and minimizing hot water loads.

Chapter 5. Minimize the occupants' energy needs

The chapter covers selection and use of appliances, lighting, water-using fixtures and features, and household gadgets. It also addresses systems management, the connection between monitoring and behavior, and occupant education.

Chapter 6. Power the rest

The chapter reviews the major renewable energy technologies: solar hot water, solar electricity (photovoltaics), and wind power, with brief mention of less common options, such as micro-hydro. It offers information to help guide your investigation of the alternatives, and resources for learning more.

Appendices

The appendices contain an array of supporting information and resources that are referenced throughout the book.

Final Thoughts

In the months following the fall 2008 market crash – which occurred, coincidentally (or perhaps not) around the time I began thinking about this book – many people lost their jobs and had to give up their homes, their pets, other things precious to them. Just as, shortly after the birth of my son, I became suddenly acutely aware of my mortality, early in 2009 I became abruptly more aware of the vulnerability of our economic system as a whole, and of the comfort and stability that I had experienced for my entire life. I realized it was possible for us to have not enough money to pay all our bills. Naïve as this may seem, I had never before entertained this as a real possibility. I comprehended how shackled we were by our ongoing expenses. Not free.

I began to examine seriously the expenses that we could reduce or eliminate. Utility bills were an obvious target. We had already reduced them substantially when we completed a comprehensive energy retrofit and photovoltaic installation three years earlier, but we could make more changes. We're not finished yet, but we've made some headway. Meanwhile, several of our clients have begun building zero energy homes, adding to the body of experience even as I write this account.

I can't offer solutions to the problem of astronomical housing costs or escalating mortgage payments, but I do have some confidence, gained from doing research for this book, that we can dramatically reduce the costs, both financial and environmental, of powering our homes and our lives. I hope you take inspiration and courage from this book, not because it provides all the answers but because it conveys the experience of others, provides guidance for your efforts to design and build energy-free homes, and offers reassurance that your labor will bear fruit of the most rewarding kind – you will be crafting solutions with profound personal and social benefits.

One Last Thing

Energy Free is not absolutely current. Because the field is evolving so rapidly, no book on this topic could still be current by the time a reader opens its pages. However, I hope I have provided enough direction for you to find the newest information when you begin your own quest.

1

What's It All About?

Why ZEH?

The growing desire for homes that are zero energy – or more accurately, net-zero energy (NZEH) – is being driven by a number of converging influences. First and arguably foremost among them is climate change – increasing levels of greenhouse gases in the atmosphere that are disrupting global ecosystems at an alarming and quickening pace, threatening life as we know it on this blue-green planet. No longer is there any legitimate, rational resistance to the patently obvious fact that climate change is driven principally by human activities, notably our penchant for burning fuel at an ever more furious rate.

Second is the phenomenon known as peak oil, based on the belief that humanity has passed (or will soon pass) the point at which it can continue to economically extract oil from the Earth's crust. Our population continues to grow, as does our demand (both absolute and per capita) for power to drive all our daily processes; yet there is less and less oil that we can readily access to fuel those demands. The inevitable outcomes are a constrained and erratic supply and increased prices. Other outcomes – highly likely if not inevitable – may include mandated conservation (rationing), brown-outs, rolling outages, and more wars over this most coveted of resources. (Whether it will remain the most coveted is a topic of great speculation, as water, forests, and arable lands represent other, future frontiers of scarcity – and conflict.)

These two powerful forces are compelling reasons enough to curb our energy appetite. There are positive motivations, too, though. In refreshing contrast to the

► Even the US military is now finding reason to be concerned with climate change. As reported recently in the *New York Times*, "The changing global climate will pose profound strategic challenges to the United States in coming decades, raising the prospect of military intervention to deal with the effects of violent storms, drought, mass migration and pandemics..."[1]

sticks of climate change and peak oil are the carrots of local self-reliance, more vibrant and cohesive communities, and healthier, more active selves. All these are tantalizing rewards for decreased dependence on fossil fuels. How do they follow from zero-energy homes?

- As households become energy-free, they cease to rely on power plants and pipelines, realize financial savings in the form of diminished or eliminated utility bills, and liberate income to be spent in local communities.

- Money spent locally translates into greater local control and improved community resources (libraries, schools, public safety, recreational and cultural facilities and activities, support infrastructure for working families, children, and seniors). Communities with strong local funding bases are less vulnerable to budget cuts from county, state, and federal governments.

- While reduced residential energy consumption does not necessarily translate into greater use of muscle-powered forms of propulsion, many of the strategies that communities need to implement – and individuals and households to employ – involve decreased use of automobiles for personal transportation, replaced by walking, biking, carpooling, and public transit. More footsteps equal not only reduced vehicle miles traveled, they equal more calories burned and improved physical fitness. Pedestrians and bicyclists are often advocates for traffic-calming strategies, improved public transit systems, and other improvements aimed at transforming communities from auto-centric to people-centric.

- Understanding home energy use leads naturally to the consideration of one's interrelationship with one's neighborhood, the local environment, and the natural world in general. Consider growing your own vegetables – kids learn that food comes from the earth and not from packages created somewhere else by a mysterious process.

Which Energy Use?

► To find out how pedestrian-friendly your home is, check your "Walk Score" at **www.walkscore. com.** My home's score is 22 out of 100 — "car-dependent." That's pretty accurate (unfortunately).

Not just homes but, more accurately, *households,* are the target for net-zero energy use. What's the difference? People.

Inevitably, when we talk about *real* energy use – not modeled, simulated, or predicted energy use – we have to consider occupants – people, doing stuff, in and around their homes. The most efficiently-designed home and expertly-sized renewable energy system, if coupled with high-demand energy users, can fail to achieve net-zero energy use. In any event, the attainment of net-zero energy – energy-free living – can't be assessed until the occupants have been in residence throughout a four-season cycle after construction or remodeling is complete. Then, the energy use that is measured will be a function of the home's *design,* the occupants' energy-using *stuff,* and their *behavior* patterns.

The ability of a building project to meet (or exceed) the energy needs of the household will depend on several factors:

- The accuracy of predicting energy loads in the completed structure;

- The success of the design;

- The quality of construction, particularly as regards airtightness and insulation;

- The size of the renewable energy system that the project can accommodate;

- The availability and commitment of financial resources;

- The occupants' behavior.[2]

FIGURE 1-1.
"STUFF"

Courtesy of Mona Helen Renney

Given a fixed number of occupants and amount of stuff to be powered, it will be much easier for a project with lots of real estate to meet its demands than it will be for a project with relatively little real estate. (Real estate can include roof space as well as land space, if PVs – photovoltaic arrays – are used.) Of course, the former condition is almost always associated with a high-budget or rural project, whereas the latter, except in high-density urban areas where real estate is very expensive, is almost always associated with a lower-budget project. Hence the greater number of NZE case studies to date for single-family custom homes, as opposed to multi-family affordable housing – or even midrange production homes. Hence, too, the more frequent adoption of aggressive NZE definitions by single-family custom home projects, vs. multifamily affordable projects.

Components of household energy use

In a talk delivered at West Coast Green in 2006, Professor Ray Cole of the University of British Columbia identified five principal components of household energy use:[3]

1. Home power

2. Personal transportation

3. Consumables (food, cleaning supplies, clothing, etc.)

4. Durable goods (furniture, vehicles, etc.)

5. Vacations

Conventional discussions of home and household energy use, and conventional NZE definitions, only look at the first of these five, which is also the central focus of this book. However, the interplay between the other components and home design deserves consideration before we move on.

Personal transportation

Two aspects of personal transportation are relevant to net-zero energy home design. The first is location: where one lives has a lot to do with the amount of transportation energy one uses; that in turn has a very large influence on one's overall energy use. Urban dwellers use by far the least transportation energy, and rural residents use by far the most, reflecting their degree of reliance on personal motorized vehicles to meet daily needs (getting to and from work, shopping, recreation, etc.). This connection is known as *location efficiency*.

Personal transportation energy is not reflected in any of the conventional metrics used to assess home or energy use, yet it is nevertheless a very important part of the household energy equation. Research by the Canada Mortgage and Housing Corporation (CMHC) found that personal transportation energy use (excluding vacations) for a typical suburban Canadian household represented 23 percent of overall household energy use for all of Cole's categories except durable goods; vacation air travel represented 35 percent. CMHC's analysis showed that if the same family adopted dietary changes and moved to a net-zero energy home downtown where they could walk to work, school, and shops, their household energy impacts would be reduced by 74 percent; retrofitting their existing home would yield a reduction of just 12 percent.[4]

Selecting a location-efficient building site has other benefits, too. The first grant made to support the Leadership in Energy and Environmental Design for Neighborhood Development (LEED-ND) program created by the US Green Building Council, Natural Resources Defense Council, and Congress for the New Urbanism was given by the Centers for Disease Control. The reason? The CDC had found that people who lived within walking distance of basic community services had lower incidences of heart disease, diabetes, and other major health problems. Urban locations are also typically more "senior-friendly," allowing elderly people to continue to live in their own homes, walk to services, and remain near long-time friends and neighbors after they can no longer drive.

The second aspect of personal transportation potentially of interest in a net-zero energy project is the extent to which vehicle power demands may be met with the home's renewable energy system. A number of developers have included electric-vehicle charging stations in their residential projects (both single- and multifamily), and some of those projects have included renewable energy systems (typically PVs). In at least one instance the PV array was sized to provide for the energy needs of the family's automobiles as well as their home power needs.[5]

Other components of household energy use

In theory, a home's renewable energy system could be sized to also offset the energy use and/or emissions associated with the remaining major components of household energy demand: consumables, durable goods, and vacations. And conversely, those components of energy demand may be diminished, in some measure, by the home's design. Onsite food production, for example, can reduce the household's energy use associated with consumables. More and more green building and sustainability advocates are promoting the use of not just rooftops but vertical surfaces, too, as sites for growing. Building sites that are land-rich can also adopt permaculture[6] practices, for example, coppicing[7] to produce willow canes for use in making furniture, fences, and baskets. Permaculture practices may be adopted successfully in smaller projects as well, even urban ones. Further, the more beautiful, holistic, and experientially rich our homes are, the less we may feel the need to vacation elsewhere. Pipe dream? Perhaps. Inevitable future? That remains to be seen.

▶ To learn more about permaculture, see the resource listings in Appendix A.

In addition to those major components of household energy use identified by Cole and investigated by CMHC, a comprehensive analysis of household energy impacts would address incidental operations such as mowing the lawn (if you have one), your household waste stream, and the embodied energy of your home construction or remodeling project itself. Embodied energy is the total energy necessary for an entire product lifecycle, including raw material extraction or harvesting, production, assembly, installation, use, disassembly or deconstruction, disposal or decomposition, and all associated transport.

In 1998, a group of Swiss scientists founded the 2,000 Watt Society, an organization based on the premise that a globally sustainable rate of human energy consumption would be 2,000 Watts, or 17,520 kilowatt-hours per capita per year – the equivalent of twenty 100-Watt light bulbs running 24/7 for a full year. Although this level of energy consumption is approximately the current global average, it is many times higher than energy use throughout the developing world. As shown

▶ Ideally, your landscape or garden will require minimal maintenance. A monoculture such as a conventional lawn arguably has no place in a zero energy building project. See **www.sustainablesites. org** for guidance on low-impact landscapes, as well as information on water in Chapters 4 and 5.

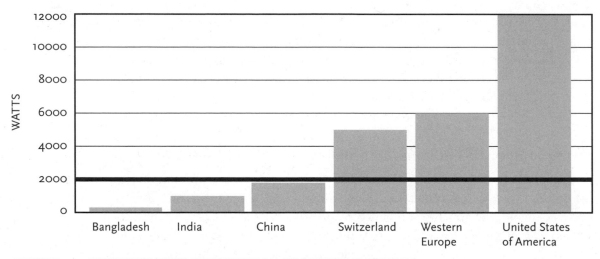

FIGURE 1-2. CURRENT ENERGY CONSUMPTION OF DIFFERENT REGIONS

in Figure 1-2, US average energy consumption is about 12,000 Watts, or six times greater than the proposed "sustainable" level. (Note that these figures represent total energy use across all sectors, divided by population, not just household energy use.)[8]

As astounding as this discrepancy may appear, the Swiss Federal Department of the Environment, Transport, Energy, and Communications has endorsed the aims of the 2,000 Watt Society. The department's head, Mortiz Leuenberger, has said, "At first glance, the objective of a two-thousand-watt society appears unrealistic, but the necessary technology already exists."[9]

In her *New Yorker* article about the 2,000 Watt Society, Elizabeth Kolbert reports, "A few years ago, a group of Swiss scientists published a white paper … on the feasibility of a 2,000 Watt Society. Relying on widely agreed-upon figures, the scientists estimated that two-thirds of all the primary energy consumed in the world today is wasted, mostly in the form of heat that nobody wants or uses … . This same paper concluded that, with currently available technologies, buildings could be made eighty per cent more efficient, cars fifty per cent more efficient, and motors twenty-five per cent more efficient."[10]

In her research for the article, Kolbert asked many people if they were living 2,000-Watt lives. While most of her interviewees responded that air travel was the biggest impediment, she did meet one person, Robert Uetz, an engineer who was living a

2,000-Watt lifestyle. He told her, "We don't experience it as a restriction. On the contrary. I don't feel that we're giving up anything." He, his dentist wife, and their two children live in a modern, highly efficient, 2,000-square-foot house with a solar electric system and a solar hot water system on the roof. Their principal concessions: they don't own a car, and on vacations they travel by rail, not by air.

Swiss researchers believe that this vision is achievable through strategically targeted research aimed at development of new technologies and methods, including refurbishment of existing building stock to low-energy standards, further development of renewable energy sources, and district heating, among others. Multi-stakeholder efforts involving industry, universities, research institutes, and government agencies, working to develop and commercialize some of the relevant technologies, are underway in the metropolitan areas of Basel, Zurich, and Geneva.[11]

The Swiss are legendary for their pacifism, watches, trains, engineering, and general rationality. Their embrace of this concept is at once inspiring and reassuring, a strong shoulder to the wheel of the sustainability movement. In concert with Architecture 2030 and the Passive House movement (both of which are profiled elsewhere in this book), along with so many other sustainability-focused organizations, the 2,000 Watt Society represents a beacon of progress.

So, what to include?

Clearly, the client's budget and priorities will be the primary determinants of which components of occupant energy-consuming activities and behaviors are addressed within the scope of a residential design project. The scope may be ambitious or relatively modest. It is an unusual client who opts to engage with more than the usual set of concerns – home operating energy, the first of Cole's five components. Nevertheless, the efforts underway in Switzerland and elsewhere are harbingers of a time in the not-too-distant future when more of us will look at a wider scope in our design endeavors.

▶ Check out the Union of Concerned Scientists' *Getting There Greener: The Guide to Your Lower-Carbon Vacation,* **www.ucsusa.org/clean_vehicles/solutions/cleaner_cars_pickups_and_suvs/greentravel/getting-there-greener.html.**

What Does It Mean to Be Net-Zero Energy?

Off-grid, on-grid?

This book does not address off-grid homes. Although such homes may be viewed as energy free, they represent a design challenge significantly different from that of creating grid-tied net-zero energy (NZE) homes. There are three reasons for my focus on grid-tied homes and exclusion of off-grid homes:

- The vast majority of North American residences are grid-tied.

- Most off-grid homes are rural and have significant location-associated energy impacts (primarily, personal transportation) that cannot be completely remedied by renewable energy production nor by energy efficiency, using current or emerging technologies and strategies.

- Off-grid homes typically have renewable energy systems that are significantly larger than their grid-tied cousins, simply because they need to be able to provide for their own peak usage; they do not benefit by the load-sharing capacity that the grid provides.

This isn't to say that there won't or shouldn't be a role for off-grid living in a sustainable energy future; there very well may be. However, if we are to be as frugal as possible with our resources – and I believe that is imperative – those off-grid homes may instead need to become standalone mini-grids serving multiple homes or even small communities, to avoid the need for such large renewable energy systems serving each individual structure. Creative groups are starting to address the challenge of community-scale renewable energy production (district energy) and net-zero energy living,[12] but that subject is beyond the scope of this book. Here I simply address net-zero energy living at the scale of the individual residential structure.

Notwithstanding my preference for the concept of energy freedom over that of net-zero energy, energy freedom equally requires us to adopt a framework for assessing the energy performance of the home or household. Numerous NZE definitions are available for consideration. In the interest of moving toward consensus on these definitions, I use those provided by the US National Renewable Energy Laboratory (NREL) in *Zero Energy Buildings: A Critical Look at the Definition*.[13]

The central points of distinction among the different definitions relate to where the energy is produced and how the energy is measured.

Where is the energy produced?

The first point – the location at which the energy production takes place – deserves thoughtful consideration. The NREL paper's authors prioritize production locations based on generalized assumptions about their relative reliability as long-term sources of energy, in the following order of preference:

Onsite sources

1. Within the building's footprint.

2. Outside the building's footprint.

Offsite sources

3. Imported to and used onsite – e.g., biomass, wood pellets, ethanol, or biodiesel (oddly enough, they also include in this category waste streams from onsite processes).

4. Offsets or renewable energy credits (RECs) purchased for renewable power produced elsewhere.

In general, NREL bases this hierarchy on the presumption that competing demands in the future might jeopardize sources not within the building's footprint; the farther removed from the building owner's control, the more risky the source in the long term.

This reasoning holds that each project should strive to achieve its zero-energy goal as high within this hierarchy of options as possible, reverting to less-preferable options only if the others prove unattainable. Although this seems a reasonable approach, I also believe there will be many exceptions to these "rules" – situations in which options 2 and 3 are as likely to produce long-term net-zero energy performance as option 1. On the other hand, I view option 4 – offsets or RECs – as questionable under most circumstances. This is because we have yet to arrive at a consensus-based standard in North America for what constitutes an offset method that assures the real reduction of fuel usage and/or emissions systemwide.

This book deals principally with *onsite* renewable energy sources, both within and outside the building's footprint. Imported offsite sources such as biomass or pellets, while entirely appropriate in some circumstances, have more limited applicability, are not typically emissions-free, and do not pose the same sort of design challenges that onsite renewable energy systems do. They are therefore outside the scope of this book.

How is the energy measured?

Now, moving to the question of how the energy is being measured, our friends at NREL offer four definitions by which "net-zero" can be assessed:

- By energy usage at the site
- By energy usage at the source
- By energy cost to the purchaser
- By emissions associated with energy used and produced by the home

NREL's complete definitions are given below. I have restated each in my own words, in brackets, in the hope that providing alternate definitions will assist in clarifying the differences. In each case, I refer to the renewable energy the project produces annually.

Net-zero site energy (Definition 1). A site zero energy building (ZEB) produces at least as much energy as it uses in a year, when accounted for at the site. [The amount you produce equals the amount you use.]

Net-zero source energy (Definition 2). A source ZEB produces at least as much energy as it uses in a year, when accounted for at the source. Source energy refers to the primary energy used to generate and deliver the energy to the site. To calculate a building's total source energy, imported and exported energy is multiplied by the appropriate site-to-source conversion multipliers. [The amount you produce equals the amount that is *consumed* in delivering to you what you use. In other words, the efficiencies of the generating facility and the delivery system must be factored in, since roughly two-thirds of primary energy is lost in conversion, mostly in the form of heat produced during fuel combustion.]

Net-zero energy costs (Definition 3). In a cost ZEB, the amount of money the utility pays the building owner for the energy the building exports to the grid is at least equal to the amount the owner pays the utility for the energy services and energy used over the year. [The price the utility pays you for the energy you produce equals the price you pay them for the energy they supply you.]

Net-zero energy emissions (Definition 4). A net-zero emissions building produces at least as much emissions-free renewable energy as it uses from emissions-producing energy sources. [The amount of energy you produce equals the amount you use from emissions-producing sources. Because hydro and nuclear are considered emissions-free, for example, you would not need to offset the portion of your utility power mix that comes from those sources.]

The NREL team explains how the choice of definition affects the size of the renewable energy system needed to meet the net-zero energy goal. The impact of that choice of definition may be substantial: for the seven buildings[14] they studied for the NZE definitions paper, the photovoltaic arrays needed to achieve net-zero *site* energy ranged from 1 percent to 72 percent larger than the arrays needed to achieve net-zero *source* energy. (Because both imported and exported energy is multiplied by the same site-to-source multipliers, for the all-electric buildings source energy equals site energy; hence there is no difference in array size.)

The relative magnitude of these size differences was due to the power mix supplied to the building – the more natural gas each building used, the less renewable energy was needed to offset it to achieve a net-zero source energy goal. This is because the more of your imported (grid-supplied) energy is supplied by natural gas, the more of that energy input is provided at a lower conversion rate – the average site-to-source conversion multiplier for natural gas is approximately 1.1, while the average multiplier for electricity is approximately 3.4.

If you have limited space and plan to use PVs to provide your power, your choice of definition and your PV array size are significant factors in whether or not you will be able to achieve net-zero energy. Similarly, if you have a limited opportunity to generate wind power, the amount of generating capacity and your choice of net-zero definition will also be important.

▶ Site-to-source conversion factors vary by source energy type, place, season, and even time of day. National average factors are 3.37 for electricity and 1.12 for natural gas.[15] More localized factors can be found in *Source Energy and Emission Factors for Energy Use in Buildings.*[16]

TIME-DEPENDENT VALUATION

The California Energy Commission requires buildings within the state to comply with a minimum standard of energy efficiency. That standard includes a construct known as time-dependent valuation, or TDV. TDV is a mechanism whereby hour-by-hour energy use is computer-simulated; a building's predicted hourly usage is multiplied by a factor representing the cost to the utility grid of providing energy *during that hour.* The TDV multipliers, as the term implies, vary over time as the cost of generating power varies over time; at times of peak demand, for example, when additional power plants may need to be fired up, generating costs go up dramatically. Thus, at those times, the TDV multipliers are higher than they are during off-peak periods. This creates an incentive to select systems that draw less power during peak times and more during off-peak times.

TDV simulation yields a comparison of the project as designed with a minimally code-compliant project of the same size and configuration and in the same location. While the "energy" values the model produces are fictional, they are a proxy for the building's energy demand on the grid.

If your goal is net-zero *site* energy, the gas and electric fractions will have no impact on the size of the array you will need to achieve net-zero, because no multiplier is applied to them. Figure 1-3 illustrates the effects of different gas and

FIGURE 1-3.

IMPACT OF DIFFERENT GAS AND ELECTRIC FRACTIONS ON SOURCE AND SITE ENERGY REQUIREMENTS

In each of the scenarios pictured below, energy inputs (E for electricity, G for gas) from the grid are shown delivered to the left side of the home; renewable energy produced onsite (E) is shown feeding into the grid from the roof on the right-hand side. Three different net-zero site and net-zero source fuel mixes are shown: all-electric, 50-50 gas and electric, and all-gas. The respective site-to-source multipliers for electricity and gas are 3.4 and 1.2, the national averages. The effects of those multipliers are shown in the space between the horizontal lines representing the power plant and the grid. The relative size of the renewable energy system needed to meet net-zero energy in each case is indicated by the size of the arrow pointing from the roof into the grid.

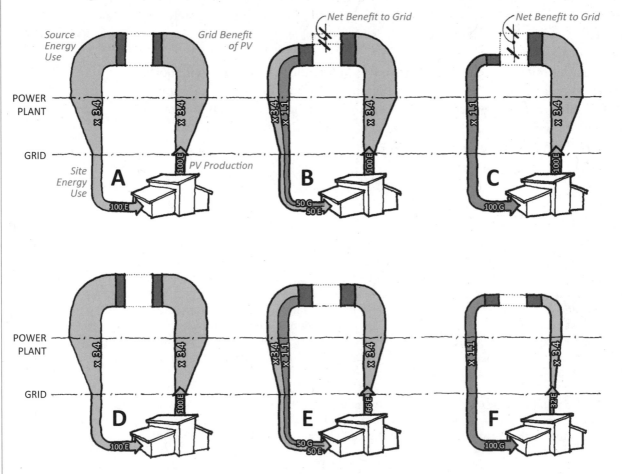

electric fractions. At left are shown all-electric scenarios, at right all-gas scenarios, and in the middle an even split between gas and electricity.

With a given level of site energy demand for your home, all of the following are true, as Figure 1-3 illustrates:

- The larger the fraction of your grid-supplied energy that is supplied by electricity, the larger your source energy use, hence the larger the renewable energy system you will need to achieve net-zero source energy use (scenario D);

- The larger the fraction of your grid-supplied energy that is supplied by natural gas, the smaller your source energy use, and the smaller the renewable system you will need to achieve net-zero source energy use (scenario F);

- If all of your energy use is electric, the size of the renewable system will be the same, regardless of whether you choose net-zero site or net-zero source energy as your goal (scenarios A and D are the same).

▶ Chapter 6 discusses a range of renewable energy options and explains how to approximate the amount of renewable energy you will need to generate.

Note that the diagrams in Figure 1-3 address only the energy imported from and exported to the grid. Energy produced and used onsite, real-time, has no effect on the site-to-source equation, because it never enters the grid.

This means if most of your power usage occurs during periods when your renewable system is producing electricity, your system sizing will be less affected by site-to-source multipliers.

Choosing a definition

Net-zero site energy is arguably a disadvantageous metric, in that it does not reflect the reality that electrical power supplied to the grid displaces the need for industrial electricity production, which is highly inefficient, with roughly two-thirds of the primary energy lost, mostly in waste heat. Thus every unit of renewable electricity exported to the grid has roughly threefold value. On the other hand, it can be argued that measuring energy at the site better reflects the demands of the project's occupants; you must produce as much energy as you use.

Net-zero source energy gives you credit for exporting electricity at approximately threefold value. This might seem like a cheat, allowing you to "discount" the amount of energy you actually use. So long as the energy you are producing is emissions-free, however, this does have a legitimate benefit, as every unit of energy you put on the grid reduces the amount that industrial power plants have to produce by a factor of three, give or take.

While there is no right or wrong definition, there are clearly different outcomes based on which one you choose. So which one makes sense? It depends on your fuel mix, on how grid-supplied electricity is generated in your area, and on your perspective.

If you want to offset or compensate for:	Then you will likely choose net zero:	Relative amount of energy you will need to produce:
Your power bill	Energy **cost** (Definition 1)	Probably the least, unless you have high peak electric usage, but this is very uncertain and will fluctuate over time
Industrial production associated with your power usage	**Source** energy (Definition 2)	*Typically* more than NZE cost (Definition 1)
Your actual on-site power usage	**Site** energy (Definition 3)	More than NZE source (Definition 2) or equal to NZE site (Definition 3), if project is all-electric
Emissions associated with your power usage	Energy **emissions** (Definition 4)	May be more or less than NZE source (Definition 2) or site (Definition 3); depends mostly on fuel mix and how grid-supplied electricity is generated

FIGURE 1-4. CHOOSING A NET-ZERO DEFINITION

It may also be a pragmatic decision based on how much real estate you have to devote to your renewable energy system.

Here I want to reiterate a key point: **for an all-electric home, source energy equals site energy.**

As noted above, this means that for an all-electric home, whether the project is net-zero based on site or on source energy makes no difference in the renewable energy system size. It also means that getting to net-zero will mean installing a larger renewable energy system than if you have some fossil-fuel usage. However, it also somewhat simplifies your choice of definition – you get two for the price of one!

Many advocates working to reverse climate change believe that not only do we need to make our buildings net-zero energy users, we need to free them from dependency on fossil fuels. While the logic of this may be obvious, it is perhaps worth reviewing the rationale for this position:

- All fossil fuels – not just petroleum but also natural gas, propane, etc. – are in finite supply, as measured in human rather than geologic time intervals.

- All fossil fuel combustion, no matter how clean, adds some carbon, along with other pollutants, to the atmosphere.

- The transport of fossil fuels represents significant environmental impacts: ecosystem disruption and habitat loss due to pipeline construction, energy use, and emissions associated with pumping, infrastructure, trucking, etc.

Therefore, for many developers of NZE homes, the definition of choice is that of **net-zero site energy *and* an all-electric home.** This sets the highest performance bar, driving greater renewable energy production than any of the other definitions, and it is arguably the definition that is truest to the ultimate aim of a sustainable energy future.[17] However, cautions one of my engineer colleagues, it's also important to bear in mind that an all-electric project, even a net-zero energy user, may require more natural gas to fuel the industrial power plant than would be used in lieu of electricity in the home.

ENERGY PRIMER

The most common units of energy used in discussions of residential energy use are **British thermal units** (Btu) and **kilowatt hours** (kWh).

One Btu is the amount of heat needed to raise the temperature of one pound of liquid water by one degree from 60° to 61°F at a constant pressure of one atmosphere. It is equivalent to approximately 1.06 kilojoules (1,060 joules). (Joule is the preferred unit of energy in the International System of Units, defined as the work required to continuously produce one watt of power for one second.) Btu's are used to describe both the energy content of fuels, such as natural gas and propane, and the power of heating and cooling equipment (furnaces, air conditioners, etc.); in the latter context, the more accurate term would be Btu per hour (Btu/h), though "per hour" is often omitted.

MMBtu is often used to represent one million Btu.

One therm, a unit often used by utility companies to bill for natural gas usage, is 100,000 Btu.

One quad, or quadrillion Btu, is 10^{15} Btu. This unit is used when talking about energy used by an entire country.

One kWh is equal to 3.6 mega (million) joules. Electrical energy is usually described in kilowatt hours – i.e., the product of power in kilowatts and time in hours.

Analyzing home energy use frequently requires converting Btu to kWh or vice versa, to allow the use of consistent units. The conversions are given below.

1 kWh = 3412.3 Btu, so # of kWh x 3,412.3 = # of Btu

1 Btu = 0.000293 KWh, so # of Btu x .000293 = # of kWh

Many *energy-free* homes will be net producers – that is, they will generate more energy than they use – and those homes will not only meet the NZE site definition, they will further serve the transition to a sustainable energy future by putting clean electricity onto the grid and thereby reducing the demand for power from industrial sources even beyond their own project's needs.

About net-zero energy emissions – NREL may view hydro and nuclear as "emissions-free" but, depending on the system boundaries (are we taking into account the loss of vegetation caused by dams, for example, or the emissions associated with their construction?), that stance is debatable. Since hydro and nuclear power create other environmental problems, treating them as emissions-free seems somewhat equivocal.

How Do You Get There?

The name – also the motto – of the organization Efficiency First (**www. efficiencyfirst.org**) sets the critical agenda for creating energy-free homes. Only by maximizing efficiency in design and operations can most projects afford to reach net-zero energy by any definition. The remainder of this book lays out, generally in chronological order, the steps or phases in the process of developing an energy-free home, beginning with questions of NZEH economics, then following with process guidance and specific strategies for pursuing an efficient design, efficient operations, and renewable energy production.

Your choice of definition is a critical first step, as it will influence budget, the rigor of your efficiency and conservation efforts, renewable energy system sizing, and not least of all your success in meeting your NZE goals. There is no "right" definition, no correct outcome; yet you and others will derive the greatest benefit by establishing clearly defined goals at the outset of your journey.

ENDNOTES

1 John M. Broder, "Climate Change Seen as Threat to U.S. Security," *New York Times*, August 8, 2009, http://www.nytimes.com/2009/08/09/science/earth/09climate.html?_r=1&pagew

2 In many instances homes have been retrofitted to be more energy-efficient, and yet energy usage has not decreased – perhaps because the occupants were reluctant to turn up the furnace before the retrofit but will do so now that they can actually make the home comfortable.

3 Ray Cole (keynote presentation, West Coast Green, San Francisco, California, 2006).

4 Don Fugler, Canada Mortgage and Housing Corporation, "Climate Change & the Residential Sector: Concepts & Terms" (Powerpoint presentation, Affordable Comfort Conference, Pittsburgh, PA , 2008).

5 See Tah.Mah.Lah. listing in Appendix B.

6 "Permaculture is an approach to designing human settlements and perennial agricultural systems that mimic the relationships found in the natural ecologies. It was first developed by Australians Bill Mollison and David Holmgren and their associates during the 1970s in a series of publications. The word permaculture is a portmanteau of permanent agriculture, as well as *permanent culture*." (Wikipedia contributors, "Permaculture," *Wikipedia, The Free Encyclopedia,* http://en.wikipedia.org/w/index.php?title=Permaculture&oldid=314338045 (accessed September 16, 2009.)

7 "Coppicing is the art of cutting of trees and shrubs to ground level allowing vigorous regrowth and a sustainable supply of timber for future generations." (*The Ancient Art of Coppicing,* www.coppicing.com.)

8 Wikipedia contributors, "2000-watt society," Wikipedia, The Free Encyclopedia, http://en.wikipedia.org/w/index.php?title=2000-watt_society&oldid=306600067 (accessed August 7, 2009).

9 Elizabeth Kolbert, "A Reporter at Large: The Island in the Wind," *The New Yorker,* July 7, 2008, www.newyorker.com/reporting/2008/07/07/080707fa_fact_kolbert?printable=true.

10 Ibid.

11 Eberhard Jochem, et al., *Steps towards a 2000 Watt-Society* (*Novatlantis*, December 16, 2002), http://www.efficientpowersupplies.org/pages/Steps_towards_a_2000_WattSociety.pdf.

12 Kolbert, "The Island in the Wind."

13 P. Torcellini, et al., National Renewable Energy Laboratory, *Zero Energy Buildings: A Critical Look at the Definition*, preprint. Conference paper, June, 2006, http://www.nrel.gov/docs/fy06osti/39833.pdf.

14 All seven buildings studied by NREL were commercial buildings; therefore, conclusions that may be drawn from them relative to homes are somewhat limited.

15 Torcellini, et al., *Zero Energy Buildings: A Critical Look at the Definition*, pg. 7.

16 M. Deru and P. Torcellini, *Source Energy and Emission Factors for Energy Use in Buildings,* National Renewable Energy Laboratory, June, 2007, http://www.nrel.gov/docs/fy07osti/38617.pdf, page 1.

17 Note that if you choose the all-electric route, you will need to be attentive to state and/or local code regulations and policies pertaining to electric power, such as the California Energy Commission's rules regarding energy modeling (see time-dependent valuation sidebar in this chapter).

2 Net-Zero Home Economics

An energy-free home is a high-performance home, a higher-quality home than its status-quo counterpart. It's no longer the same product, so it stands to reason that it's not going to come at the same price as its lesser-performing cousin (or prior incarnation, if you're doing a retrofit). Or is it?

In the case of a retrofit, this is self-evident; what you start out with is not energy-free, so getting it to be energy-free is going to require some investment. However, since investments that reduce dependence on imported energy will inevitably reduce your utility bill, they are investments with a payback. I'll cover paybacks a bit more later in this chapter. Meanwhile, it's important to understand that achieving energy independence isn't always, or only, about spending more; first and foremost, it's about making choices.

In the case of a *new* residential project, one might ask whether an energy-free home can be built for the same price as a "normal" home. Indeed it can, with some trade-offs – once again, it's no longer the same home we're talking about.

I have yet to find anyone who has put this case more clearly or completely than Bruce Coldham of Coldham & Hartman Architects, Amherst, MA, in his *Northeast Sun* article, reprinted in its entirety in the following pages.

Making Choices Instead of Paying Premiums for Greener Buildings

By Bruce Coldham, Northeast Sun, *Fall 2008, reprinted with permission from the Northeast Sustainable Energy Association (NESEA); photos added.*

It is often presumed that "green" resourceful building involves a cost premium. This is not a universal truth. Though it is reasonable to assume that a superior product should come at a premium, good performance enhancing design is more a matter of examining design goals and objectives with a view to redirecting investment. On this basis, a performance enhancement can be seen as favoring one option over another – a choice rather than a cost premium. Unfortunately, due to the rather extreme conservatism in the building industry, many choices are never made explicit. They are never discussed, never offered.

In this article I will address a particular residential opportunity for improving green resourceful building performance by means of conscious choice rather than cost premium. It involves improving the thermal envelope at the expense of committing to a central heating system. Let's begin with three questions:

1. Can compact, open-planned houses with well designed, well constructed, thermally-efficient building envelopes achieve a reasonable standard of comfort by relying solely on the natural convection air circulation within the house to distribute heat throughout the interior spaces?

2. Can a single space heater located in the first floor living space provide comfortable heating for the whole house?

3. Can the envelope upgrade cost be covered by savings generated by the elimination of the heating ducts/pipes and the associated fans/pumps?

The evidence of recent projects completed by our office is that we can confidently answer YES to each of these three questions.

With the savings from not investing in central heating, we are able to afford better windows (at least up to a U value of 0.25[1]), improved insulation (a strapped 2' x 6' framed wall with 7" of DensePak blown-in cellulose) and enhanced air tightness (2 ACH at 50 Pa[2]). We modeled the annual heating fuel costs to be approximately 35% lower year-on-year. The cost of electricity to power the heating system (in the absence of the typical fans, pumps and burners) adds around $60 to $100 to those annual energy savings. To this we can add reduced annual maintenance costs: The space heater can be treated as an appliance whereas a central system really requires a technician to perform an annual service.

But the envelope-enhancement-with-space-heating (EESH) solution concept has certain lifestyle implications requiring explicit declaration and thorough consideration.

The space heater (usually gas, but always with a small electrically-powered fan) is located within the first floor living area and space will be required for this purpose. Whereas the rumble in the basement is gone, there is the fan in the living space. It is quiet, but some

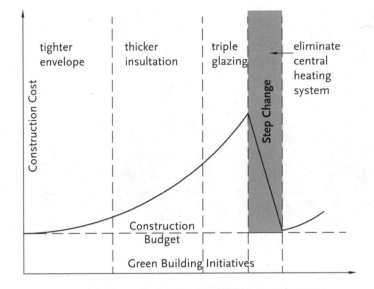

FIGURE 2-1. COST AND GREEN BUILDING INITIATIVES

people may still find it distracting – especially during late evenings when masking ambient noise levels are at a minimum. Basement spaces and first floor addition bedroom spaces, which are "outside" of the simple, connected interior volume require special consideration – usually some supplementary heating. This can be achieved inexpensively using baseboard or radiant electric devices if the use is infrequent, or using a second, smaller space heater if a constant occupancy is envisaged.

In order for the heat to distribute evenly through the upstairs, bedroom doors need to be left open or ajar throughout the bulk of the day. If they are left ajar, one can expect a temperature differential of no more than 5° F during the coldest days. If upper floor doors are closed, a 10° F differential is to be expected. We used a single unit prototype constructed a year earlier for a separate client to determine this with some certainty. So we felt confident in our design counseling.

Note: The coldest days are an infrequent occurrence. For Westover, MA:

• 630 hours each year below 20° F

• 190 hours per year below 10° F

• 45 hours per year below 0° F

Again, electric resistance heating (strip baseboard or ceiling mounted radiant panels) [see Figures 4-12 and 4-13] can be added to spaces where there is any

© Scott Barrow

FIGURE 2-2. ROCKY HILL CO-HOUSING COMMUNITY

concern – or even just the electrical wiring capacity to install these if the need arises. It is usually necessary to think through just how frequently this supplementary heat might be needed because it may be less frequently than initially imagined. We remind our clients that they are in an "enhanced enclosure" – one that is not drafty, one with better insulation and therefore warmer interior surfaces, one that is inherently more comfortable, and one in which the annual cost of operating the electric resistance heating supplement in a couple of bedrooms under these conditions may be less than $40. Because it is not a typical house, we assist our clients in making some assumptions and doing the calculation before abandoning the whole idea. (Also – increasingly, the cost of electric resistance heating is cheaper than propane, and the space heaters are typically fueled either by natural gas or propane, so that $40 may turn out to be a bargain.)

Our firm offered this choice to 28 residents at the Rocky Hill co-housing community in 2004. We spent considerable time explaining the proposition and evaluating the implications of the trade. We noted for example that families with infants or teenage children are more likely to have problems with the closed bedroom-door condition than the empty nesters or young families. We developed options for supplementary heating. Eight of the 28 – those with the smaller more compact units mostly – decided to take the space heating option. After two winters during which we installed basic temperature monitoring with assistance from Integrated Building and Construction Solutions (IBACOS) in Pittsburgh, Pennsylvania, and after which we had visited these early adopters, there appears to be complete satisfaction. People are comfortable, and they are saving fuel – and they did not pay any premium. They simply made a choice, and (it should be said) they stood their ground when, as usually happens, their friends and families and the mechanical sub-contractors (who are used to the inevitability of central heating and the guarantee of temperature uniformity under any condition) told them that they were nuts.

On the basis of these recent successes, other progressive housing projects are in construction that have a total commitment to this cost shifting that favors enhancing building envelopes at the expense of conventional central heating systems. These include the 30-unit Northeast Creek housing development in Bar Harbor, ME, that our office is completing with Gordon Stanley Architecture, the Mosaic Commons co-housing now in construction in Berlin, MA (Kraus Fitch Architects and Marc Rosenbaum providing building performance consulting support), and the recently-completed Jenny Lane affordable housing development in Edgartown on Martha's Vineyard by South Mountain Company. This shift has widespread applicability in this climate zone – especially if houses are simple, single volume affairs.

The next step for us is to move to non-fossil fuel space heating. The Mosaic Commons is using electric radiant and baseboard heating which ultimately allows for a renewable power source. In Europe (but unfortunately not here yet) are micro-silo, auto-feed, wood pellet space heaters that more or less duplicate the performance characteristics of the current crop of gas space heaters that the likes of Rinnai and Takagi are selling in the local market. One model produced by Wodtke has a direct vent device that had the admirable quality of turning the now redundant flue into the pellet storage silo – the same formal components used differently. I hope that we can buy something like that here soon.

END OF REPRINT

Courtesy of Wodtke, wodtke.com

FIGURE 2-3. WODTKE DIRECT-VENT HEATER

Coldham has provided a very concrete illustration of how achieving high performance necessitates trade-offs. The other way of thinking about this is to consider what the project's fundamental goals are. As Coldham stated above, "It is often presumed that 'green' resourceful building involves a cost premium." I believe this is relatively easily eliminated as a problem by taking a somewhat unusual approach to articulating project goals. (Keep this in mind in the context of how the integrated design process unfolds, described in Chapter 3.)

An architect generally understands his or her obligations to the client to include delivering a design that is:

- Functional,
- Aesthetically pleasing,
- On budget, and
- Safe.

These obligations may be unspoken or addressed only indirectly, yet every architect understands them to be part of his/her charge. There are several additional basic

SETTING PRIORITIES

One of the exercises I like to do with new clients who have high performance goals is to have them prioritize the following attributes (or objectives), from most to least important to them:

- Beauty
- Comfort
- Budget
- Environmental responsibility
- Schedule
- Function
- Durability
- Maintenance

This is very instructive, and becomes a very useful tool as design progresses and decision-making ensues. Time and again, prioritizing provides a touchstone for the design team. It can be used to compare basic design options, from such basics as one-story vs. two-story, to much more detailed issues such as Flooring A vs. Flooring B. It should be noted, though, that prioritizing can create frustrating dilemmas – few clients would want to choose between beauty and cost, yet this is the reality of design. It's also worth noting that the order of priorities may shift depending on the particular issue at stake. That's OK; it's just important to be clear about the trade-offs that are being made, and not to overlook any of the key criteria.

obligations that are almost always *un*spoken, yet nonetheless important. The building design should also be:

- Durable,
- Healthy for occupants and workers, and
- Environmentally responsible.

It is critical that these last three criteria be made explicit and be agreed upon. Once they become part of the covenant between owner or developer and architect, "green" is no longer an extra. It's part of the design charge, and it gets treated as such; when trade-offs have to be made – which is, after all, what the entire design process is all about – *all* the project's fundamental goals become lenses through which the decisions are scrutinized. If high performance is treated as an add-on or option, it is all too easily eliminated when budget concerns arise.

DOE's Building America program approaches the challenge of achieving net-zero energy from a different perspective. Their goal is to identify building measures that will result in NZE homes for *neutral* cost – no change in the total cost of mortgage and utilities. Similarly, the State of California, which is the nation's leader in pursuing net-zero energy goals and has mandated that all new homes will be net-zero energy by 2020, has been investigating whether this mandate is economically viable.[3]

Navigant Consulting, researching on behalf of California's PIER (Public Interest Energy Research) program, has arrived at a number of interesting conclusions, among which are the following:[4]

- Today's NZEH communities reduce energy use by at least 30 to 50 percent through a combination of energy efficiency and onsite solar energy systems.

- It is technically possible to construct NZEH, but the cost premium for NZE (as of August 2008) is $40,000 to $70,000.

- Neutral-cost NZEH will require source energy savings of about 40 to 45 percent from energy efficiency, with the remaining energy needs met by onsite renewable energy systems (typically 3-5 kW).

- In order to meet NZEH goals at neutral cost in all climates, a number of technologies and strategies that do not yet exist are needed, and a number of existing technologies will require further research and development to bring their costs down, as shown in Figure 2-4.

The report makes the following significant assumptions about developments needed in order to achieve NZE at neutral cost:

- 20+ SEER (seasonal energy efficiency ratio) air conditioners available at reduced cost and lower cooling capacities than currently exist;

Rooftop PV System @ $3.30/Watt*

30% Reduction of Miscellaneous Electric Loads*

20+ SEER/ EER AC with Low Cooling Capacity

EF 0.8+ Gas Tankless Water Heater

90% Market Penetration of Compact Fluorescent Lights for All Applications*

R-10 Windows*

High Efficiency Pool Pumps when Applicable

* = Technologies that do not yet exist; others require further research and development.

FIGURE 2-4. ADVANCES NEEDED TO ACHIEVE NZEH GOALS AT NEUTRAL COST

Note: All acronyms in the figure above are listed in the Table of Acronyms and Abbreviations and defined in Chapter 4.

Data courtesy of Navigant Consulting, on behalf of California's PIER (Public Interest Energy Research) Program

- R-10 windows available at $20/sq. ft. (note that Figure 2-4 shows R-10 windows as a future technology, but Serious Windows has since introduced their line of windows rated up to R-11; costs for their high-R-value windows are in the range of $40/sq. ft. and up, with prices expected to come down as the market matures);

- 30 percent reduction in miscellaneous electric loads achievable at incremental cost of $1,000;

- PV systems available at $3.30/Watt (versus current cost of $7.50/Watt).

Depending on the project, climate, commitment, and budget, these are not necessarily impediments to a residential project achieving net-zero energy today. They are, however, useful data points to inform the design (and financing) process.

Other interesting findings from the report include:

- The cost of a California ZEH per square foot is dependent on building size but not on climate, ranging from ~$9/sq. ft. for a 3,500-sq. ft. home to ~$13/sq. ft. for a 1,500-sq. ft. home.

- Also, not surprisingly, the percent increase in cost for NZEH is larger in less expensive housing markets and for smaller homes.

- As square footage increases, energy efficiency measures account for a greater percentage of energy savings, mostly from larger reductions in heating, ventilating, and air conditioning (HVAC) consumption; the corollary to this is that for smaller homes, a larger fraction of the load is met by renewable energy systems.

- Using regional average energy costs, DOE found that NZEH is achievable with 50 to 70 percent energy use reduction, supplemented by PV, as shown in Figure 2-5.

- DOE also evaluated the incremental cost, which is roughly $30,000 for a 2,500-sq. ft. home, except in the cold climate, where it is much higher. See Figure 2-6.

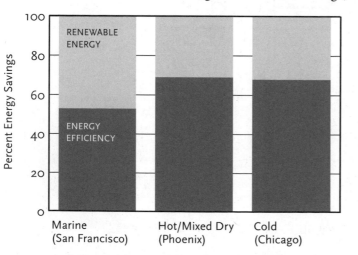

FIGURE 2-5. POTENTIAL FOR ZERO ENERGY HOMES
Data courtesy of Navigant Consulting, on behalf of California's PIER (Public Interest Energy Research) Program

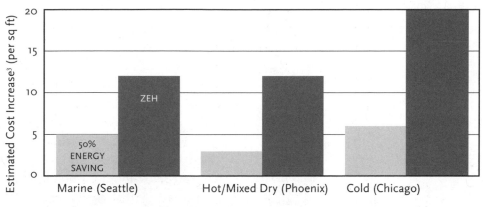

FIGURE 2-6. INCREMENTAL COST OF NZEH
Data courtesy of Navigant Consulting, on behalf of California's PIER (Public Interest Energy Research) Program

- Without rebates, a ZEH's incremental cost would need to decrease to approximately $12,500/unit for the benefits to equal the costs. In other words, until advances in technology bring down costs, the savings you will accrue from incorporating energy efficiency improvements will not balance out the additional investments made to reach net-zero energy. However, it's important to keep these findings in DOE's context, which is somewhat different from that presented by Bruce Coldham earlier in this chapter.

Increases in energy costs may ultimately have as much effect on this equation as decreasing technology costs.

Net Cost of Ownership – Who Pays, Who Benefits?

A key concept in the energy-efficient building community – similar to the idea of cost neutrality introduced above – is the net cost of ownership. This refers to the fact that the *real* cost of a home isn't just the capital cost – the purchase price and/or the amount invested in remodeling – or even the real estate industry's PITI (principal, interest, taxes, and insurance); it includes *all* the ongoing costs of owning and operating the home (OOO costs). Besides interest, taxes, and insurance, OOO costs include:

- Utilities (electric, gas, water, sewer, waste)

- Fuel (if not utility-supplied – propane, wood, pellets)

- Maintenance (replacing filters, lubricating motors, repainting, etc.)

In an energy-free home, the costs of utilities and/or fuel are reduced, as compared to the *non*-energy-free home. Some capital costs (such as the heating plant, as described in Bruce Coldham's article above) may even be eliminated or traded off for other features in an energy-free home. Additionally, a genuinely high-performance home will have been designed with consideration for enhanced durability and reduced maintenance. These performance enhancements translate into month-to-month, year-to-year savings that should be weighed alongside the "first" or capital costs of the construction project, whether building new or remodeling.

To make this more concrete, Figure 2-7 shows a simplified calculation of the net cost of ownership for a LEED Home and a conventional home, adapted from the US Green Building Council's marketing and outreach effort for LEED for Homes Rating System, a green/high-performance building program.

	CONVENTIONAL HOME	LEED HOME
Baseline construction cost	$300,000	$300,000
Upgraded performance features		$7,000
Verification/quality control		$3,000
Selling price	$300,000	$310,000
Monthly mortgage payment (6.5%, 30-year fixed rate)	$1,896	$1,959
Monthly energy cost (30% overall energy savings)	$130	$91
Net cost of ownership / month	$2,026	$2,050
Additional monthly cost for high performance		$24
Additional daily cost for high performance		$0.81

FIGURE 2-7. SAMPLE NET COST OF OWNERSHIP CALCULATION FOR LEED HOMES

Here's where it gets tricky. In many scenarios, the party who pays for construction (the "builder" in the discussions below) is not the same as the party who pays for operating costs (the "operator"). If those parties are not the same, do not share the same priorities (and it's very likely that they don't), or are financially constrained in certain ways, it can be challenging to reallocate operating cost savings into the construction budget. A few representative scenarios are described below.

Homeowner-builder/long-term owner

Many of the pioneers in energy-free or net-zero energy projects are private individuals developing custom homes as their personal residences – either primary or vacation homes. In this scenario, the builder and operator are one and the same, so these individuals are have complete liberty to view the construction budget and the ongoing ownership and operating budget as one seamless resource. They can choose any time horizon that suits them and add the OOO cost savings from that period to their construction budget, recognizing that at the end of that period, they will be in the same position financially as if they had *not* invested in the energy improvements. In many cases, the net cost of ownership – the capital outlay plus OOO savings – of an energy-free project may be lower than the net cost of ownership of a conventional project, so the savings continue to accrue even after they have "paid off" the initial investment. In other cases, the net cost of ownership of the energy-free project may indeed be higher than the cost of its conventional counterpart, but the incremental cost of the higher-performing project provides disproportionately high value for that marginal investment. And as utility costs change over time (the overall trend being inevitably upward), the equation becomes ever more favorable.

Speculative builder

To date, only a few NZEH projects have been built by speculative builders – that is, built for sale to unknown future buyers. When the future operating savings will accrue to someone other than the builder making the investment in the home construction, it becomes more challenging – and yes, speculative – to invest added capital into an energy-free home. Building for an unknown buyer also makes it riskier to decide on the trade-offs Bruce Coldham discussed in his article, which could otherwise make it possible to hold the cost at the same level as for a conventional-energy home.

Tackling this specific problem head-on was the aim of an NZEH project sponsored by the Sacramento Municipal Utility District (SMUD) in California, working in collaboration with the National Renewable Energy Laboratory. The project, dubbed "Home of the Future," incorporated many of the features discussed later in this book:

- A well-insulated, well-sealed building enclosure
- High-performance windows
- Well-sealed ducts, inside conditioned space
- Solar-assisted hydronic space heating
- Solar water heating with a high-efficiency backup boiler
- Efficient air conditioners, lighting, and appliances
- Solar electric panels

Specific design parameters for the Home of the Future are available in the case study resources. See Appendix B for more information.

Modeling indicated above-code performance including 89 percent lower source energy use and 50 percent lower gas use. The home was designed to be a net exporter of electricity. Based on these predictions, utility bills were projected to be $24 per month, versus $140 per month for a comparable code-compliant home. However, Mike Keesee, SMUD program manager, reports that the home is not operating at net-zero source energy use, likely due to higher-than-anticipated plug loads.[5]

Keesee offered a number of observations about the project and its outcomes:

- SMUD's primary interest is in reducing peak electric demand, not necessarily achieving net-zero energy, per se, because they have power plants that are needed for less than 50 hours per year at peak system load. Needless to say, this is very expensive!

- Chief drivers of peak demand in homes are cooking, water heating, and clothes drying.

- Solar and efficiency features do make economic sense.[6]

- NZE homes should be all-electric and should include solar thermal systems, heat pump water heaters, and mini-split heat pumps for space conditioning.[7]

Is there in fact a viable market for speculative energy-free or NZE homes? SMUD is betting there is, and so am I. Perhaps the bigger questions are when, and how large a market? The factors shaping that market include the economy in general, of course, but also regulatory developments and the mindset of the prospective homebuyers. Will they be like the eight households at Rocky Hill co-housing who chose space heating, or will they have more mainstream tastes and expectations?

Judy Lew-Loose photographer, courtesy of SMUD, smud.org

FIGURE 2-8. SMUD HOME OF THE FUTURE

In some markets, speculative builders have been able to obtain a premium price for homes that were more energy-conscious than their competitors' (e.g., built to ENERGY STAR or LEED standards), so to that extent they have benefited from the savings in OOO costs that their buyers later experienced. However, the ability to reap a premium price is entirely at the whim of the marketplace. When the housing market is poor, as it has been for some time as of this writing, it's more likely that the reward for builders of high-performance homes will be a faster sale (and therefore lower carrying costs) rather than a premium price. This was the experience of Grupe Homes in Rocklin, California, near Sacramento, when they developed Carsten Crossings, their first LEED for Homes subdivision of 144 single-family homes. Although their prices were on a par with those in adjoining developments, they outsold the competition by more than double during the same time period. Mark Fischer, senior vice president at Grupe, estimated that this quicker sales pace represented a $13 million savings to Grupe, and further stated, "If just 20.3% of the acceleration was due to the GrupeGreen features the program has paid for itself. Put differently, if GrupeGreen features shaved 8.4 months off the sales period, the program has paid for itself [in] 8.4 months."[8]

Citing *The Ryness Report,* June 2008, Fischer reports similar experiences in other solar communities, compared with non-solar communities in California, as shown in Figure 2-10.[9]

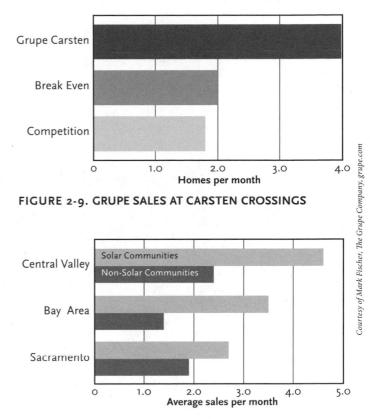

FIGURE 2-9. GRUPE SALES AT CARSTEN CROSSINGS

FIGURE 2-10. SOLAR VS NON-SOLAR COMMUNITY SALES

Courtesy of Mark Fischer, The Grupe Company, grupe.com

Multifamily affordable housing projects

With the exception of a duplex project in Canada and a student housing project in Maine, I am aware of only two NZE multifamily projects to date, both of which are affordable housing developments in Southern California. In light of California's policy mandate for all new residential construction to be net-zero by 2020, we are likely to see more such projects in the near future. Projects of this type present yet a third financial scenario, described below:

- The housing developer (often a nonprofit organization) is typically also the building operator.

- Rents are based on residents' income and a utility allowance, which together may not exceed a given amount.

- Utility allowance schedules (UAS) are set uniformly by the local housing authority based on costs for their entire housing stock, resulting in allowances that may be higher than necessary to cover utility costs in an energy-efficient building.

- Unless a project-specific utility allowance is assigned for a project, thereby allowing the housing developer to charge higher rent, the developer has no financial incentive to incorporate energy improvements in the building.

This situation represented a significant challenge to California's first NZE multifamily project, SOLARA in San Diego. Since then, advocates successfully lobbied the state's housing finance agency to create a new, project-specific method for setting the utility allowance. This change went into effect in 2009, and the second multifamily NZEH project in California, Los Vecinos in Los Angeles, is now benefiting from that new mechanism.

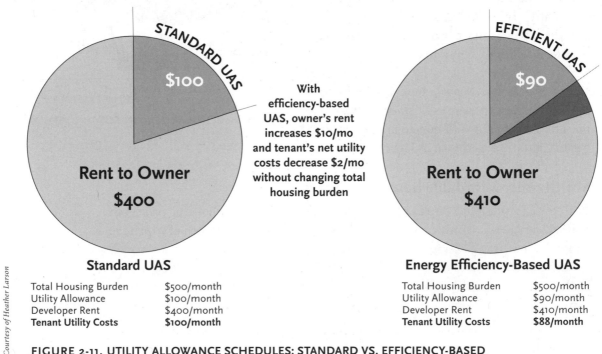

Courtesy of Heather Larson

Standard UAS	
Total Housing Burden	$500/month
Utility Allowance	$100/month
Developer Rent	$400/month
Tenant Utility Costs	**$100/month**

Energy Efficiency-Based UAS	
Total Housing Burden	$500/month
Utility Allowance	$90/month
Developer Rent	$410/month
Tenant Utility Costs	**$88/month**

FIGURE 2-11. UTILITY ALLOWANCE SCHEDULES: STANDARD VS. EFFICIENCY-BASED

A second obstacle SOLARA encountered was that the utility would only allow net metering to a single customer on the project site. This problem was tackled by lobbying the Public Utilities Commission, which, via an administrative tariff-setting process, amended its rules to allow "virtual net metering," which is now in effect, also benefiting Los Vecinos.

Virtual net metering makes it possible for net-metered photovoltaic arrays to have power production as well as grid-supplied power consumption allocated by contract (rather than with separate physical meters) to individual units in a multifamily project. Before this was allowed, the requirement to meter dwelling units individually limited the use of renewable energy systems in most multifamily projects[10] to supplying power only to the project's common areas and not the individual units.

Because the investor-owned utilities in California also only allow net-metering PV customers to be credited to the extent of their *monetary* contribution to the grid, not to the extent of their *energy* contribution (this is more thoroughly explained in Chapter 6), this has discouraged placing larger systems on multifamily projects

Courtesy of Community HousingWorks, Owner/Developer

FIGURE 2-12. SOLARA NZE COMMUNITY

▶ October 11, 2009, Governor Arnold Schwarzenegger signed a bill that will require utilites to pay for any surplus electricity produced by a customer's renewable energy system. The law will go into effect January 1, 2011.

even when roof space might have permitted it. I hope to see other states follow suit, thereby making it easier and more attractive for multifamily projects to target energy-free production capacity.

Bottom line

In the financial realm, what you have to work with is inextricably tied to who is footing the bill for construction and who is footing the bill for operations. Those two pots of money may both be available in the pursuit of an energy-free project, or only the construction pot may be available. If it first appears that the OOO budget is not available, you may want to investigate further, lobby, haggle, or engage in other means of persuasion to have that pot made available to benefit the project. And yet there is no guarantee of success.

Unfortunately, there is no one-size-fits-all solution. At this early stage in the emergent energy-free era, your best bet is to make use of available case study data, interview project principals for more information, and get creative (and persistent). The case of SOLARA and the outcomes for Los Vecinos bear witness to the value of this approach.

▶ See Appendix B for case study resources.

Other Multifamily Findings

Ted Bardacke of Global Green, who was involved with the SOLARA project and with Los Vecinos (both of which are located in notably mild climates), offers these observations based on his experience with the two projects:[11]

- It's possible to achieve net-zero *electrical use*; achieving net-zero by other definitions represents significant practical challenges. (Both projects use natural gas for heating, domestic hot water, and communal clothes dryers; Los Vecinos also uses gas for cooking.)

- Two stories is the maximum for projects with air conditioning, three stories without.

- In this "paradise climate," the effect of improvements in the enclosure will be quite small; what's left is lighting, appliances, and plug loads. These projects used all compact fluorescent lights and all ENERGY STAR appliances. Plug loads are difficult to control (with TVs and game consoles factoring in prominently). Further load reductions – and achieving net-zero *energy* – will rely on significant improvements in lighting, appliance, and PV efficiency.

However, future prospects for achieving NZE in multifamily projects appear bright, based on expected technology improvements and Navigant's analysis, which indicates that "with energy efficiency gain of 50-70% over Title 24 - 2008, the maximum height achievable in 2020 for a multifamily ZEH with rooftop PV is 10 to 25 stories, depending on climate and energy intensity."[12] Since more than 97 percent of California's multifamily residential buildings are four stories or lower, and two-thirds of them are only two stories, NZE for multifamily projects seems well within reach in the coming decade.

Incentives and Innovative Financial Arrangements

One financing option that has been around for a while but is little-used is an energy-efficient mortgage (EEM). EEMs are offered to homebuyers who demonstrate that their utility expenses will be lower than normal because of the energy-efficiency of the home; the lender will then allow the buyer to qualify for a larger loan amount. Learn more about energy-efficient mortgages at the following websites:

- **www.energystar.gov/index.cfm?c=bldrs_lenders_raters.energy_efficient_mortgage**

- **www.disasterhousing.gov/offices/hsg/sfh/eem/energy-r.cfm**

- **www.natresnet.org/ratings/overview/faq_mortgage.htm**

Increasingly, public agencies are devising ways to encourage the development of NZEH projects. The means they are employing fall into three broad (and not altogether distinct) categories:

- **Mandates.** Some counties and municipalities *require* construction projects to incorporate energy efficiency and/or other green building measures. While this may not directly benefit your project, it may mean that there are more resources in your area than would otherwise be the case. Moreover, where there are mandates, there are often incentives.

- **Incentives.** Many communities also offer green building, energy efficiency, and/or water conservation incentives. Examples include expedited permit processing, quicker turnaround on building inspections, or fee reductions to projects that meet specific performance guidelines. There are also federal tax incentives, as well as state-level incentives in many states, for both renewable energy and efficiency measures. In addition, public utilities frequently offer incentives ranging from equipment, appliance, and fixture rebates, to free CFLs, to free or discounted low-flow showerheads and faucet aerators.

▶ An extensive database of incentives and rebates is available at **www.dsireusa.org.** Also check with your local utilities, your city and county government offices, and your tax advisor for specifics.

• **Assistance.** Innovative financing options are beginning to appear. A program pioneered in Berkeley, California is now being replicated by other California communities; in this arrangement, property owners have an opportunity to borrow money from the City's Sustainable Energy Financing District to install solar electric systems and repay the cost over 20 years through an annual special charge on their property tax bill. The State of California recently enacted legislation (referred to as AB 811) which allows other cities and counties in California to provide a similar program for their residents. Some local communities, such as the Town of Portola Valley in California, have established "bulk buy" programs that give their residents access to discounted pricing on renewable energy systems, energy audits, or other relevant products and services.

Leasing arrangements have recently been developed that may make it easier to incorporate renewable electric systems – PVs in particular – in NZEH projects. One type is a conventional lease, in which a private company (not the homeowner) installs a PV system on a residence but retains ownership of the system. The homeowner makes fixed lease payments on the system over time. The other lease option is known as a Power Purchase Agreement (PPA). In a PPA, the homeowner makes variable payments over time based on the amount of energy the system produces.

Under these arrangements, the building owner has renewable energy without having to come up with the system's up-front cost. It also means someone else is responsible for maintenance. Both arrangements include a purchase option after a number of years.

These financial arrangements are offered by solar financers, which typically market to customers via solar installers. Solar City (**www.solarcity.com**) and Sun Run (**www.sunrunhome.com**) both offer leases; Sun Run also offers PPAs.

Payback – the Relative Cost-Efficiency of Various Options

First, the conventional wisdom

"Efficiency first" has become the mantra of proponents of low-carbon-footprint homes, and this perspective is echoed by Peter Amerongen, the designer of Riverdale NetZero, a winning entry in the Canada Mortgage and Housing Corporation (CMHC) EQuilibrium™ Sustainable Housing Demonstration Initiative: "We ran seven gazillion iterations of the [modeling] program. Since zero energy was the goal, it didn't make any difference whether we conserved or collected the energy:

a kilowatt-hour is a kilowatt-hour either way. Since the PV is our most expensive system – between $7 and $8 per annual kilowatt-hour – we calculated that we could afford any conservation measure that costs less per kilowatt-hour than the PV."[13]

A contrarian view

In many circumstances it will be less expensive, per Btu/kWh saved, to incorporate efficiency measures than it will be to purchase additional Btu/kWh in renewable power-generating capacity. This assumes, of course, that achieving an energy-free design is a principal goal of the project and that it has been part of the design charge from the outset. Naturally, like all generalizations, there are exceptions to this rule – notably in retrofitting existing homes, also when adopting some advanced efficiency options.

For example, in a home that already has been air-sealed and insulated in all the readily accessible places, and where the windows have already been replaced, it may be more cost-effective to install generating capacity sufficient to get to net-zero than it would be to do further retrofits. For instance, a retrofit might be too expensive if the home has a forced-air heating system that is not terribly old or inefficient but has ducts in unconditioned space, situated to make them very difficult to insulate or move into conditioned space.

Particularly since part of any energy-free strategy will entail installing renewable energy, simply adding an increment to the system's generating capacity *may* represent lower marginal cost than tackling some of the more challenging and costly efficiency retrofit options. Of course, if attaining the NZE goal is truly of paramount importance, the amount of space available for renewables also factors in, as described a bit later in this chapter.

Another scenario in which it may be more cost-effective to bump up the size of the renewable energy system is when the decision to go energy-free is reached somewhat late in the design process. Sometimes there is just too much investment – financial and/or psychic – in the design as it has evolved to go back and revisit basic factors that *would* have represented low-cost ways of improving energy performance, had they been addressed earlier in the process.

We have found this to be true on several of our clients' projects over the last couple of years. They started out wanting to build green, *then* decided to up the ante and earn a LEED rating, *then* decided they could stretch to LEED Platinum (the highest available LEED rating), and eventually decided to shoot the moon and go for

OPPORTUNISTIC REMODELING

There are readers among you, I'm sure, who will undertake a retrofit project solely for the purpose of moving your home toward energy independence. However, the opportunities for deep energy or energy-free retrofits are much greater than that pool of dedicated individuals. During the first half of 2009, re-modeling represented nearly half of all residential construction activity in the United States, up from about 25 percent in 2002-2008; in other words, almost as much money is being spent on remodeling as on building new homes.[14] Put in yet a different way, for every one new home built, several others are undergoing remodeling. Many remodeling projects present the opportunity to incorporate significant energy improvements at zero or very low incremental cost, provided that the opportunity is identified early enough and strategically exploited.

Our home is a good example. Having the designer's constant yen to better my surroundings, for years I had wanted to make a number of architectural improvements. I had also, for years, considered it imperative to make certain energy improvements. Thus it's hard to say, really, which was the principal goal: improved energy performance or improved design. But let's say for the sake of argument that the primary driver was to improve the design. High on my list of priorities for change were the windows in the two downstairs bedrooms. The existing windows were small and ill-placed; they were also energy hogs, single-paned and aluminum-framed. Off with their heads! Replacing them meant not just putting in better-performing windows (dual-paned, wood-framed, low-emissivity); it also meant enlarging and moving them to provide better daylighting, passive solar heating, and visual connection to the outdoors. This in turn meant that a substantial portion of the exterior walls would be opened up, creating a very low-cost opportunity to install insulation – and do a much better job of it than would have been possible by other means.

With every remodeling project you approach, consider what energy improvements can be added with very little effort to create a much better project. This effectively reduces the cost of those improvements.

energy-free … but their designs were already quite well-developed. At that point a number of enclosure measures can still be tinkered with – air sealing details, quality and (sometimes) quantity of insulation, window specs, equipment efficiencies – but some critical factors like massing and orientation are no longer on the table. And so it's possible to get only so far with efficiency. What's left to work with is the size of the renewable system.

I realize this stance flies in the face of conventional wisdom, and I don't want it to be misunderstood. I *always* advocate identifying and evaluating every opportunity for improving efficiency and otherwise reducing demand – via behavior changes, for example. However, in your evaluation you may find that the "efficiency first" mantra doesn't apply *under your specific circumstances*. To every rule there are exceptions.

What about your project?

At the risk of antagonizing the efficiency mavens, my point is that while "efficiency first" is a fine rule of thumb, efficiency exists on a spectrum and is influenced by many, many variables, as this book and others illustrate. Depending on a variety of factors, you may decide that you've gone as far along the efficiency spectrum as is practicable for your project and you need to make up the difference with renewables.

The compelling argument for taking efficiency as far as you reasonably can is that renewables are more expensive (in general), and you may simply not have enough roof space to devote to solar to get you to energy-free, if you don't reduce your loads as much as possible *first*. Of course, if you're among the lucky souls who can use wind energy to good advantage, you may not be so constrained. However, for the vast majority, PVs – for the time being – will be the renewable power option of choice, and the amount of roof real estate you have available will be a dominant consideration.

This is nowhere more true than in multifamily projects, which tend to be relatively tall and thin, not low and wide, with roof area much smaller in proportion to the living area it covers. The diagram shown in Figure 2-13, developed by Ted Bardacke at Global Green, illustrates the point nicely. The same PV production area, serving three stories instead of one, provides one-third as much energy per floor. (That same volume, because it is stacked, may also be somewhat more efficient, all other things being more or less equal, but probably not three times more efficient.)

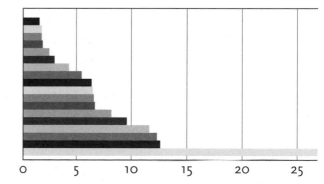

Courtesy of Ted Bardacke, Global Green, globalgreen.org

FIGURE 2-13. PV OUTPUT BY NUMBER OF STORIES

Figure 2-14 shows data compiled by Andrew Webster for a homework assignment he gave in the zero-energy homes class he and his colleague Tom Hartman teach for Boston Architectural College. The question they posed was, "How many rooftops would it take to provide enough PV to supply your home's current energy demands?" The results are quite telling, ranging from a low of 1.5 rooftops to a high of 371. Even omitting the outlier on the assumption that the

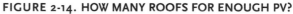

FIGURE 2-14. HOW MANY ROOFS FOR ENOUGH PV?

calculation may have contained an error, the next highest value was 28.4 and *the average was 7.26 roofs*. The assignment did not require students to factor in things like shading, roof pitch, or vent stacks and other obstructions which would render some roof area unavailable – every square foot of south-facing roof was assumed to be available for PV installation. Even under those unrealistically favorable conditions, no one in the class had a roof that provided enough space to meet their existing loads.

These illustrations underscore the importance of taking efficiency as far as you reasonably can.

THE NET-ZERO-COST PARADOX

Because peak production for PVs typically occurs at times of high demand, when some utilities' rates are higher, it may be possible to get to net-zero cost with a level of production that is considerably below net-zero site (let alone source) energy. This is great inasmuch as you're buying low and selling high, but the fly in the ointment is the monetary cap – many, maybe even most utilities won't pay you more for the energy you send into the grid than you pay them for the energy you pull from it. This scenario is shown in Figure 2-15. In that scenario, the utility sells power at an average price of $.09/kWh, charging $450 for 5,000 kWh. If the utility buys peak power you produce at an average price of $.30/kWh and they will only buy $450 worth of power from you, that's 1,500 kWh, less than one-third of what you would supply to the grid in your net-zero scenario.

This gives you two choices:

- Donate the monetary value of your "excess" production to the utility; or

- Size your production capacity so you supply no more power to the grid than your utility will buy from you.

This situation creates a perverse incentive for affordable housing developers in particular, or anyone else who must make their production budget go as far as possible, to minimize, not maximize, the size of their PV arrays. Instead of encouraging projects to strive to be energy-free (i.e., net-zero site or source, as you choose), it encourages projects to underachieve, to merely target net-zero cost.

The situation is also unfortunate in that it discourages more wide-spread adoption of distributed generation, which might allow the utilities to forestall or even eventually eliminate the need to develop more power plants. Development of new plants would be far costlier, subject to massive transmission losses, and increasingly politically problematic to site, as residents in many areas object to having power plants located in their communities.

Annual	Amount	
kWh fed to grid	5,000 kWh	A
Average price paid by utility (peak)	$ .30 / kWh	B
Value of energy fed to grid	$1,500	C (A x B)
kWh bought from utility	5,000 kWh	A (assume equal amounts bought and sold in exact net-zero energy home)
Average price paid to utility (off-peak)	$ .09 / kWh	D
Cost of energy bought from utility	$450	E (A x D)
Credit from utility	$450	E (cannot exceed E per utility rules)
Value of energy "donated" to utility	$1,050	C – E

FIGURE 2-15. NET-ZERO ELECTRICITY BUY-SELL SCENARIO

There is, of course, another side to this. Utilities are reportedly struggling with rate structures that incentivize the development of residential-scale renewable power installations, in effect being subsidized by regular ratepayers. These rates are predicated on a certain level of adoption which, if exceeded, will create a budget shortfall for the utilities, along with other management challenges. In California, at least, evidently the major investor-owned utilities are actively considering how to restructure rates so as to eliminate this disincentive to larger residential PV and wind installations.[15]

Relative cost-effectiveness

There is no universal prescription as to the relative cost-effectiveness of different efficiency measures. Clearly, in principle, what every energy-free project team should do is to make the greatest use of least-cost measures, proceeding down through the hierarchy in steps only as each low-cost opportunity has been capitalized upon to the greatest practicable degree.

The hierarchy of cost-effectiveness will vary from project to project, climate to climate, building type to building type. The most reliable guideposts to cost-effective design measures for *your* project will be local experts (particularly experienced passive-design professionals) and building-specific energy modeling, expertly conducted.

▶ See the "Energy Modeling" sidebar in Chapter 3.

However, there are some general guidelines you may wish to consult in addition to your experts and/or to assist them in their investigations.

One oft-cited resource is the McKinsey report, "U.S. Greenhouse Gas Emissions: How Much at What Cost?"[16] The report ranks a wide range of measures for reducing greenhouse gas emissions (GHG) by their cost per ton. While in its scope the report goes far beyond residential building opportunities, it contains some findings worth noting, highlighted in Figure 2-16.

As shown in Figure 2-16, four types of residential energy efficiency measures – shown below the horizontal line representing cost-neutrality – offer greater payback than cost. In other words, they generate more savings in operating costs than they cost to implement up front. Those measures are:

- Electronics

- Lighting

- Shell improvements

- Water heaters

The graph shows two additional strategies (above the line) that, while they don't offer positive cost savings, are still quite cost-effective by the metric utilized for this analysis – they cost less than $50 per ton of avoided GHG emissions:

- Building shell retrofits

- HVAC equipment efficiency improvements

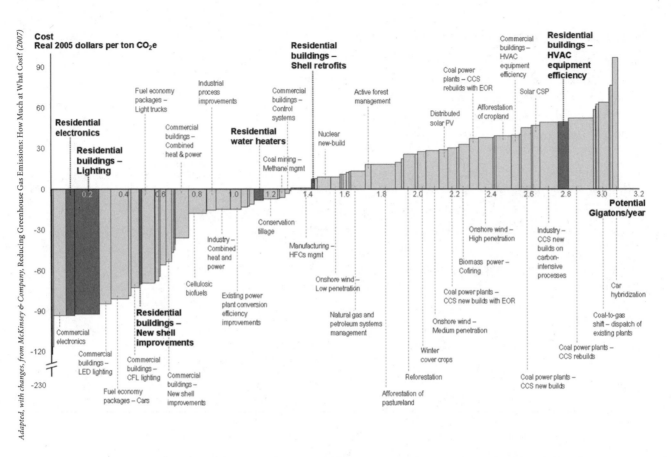

FIGURE 2-16. RELATIVE COST-EFFECTIVENESS OF DIFFERENT OPTIONS TO REDUCE GHG EMISSIONS

Another helpful resource is *Maximizing Residential Energy Savings: Net Zero Energy Home Technology Pathways*, by R. Anderson and D. Roberts. The report, published by NREL, describes reference packages of climate-specific energy-saving measures that the Building America program has found to be highly cost-effective for single-family homes in each of the climates identified in the report.

Building America is a federal program, developed by the US Department of Energy as a public-private partnership initiative to identify next-generation housing technologies that are highly cost-effective. The Building America program has been working toward the goal of NZE for some time.

The Building America reference packages are shown in Figure 2-17. The NREL report states about the packages that "an additional 20% in whole-house efficiency savings relative to the Building America benchmark (equivalent to 40% in additional savings relative to a 50% house[17]) is required to achieve net ZEHs by 2020. The 50% technology packages combine a ZEH-ready envelope with best available equipment … These packages are provided as examples, not as prescriptive specifications or requirements. Alternative or equivalent approaches may also be appropriate, depending on building type, location, and builder and homeowner preferences."[18]

Note that because their efforts are aimed at transforming mainstream construction practices, the paramount goal is *cost-effectiveness*. Thus the packages represent integrated approaches resulting in a net cost of ownership equal to or only slightly greater than that of conventional homes of the same size, in the same region. These packages are therefore an excellent starting point for considering what *your* package of efficiency measures might be.

▶ See **www.eere. energy.gov/buildings/ building_america/** for more information about Building America.

	Marine (Seattle)	Hot Humid (Houston)	Hot/Mixed Dry (Phoenix)	Mixed Humid (Atlanta)	Cold (Chicago)
HDD / CDD	4,854 / 191	1,430 / 2,346	1,117 / 3,888	2,763 / 1,310	5,984 / 668
Wall assembly	2x6, R-21 cavity + 1.5" continuous	2x6, R-21 cavity	2x6, R-19 cavity	2x6, R-21 cavity	2x6, R-21 cavity + 1" continuous
Ceiling assembly	R-50	R-30	R-30	R-40	R-50
SLA / ACH50	.00015 / 2.6	.00015 / 2.6	.0003 / 5.3	.00015 / 2.6	.00015 / 2.6
Glazing	low-E/std SHGC, argon fill (U-0.29, SHGC 0.30)	low-E/low-SHGC (U-0.30, SHGC 0.26)	low-E/low-SHGC (U-0.30, SHGC 0.26)	low-E/low-SHGC (U-0.30, SHGC 0.26)	triple-pane low-E (U-0.25, SHGC 0.35)
Air conditioning	SEER 15+	SEER 15+	SEER 13	SEER 15+	SEER 18
Heating	AFUE 90+ furnace or HSPF 8.8+ heat pump	AFUE 90+ furnace or HSPF 8.8+ heat pump	AFUE 80 furnace or HSPF 8.1 heat pump	AFUE 90+ furnace or HSPF 8.8+ heat pump	AFUE 90+ furnace or AHSPF 9.2+ heat pump
Water heating	gas tankless, EF 0.8+ or premium electric, EF 0.95+ w/64-sf closed-loop solar thermal system	gas tankless, EF 0.8+ or premium electric, EF 0.95+ w/32-sf integrated collector/ storage solar thermal system	gas tankless, EF 0.8+ or electric, EF 0.9+	gas tankless, EF 0.8+ or premium electric, EF 0.95+ w/64-sf closed-loop solar thermal system	gas tankless, EF 0.8+ or premium electric, EF 0.95+ w/64-sf closed-loop solar thermal system

FIGURE 2-17. BUILDING AMERICA 50% ENERGY SAVINGS PACKAGES

Note: All acronyms in the figure above are listed in the Table of Acronyms and Abbreviations and defined in Chapter 4.

ENDNOTES

1   U stands for thermal conductance of windows and is defined in Chapter 4.

2   ACH stands for air changes per hour, Pa for Pascals; ACH is defined in Chapter 4.

3   Navigant Consulting, California Energy Commission, PIER Buildings Program, CPUC Zero Energy Home and Commercial Building Initiative, Final Report, August 22, 2008.

4   Navigant Consulting, Zero Energy Home and Commercial Building Initiative, Final Report.

5   Performance with respect to other net-zero definitions was not available.
Personal communication, Mike Keesee, Sacramento Municipal Utility District, September 2009.

6   Keesee presumably means that solar and efficiency features make economic sense, notwithstanding occupant behaviors that may drive energy use up beyond expectations.

7   Mike Keesee, SMUD, "Zero Energy Buildings – Transforming Sacramento's New Construction Market," presented at ASHRAE Net-zero conference, San Francisco, March, 2009.

8   Mark Fischer, Grupe Homes, "Selling Green to Earn Green: The Market Advantage," http://www.globalgreen.org/i/file/Green%20Urbanism/Global%20Green%20Grupe.ppt

9   *The Ryness Report*, http://www.ryness.com/p-the-ryness-report.htm

10 Housing such as single-room occupancy buildings, homeless shelters, and transitional housing are exempt from the individual electric-metering requirement; before the introduction of virtual net metering, only such projects could credit the solar electricity they generated to the dwelling units.

11 Ted Bardacke, Global Green, personal communication, September 2009.

12 Navigant Consulting, Zero Energy Home and Commercial Building Initiative, Final Report.

13 "Net Zero in Canada," *Energy Design Update*, September 2008.

14 See US Census Department reports: "Value of Private Construction Put in Place - Seasonally Adjusted Annual Rate," January 2009 through May 2009, http://www.census.gov/const/C30/privsahist.pdf, and "Value of Private Construction Put in Place - Seasonally Adjusted Annual Rate," March 2009 through July 2009, http://www.census.gov/const/C30/privsa.pdf.

15 Peter Shoemaker, Pacific Gas & Electric Company, personal communication, August 2009.

16 McKinsey & Company, *Reducing U.S. Greenhouse Gas Emissions: How Much and at What Cost?* www.mckinsey.com/clientservice/ccsi/pdf/us_ghg_emission_slideshow.pdf

17 By "a 50% house," NREL is referring to a house that is 50 percent more efficient than its code-compliant counterpart.

18 R. Anderson and D. Roberts, Maximizing Residential Energy Savings: Net Zero Energy Home Technology Pathways, Appendix A, National Renewable Energy Laboratory Technical Report NREL/TP-550-44547, November 2008.

3 Integrated Design

What Is Integrated Design, and Why Does It Matter?

Integrated design is a layered and iterative process of collaboration among design professionals, in contrast to a more typical design process, which is sequential and linear. The integrated design process recognizes that each aspect of building design influences the others. The collaboration among contributors is critical, as it enables the team to address the whole building as an integrated *system of systems*, each inextricable from the others, and to identify potential design synergies.

I like what Wikipedia says about integrated design:

> **Integrated design** is a collaborative method for designing buildings which emphasizes the development of a holistic design.

> Conventional building design usually involves a series of hand-offs from owner to architect to builder to occupant. This path does not invite all affected parties into the planning process, and therefore does not take into account their needs, areas of expertise or insights. In some cases, using the conventional method, incompatible elements of the design are not discovered until late in the process when it is expensive to make changes. In contrast, the integrated design process requires multidisciplinary collaboration, including key stakeholders and design professionals, from conception to completion. Decision-making protocols and complementary design principles must be established early in the process in order to satisfy the goals of multiple stakeholders while achieving the overall project objectives.

In addition to extensive collaboration, integrated design involves a "whole building design" approach. A building is viewed as an interdependent system, as opposed to an accumulation of its separate components (site, structure, systems and use). The goal of looking at all the systems together is to make sure they work in harmony rather than against each other.

Integrated design, to the uninitiated, may seem messy, time-consuming, and inefficient: *Haven't we been over this territory before?* However, hundreds, perhaps thousands of green building design teams have consistently concluded that it's the best way to achieve truly green, high-performance buildings.

The term "integrated" refers to two things: first the desired outcome – an integrated design *solution* that is harmonized, optimized, and considers all interacting parts and systems in a holistic fashion. It also reflects the *process* by which such a solution is achieved – a process that some call "integrative" ("performing or tending toward" integration) rather than "integrated." Either term works, but I prefer the latter because it reinforces the notion that it's not just the ultimate design but also the process itself that needs to be integrated.

The *American Heritage Dictionary, 4th edition*, defines the verb *integrate* as, "To make into a whole by bringing all parts together; unify." It defines an integrated circuit as "A complex set of electronic components and their interconnections …"

All of these definitions converge on two central points:

> **An integrated design team is one that is unified by coming together to work as a whole.**
> and
> **In an integrated building design, the building components and their interconnections are brought together into a unified whole.**

Integrated design has been embraced by some highly respected academics and is being elevated to a technical discipline. At Stanford University's Center for Integrated Facility Engineering (CIFE), director Martin Fischer and his team members practice what Fischer refers to as extreme collaboration. This is a form of integrated design in which design teams are brought together to work intensively for a concentrated period of time to produce a finished design product at the end.[1] The CIFE's objectives include partner companies achieving significant reductions in construction time, on budget, and with measurable improvements in sustainability, as measured by life-cycle costs.[2] I can't think of a better testimonial to the effectiveness of integrated design.

The Integrated Process

Seasoned members of the green building and sustainable development community talk a lot about how essential an integrated design process is to achieving a high-performance project. My experience over the past decade has borne this out. In fact, I have had two related "Aha!" moments in recent years. First, it dawned on me that a well-facilitated (i.e., integrated) design process almost can't help but yield a good project, so we should focus much more on the process, especially in the early stages of design. **Revelation #1: If the process is good, good outcomes will follow.**

A few months later, I realized that there is another essential ingredient: knowledgeable, committed people. **Revelation #2: A good process, carried out by good people, all but guarantees a good project.**

Stated the other way around, you can have a great process, but if your team doesn't have the needed expertise, you might still miss the sweet spot or take quite a bit longer to get there. What inspired this revelation? On a project I had been working on for some time, the team had done everything right – started early, involved all the players, worked collaboratively and iteratively – but just couldn't nail the energy system design . . . until we switched mechanical designers. Then it all fell into place. We had chosen a strong, qualified contributor, just not the right one for this project.

That's why this chapter precedes those that follow, which focus on the substance – the *stuff* – of the design.

Before we proceed to the particulars of integrated design, you should be aware that its positive outcomes include significant gains in efficiency and other aspects of home performance, along with cost savings. Integrated design is about spending more money up front to save money in construction and operations. There's more on this at the end of the chapter.

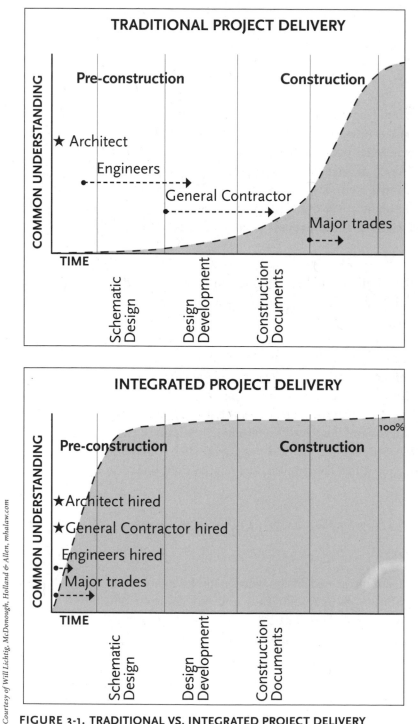

FIGURE 3-1. TRADITIONAL VS. INTEGRATED PROJECT DELIVERY

A conventional (*not* integrated) process with a full complement of design consultants (perhaps more than your project may involve) might look something like this:

1. Owner presents the design charge ("program") to the architect.

2. Architect generates the schematic design.

3. Structural engineer figures out how to make it stand up and with what.

4. Mechanical engineer or contractor figures out how to make it (marginally) comfortable.

5. Interior designer or occupant figures out how to make the interior spaces work.

6. Landscape architect figures out how to make the outdoor spaces work and/or look attractive.

7. General contractor figures out how to build it on time and on budget.

It's worth noting that steps 4-6 sometimes occur during or after construction.

The lead professional in charge of each stage of the process is also responsible – albeit indirectly – for resolving problems created at earlier stages or, at a minimum, compensating for opportunities that were missed because colleagues farther up the chain were not aware of issues that would affect his/her work.

An integrated design process involving the same set of professionals might look something like this instead:

1. Owner, architect, structural engineer, mechanical engineer, interior designer, landscape architect, and general contractor meet for a day or more to discuss the design requirements and begin to generate the schematic design. Everyone contributes, thereby forestalling potential problems and capitalizing on potential design synergies.

2. Everyone leaves with a list of issues that arose during the meeting. Each party then researches or analyzes the issues relevant to his/her discipline, and reports back to the full group about the findings.

3. When the architect has generated a schematic design, it incorporates the input received from all the other parties, and is circulated to them all for comment. Each party, while holding in mind the project's goals, reviews the design and provides comments back to everyone on the team.

4. The work proceeds in this fashion, with full and regular communication among all team members and periodic re-gatherings as needed of the whole team and/or subsets of the team, who continue to resolve collaboratively specific aspects of the design as it evolves.

5. When the drawings and specifications are complete, the builder is already completely familiar with the project and knows that it is workable within the budget and schedule because s/he has participated throughout the process.

As Figure 3-1 illustrates, a successful integrated design project requires the entire team to develop and maintain a common understanding throughout the process.

Phases of the Process

The phases of the integrated design process have been defined variously by different practitioners. I have adapted a process outline originally developed by Bill Reed, shown in the following sidebar.

INTEGRATED DESIGN PROCESS BASICS

1. Explain integrated design to the client before or as you develop the agreement.

2. Assemble team – interview with an emphasis on process and collaboration vs. individual egos.

3. Discovery – get the facts and do initial analysis before design starts.

4. Align the team around values, purpose, process (co-learning – dialogue, development).

5. Identify key form shapers – energy, water, habitat, topography, and materials systems and patterns.

6. Commit to goals and "stretch" (more ambitious) goals.

7. Map the integration process.

8. Conceptualize the *system* designs before starting concept or schematic design of the *building*.

9. Communicate system concepts, using an integrative cost trade-off approach.

10. Work towards whole system synergy using iterative workshops, research, and design steps.

11. Approach construction as a partnering effort.

12. Commission, maintain, and monitor ... forever.

Courtesy of Bill Reed, www.integrativedesign.net

All of the steps Reed identifies are important, and I encourage all readers to delve deeper (one of Reed's favorite phrases) into this topic by reading *The Integrative Design Guide to Green Building: Redefining the Practice of Sustainability*.[3] However, in the section that follows I focus on those phases or activities (paraphrased below) that have particular needs or significance in the context of NZE home projects:

- Setting goals – zero-energy definition and project boundary or scope
- Building your team
- Launching the process
- Promoting teamwork
- Working through the design

Phase 1. Setting Goals

If your great integrated design process, with all the right players, is going to yield the net-zero energy home you aspire to build, the process needs to be firmly grounded in a set of performance goals. All high-performance projects – and net-zero homes are no exception – require setting explicit performance goals. (Without them, it is impossible to know whether you are making progress toward your goals or if, at the end, you have in fact succeeded in meeting them!)

Perhaps not surprisingly, given the amount of space dedicated to the subject in Chapter 1, some of the most important goals relate to how you define net-zero:

- Where will your renewable energy come from?
- How will you define net-zero?
- Do you plan for the project to be fossil fuel-free (all-electric)?
- Which component(s) of household energy use do you plan to offset?

You may have other performance goals, too. Energy-free home developers are also often interested in water conservation, indoor air quality, resource efficiency – in short, a broad sustainability agenda. Many pursue certification or recognition under one or more programs: EPA's ENERGY STAR for Homes and/or Indoor Air Plus, LEED for Homes, the National Green Building Standard, Thousand Home Challenge, Living Building Challenge, Masco's Environments for Living, and/or a state or regional program.

Each program has a unique set of performance criteria, typically mandating the inclusion of specific features ("prerequisites" or "mandatory measures") plus, often, a set of optional measures. Programs vary as to their applicability to different housing types. Figure 3-2 provides an overview of the most widespread national programs and the types of projects to which they apply.

Program	Single-family new homes	Single-family existing homes	Multifamily new homes	Multifamily existing homes
EPA's ENERGY STAR and Indoor Air Plus	X	Gut rehabs only	Up to 3 stories	Gut rehabs only up to 3 stories
LEED for Homes	X	Gut rehabs only	Up to 6 stories incl. mixed-use	Gut rehabs only up to 6 stories incl. mixed-use
National Green Building Standard	X			
Thousand Home Challenge	X	X	X	X
Living Building Challenge	X		X	
Environments for Living	X			

FIGURE 3-2. HIGH-PERFORMANCE HOME PROGRAMS

Appendix C contains URLs and basic descriptions of each program.

It's important to understand the role of these programs in goal-setting. Ideally, the rating or label, per se, isn't the goal; it is simply the "merit badge" attesting to the achievement of the goal. However, the programs can be useful in identifying and making goals more concrete. For example, many of these programs require achieving energy efficiency that is at least 15 percent above code, reducing water consumption by a specified percentage, diverting a set minimum amount of solid waste associated with the project, and so forth.

Many owners and developers have established performance goals before assembling their project team and beginning the design process. If that has not been done for a project that is already underway, it should be done as soon as possible. (*Today.*)

Phase 2. Building Your Team

The next thing you'll need to do is put together a top-notch team. Clients often ask what's better: a design professional who is a specialist (e.g., in green building or energy efficiency) or one who's good in other ways – more experienced, shares the client's aesthetic sensibilities, is well-known, etc. Either can work, but given the choice, I'll always go with *relevant experience* unless there's a deficit in some other area.

Earlier in my career, I designed more than a hundred home remodels. During those years clients frequently asked for my advice about hiring a general contractor. They often had someone in mind. Here's how those conversations would go:

Client: My cousin's husband is a contractor and we would like to use him.

Me: Wonderful. What sort of work does he do?

Client: He installs partitions in office buildings [or he builds new homes for WalBuild].

Me: It's important to work with someone you trust, but it's also important that your contractor have experience doing the type of work you'll be asking him to do. I suggest you find out if he has done work similar to your project before you make a commitment to him.

Of course, what I really wanted to say was, "Don't do it!" Although I usually got my point across more tactfully, sometimes my advice was not heeded, and the outcomes were generally not happy (they were over budget, they were delayed, errors were made, etc.). Relevant experience is tremendously important. You wouldn't consult a podiatrist for an eye problem, right? Of course you wouldn't!

So, what's "relevant experience" when we're talking about a nascent field, with just a handful of completed projects in any given region? Project team members should have a track record doing work that is as similar as possible in nature and scope. That is, they should have experience within the same climate, developing homes of the same general type you will be designing (single-family or multifamily, high-end or more modest), that are energy-efficient and ideally include renewable energy systems. If you have other high-performance goals, their experience should include work on projects that address those added issues (water, indoor air quality, etc.).

The reason for emphasizing prior relevant experience is that achieving net-zero energy use will be challenging, and the more experience and knowledge your team brings to the process, the more smoothly that process is likely to go; you will spend less time while team members become educated and will reduce the likelihood of them overlooking either a problem or an opportunity.

Still, in all likelihood, some or all of the players involved in your project will be new to NZEH projects. Sometimes it's simply not possible to find players who meet your other qualifications *and* have relevant experience. The next best thing to an experienced contributor, of course, is someone who is new to the field but eager, open-minded, creative, flexible, and committed – to both your performance goals and an integrated design process. Because it is a new field, it will be attracting new contributors for years to come.

Past experience *as a team* can also be important. Nadav Malin, president of Building Green, LLC, says, "I've been hearing that a huge indicator of success is whether the team has worked together before (on a similar project). Lots of collaboration is about trust and knowing each other's strengths and weaknesses."

Whom do you need on your team? Much depends on project specifics, but let's assume for the moment that we're talking about one of the following two project types:

- A new, custom, single-family home with a relatively generous budget

- A new, affordable, multifamily housing project

(It may seem odd to discuss these two project types together. However, one of the non-intuitive aspects of high-performance building design is that these project types have considerably more in common than one might suspect.)[4]

I list below the key team participants, the reasons I advocate for their involvement, and what I believe are their critical qualifications. It should go without saying, but nevertheless deserves special emphasis, that in each case the individual in question should be a *skillful* practitioner of his or her discipline. Also note that although each party is referred to as an individual, in fact each may be a collective entity – a company. If that is the case, be sure that specific individuals within those companies will be consistently working on your project and that they personally have the requisite qualifications.

This roster may appear daunting, even alarming in its length; rest assured that not every project may require every one of these participants. In some cases, one party may wear several hats. Some projects by their nature – particularly smaller ones – may successfully be served by a small core team, particularly if the team is very experienced in resource-efficient design. In the vast majority of cases, finding a well-qualified architect is the crucial step; s/he will then guide you in identifying and selecting the other parties who should participate in your design process.

Owner/developer

This may seem obvious, and yet if you, reader, are someone other than the owner or developer, it is worth pointing out that attempting to design a net-zero-energy project without the unwavering commitment of the owner or developer will be an arduous, frustrating, and probably fruitless task.

Architect

Most projects of the types described above have an architect, and this is a good thing. The architect's principal job (in my opinion) is to be the chief integrator. Architects are trained to integrate various priorities – zoning, schedule, budget, aesthetics, function, structure, landscape, etc. – so even if yours is new to high-performance or NZE design, s/he already will be well-versed in the art of juggling. Your architect should be selected for his or her facility for orchestrating different issues, team members, and objectives. That improves the odds that s/he will gracefully manage the addition of another set of issues to those s/he is already juggling. If there is not an architect, someone else on the team needs to be assigned as the design team leader/ chief instigator/integrator.

General contractor or builder

Not typically thought of as part of the *design* team, the builder nevertheless *should* be included during design. S/he, more than anyone else on your team, knows what it takes to translate drawings and words into reality. This is insight and wisdom you should not be without. If you've ever baked a cake with kids, you know what a difference experience in the kitchen makes – without it, even with the best recipe, the process is sloppy and inefficient at best, downright inedible at worst. A good builder will get competitive cost proposals from subcontractors, and so protect your financial interests. Importantly, the contractor will also advise on the cost implications of various options, providing a reality check and identifying savings that you might not be aware of without this early assistance.

Early selection of a builder may require foregoing the process of getting competitive cost proposals.[5] However, many contractors will work on a pre-construction contract, which allows you to get the benefit of their expertise without locking in longer-term.

In a recent article, David Cohan of the Northwest Energy Efficiency Alliance makes a very effective case for the general contractor's early involvement: "No matter how good the design, nothing will come of it if the builders don't follow it closely throughout construction. Buildings are never built exactly according to design, because portions of the design itself are flawed, the specified materials or equipment aren't available, less expensive substitutes exist, or the builder simply thinks s/he knows a better or easier way to do it. While a modification to the design during construction doesn't always result in higher energy use, increased energy use will be the likely outcome, unless the builder has a complete understanding of the intent of the design, as well as its technical aspects."[6]

Mechanical-electrical-plumbing (MEP) consultants

Many residential projects, particularly single-family homes, do not have MEP design consultants; instead, these systems are designed by the HVAC, electrical, and plumbing subcontractors. If you do *not* engage MEP consultants, by all means get your subs involved early in the design process along with your general contractor. The mechanical (heating, cooling, and water heating) systems in particular are a huge determinant of a successful NZE design, so failing to get expert input on these systems – which interact with many other aspects of the building design, sometimes in complex ways – could result in many significant missed opportunities.

A word of caution regarding using subcontractors as design consultants: there is an inherent conflict of interest for them, as smaller systems (such as an efficient home will require) mean a smaller contract for them. Subs are also often resistant to design innovations. Another argument in favor of engaging a mechanical engineer in particular is that s/he should have knowledge of a wide range of options, whereas a subcontractor is likely to specialize in just one type of system, e.g., radiant heating *or* forced air.

Now that we've established that you should have MEP consultants involved – and early – let's talk about their qualifications. This is the tough part. In my home state of California, there aren't many MEPs who are facile with green building design; and most of those who are focus exclusively on commercial construction, so finding a creative, energy-savvy, residential MEP contributor for your team can be very, very challenging. You should try anyway, for you may find them in unexpected places. They may not identify themselves as MEP consultants but as solar

▶ A brief description of different contracting models can be found in The Engineering Toolbox, **www. engineeringtoolbox. com/contract- types-d_925.html.**

system vendors, hydronic heating contractors, or energy analysts – so persist. In some cases, if you are fortunate enough to find an architect or builder who has NZEH experience, s/he may be knowledgeable enough about building systems to act as the MEP consultant. This is rare, but an excellent alternative. If your architect has prior NZEH experience, s/he also may have experience working with MEPs on those projects and thus be able to recommend qualified candidates.

Energy analyst/modeler

The energy analyst/modeler needs to be an integral part of your team. Ideally, s/he will also be your MEP consultant or will be employed by the MEP firm. This is highly desirable because energy modeling is central to the process of arriving at a high-performance, net-zero project. If it is handled separately, the integration between design decisions and modeling can be somewhat more challenging. Either way, whether your energy analyst is part of the MEP firm or unaffiliated with it, s/he needs to appreciate fully his/her role as an active contributor *to the design process*. I emphasize this because such a role is somewhat unusual, particularly in places like California where historically energy modeling has been used primarily as a way to demonstrate regulatory compliance.

In NZE projects, since the role of the energy analyst is larger than on other projects, you can expect to pay a higher-than-normal fee for this service. It is a good investment. Your energy modeler will be instrumental in identifying the aspects of the building design that are central to minimizing building energy loads – saving you money on your utility bills. Pay now, or pay later to the utility company.

Renewables consultant/vendor

Because renewable energy is a field that is growing exponentially, there are a lot of new kids on the block. Some of them are very knowledgeable, but as in other areas, there's no substitute for experience. Admittedly, many of the technologies are relatively new, so "experienced" is a relative term. Even so, seek design-build firms that have a solid track record and, ideally, sell more than one manufacturer's products. Just as you might shy away from the investment advice of a financial advisor who sells investment products from one source alone, so might you be wary of a sole-source provider of alternative energy products – they may be biased. This doesn't necessarily make them less knowledgeable or less objective: experience may have led them to believe that certain products are superior, but how are you to know?

Another consideration in choosing a vendor is whether they offer multiple types of renewable energy systems – photovoltaics, solar hot water (sometimes called solar thermal), wind, hydro – or just one. Ideally, work with a vendor with solid

► In California, some indications that an energy modeler may be a good candidate include being a member of the California Association of Building Energy Consultants (CABEC) and/or being a Certified Energy Plans Examiner (CEPE) or Certified Energy Analyst (CEA). CEPE and CEA are credentials issued by CABEC; the requirements for CEA are greater than those for CEPE. See **www.cabec.org** for more information and for rosters of CEAs and CEPEs.

experience, a good reputation, and who sells multiple systems. Such a vendor will be neither brand-biased nor technology-biased.

Landscape architect or designer

The site and landscape can be an important element in managing energy loads. Your landscape designer should be well-versed in passive design methods, understanding orientation issues and utilizing natural forces such as wind, sun, shade, evergreen/deciduous plants, and material selections to support energy-reduction strategies. Some architects also act as landscape architects or may have sufficient landscape design knowledge to inform the project through early stages of design and/or construction.

Civil engineer

Especially for large and/or more rural sites, the civil engineer can make important contributions related to grading, infrastructure, storm water management, paving, and other land management issues.

Interior, lighting, and/or daylighting designers

Some architects and interior designers do daylighting analysis and design, though this is a relatively rare skill. Some also do lighting design, though lighting is often handled by a dedicated lighting designer. Sometimes, on single-family home projects, the electrician, the general contractor, or the homeowner is the de facto lighting designer. Thoughtful, knowledgeable daylighting and energy-efficient lighting design can be important contributions to the project.

Electrical engineer or designer

Electrical engineers are relatively uncommon on residential projects, particularly small and/or low-rise projects. Nevertheless, their specialized expertise can be immensely valuable in developing strategies to minimize power loads, size renewable energy systems, inform the lighting design, etc. Your mechanical system designer may assist in deciding whether to also engage an electrical designer and in identifying qualified candidates.

Building scientist

A somewhat sparse population, building scientists are specialized in understanding the physics of air, heat, and moisture in buildings. They are extremely knowledgeable about energy, indoor air quality, and durability, and the related systems and design issues. They're not listed in the yellow pages, however; your best bet to identify a qualified building scientist is to contact one of the Building America teams (listed at **www.eere.energy.gov/buildings/building_america/research_teams.html**)

or check the membership rosters of organizations such as the Energy and Environmental Building Association (**EEBA.org**). Also see the Chapter 4 sidebar "What Is Building Science and Why Does It Matter?" (Note that even the term "building scientist" is somewhat obscure and lacks a universal definition; the one given above is reasonably well-understood within the energy efficiency community.)

Now you know what skills are important to your NZE home project. If you have assembled a team already, you should survey the team members to find out what their experience and skills are relative to your needs, identify any voids, and fill the voids. You may be able to fill the voids from member firms that are already participating or via referrals from existing team members. Word of mouth is always the best way to find good design professionals. Resort to online referral sources or the yellow pages only as a last resort. If you find that you need to issue a request for qualifications (RFQ) or request for proposals (RFP), be sure to define your needs as precisely as possible, or you are likely to get proposals that are sufficiently dissimilar that comparing them may be difficult.

Phase 3. Launching the Process

Commit to an integrated design process

I have had the good fortune to work with a number of clients developing high-performance residential projects. Some have also made an early commitment to an integrated design process. Some have not. Some have engaged in a somewhat or partially integrated design process. Some have engaged in an integrated process, but relatively late in design. My empirical observation is that the higher the performance goals for the project, the more critical it is that the team engage in a comprehensive integrated design process, begun as early as possible. Achieving an energy-free home is a very high performance goal indeed; even the process of arriving at a satisfactory definition can be somewhat taxing. Therefore, it is wise to make a formal commitment to integrated design and to ensure that all team members are prepared to support it. Ideally, that agreement will be memorialized in everyone's contracts.

Hold a charrette

An integrated design process frequently begins with a charrette[7] or eco-charrette, an intensive design workshop, in which the entire project team comes together (often for the first time) to set goals and identify strategies for achieving the desired outcomes.

▶ Should word of mouth fail you, directories of green building professionals are available at:

www. buildingconcerns. com/nocal/ (Northern California only)

www. greenhomeguide.com/

www.directory. greenbuilder.com/ search.gbpro

A charrette is an excellent way (arguably, the *only* way) to launch an integrated design process. As mentioned above, the owner, architect, structural engineer, mechanical engineer, interior designer, landscape architect, and general contractor should all participate – as should other team members, if any.

Here are some suggestions for getting the most out of the charrette:

1. Schedule it with consideration for as many participants' constraints as possible. (**Doodle.com** is a free, easy-to-use, web-based scheduling utility that simplifies this process.)

2. Draft an agenda that includes all critical design and planning issues. Assign time blocks to your topics, and be prepared to enforce the time limits and/or adjust the schedule as needed to accommodate the direction the discussion takes. Include regular breaks, and reserve at least a half hour for a

Time		Topic/LEED category	Green consultant	Developer	City	Architect	Associate architect	Construction mgr	General contractor	MEP	Civil engineer	Landscape architect	Structural engineer
	Agenda & Consultant Participation												
9:30		Introductions	●	●	●	●	●	●	●	●			
9:45	EA	Energy & Atmosphere	●	●	●	●	●	●	●	●			
10:45	EQ	Indoor Environmental Quality	●	●	●	●	●	●	●	●			
11:30	WE	Water Efficiency	●	●	●	●	●	●	●	●	●	●	
12:15	SS	Sustainable Sites	●	●	●	●	●	●	●	●	●	●	
12:45		Lunch + intros of new arrivals, overview of green goals	●	●	●	●	●	●	●	●	●	●	●
1:45	MR	Materials & Resources	●	●	●	●	●	●	●	●		●	●
2:30	ID	Innovation & Design Process	●	●	●	●	●	●	●	●			●
3:30	AE	Awareness & Education	●	●	●	●	●	●	●				
3:45		Next Steps & Responsibilities	●	●	●	●	●	●					
4:15		Incentive Programs/Other	●	●	●	●							
4:30	LL	Location & Linkages	●	●	●								
4:45		Adjourn											

● = *Please attend; attendance during other portions is optional.*

FIGURE 3-3. SAMPLE CHARRETTE AGENDA

closing discussion. Circulate the agenda to your participants in advance, and ask for their input. (See Figure 3-3.)

3. Make sure that the right people will be present to address the issues you plan to cover. If some of your participants can only attend part of the workshop, structure the agenda accordingly.

4. Provide advance information to the design team, including goals, program, budget, client lifestyle, sensibilities, and concerns, and potential challenges such as poor solar access, noise, or views.

5. Assign a facilitator, preferably one with prior experience. This might be your architect, one of your consultants, or even yourself. Assign someone else to take notes. (An alternative is to photograph the boards or flip charts and later have them transcribed. If so, label, date, and number them so they can be put in proper sequence.)

6. Hold the charrette in a comfortable setting with good chairs, daylight and views, a place to stretch, and plenty of table space to sketch and lay out drawings, models, etc.

7. Make sure to have appropriate audiovisual aids: white boards, flip charts, markers, slide projector, etc.

8. Provide ample (and good quality) food and drink throughout – snacks, coffee breaks, meals. The event should be fun, informal, and non-stressful.

9. Establish facilitation ground rules at the beginning of the charrette. It's important to include a "bike rack" – the place where off-topic ideas get "parked" for later discussion (either later in the charrette or at a later date).

10. Have someone volunteer to serve as the "heartless timekeeper" – this person will keep the group on the assigned timetable.

11. Also make someone responsible for recording follow-up actions, each of which should be assigned to a specific individual. Review this list at the conclusion of the charrette.

▶ Architect Greg VanMechelen comments, "Sometimes it is fun to switch roles. Let the MEP have a go at landscaping." This can yield some creative and unexpected results.[8]

Phase 4. Promoting Teamwork

Have regular meetings

The charrette will get you off to an excellent start. (If you have a project already underway, it's still likely of great value to hold a charrette, even if some design decisions have already been made; you'll just need to develop an agenda that will give you the greatest leverage with the decisions still ahead.)

Post-charrette, additional targeted meetings will be needed to address specific issues and design challenges. These can either be planned in advance, with specific topics in mind (e.g., mechanical system design, materials selections, landscape design), or scheduled as specific needs are identified. How do you know when a meeting is needed? A typical signal is when an issue crops up that can't readily be answered by one party. Another signal is when the answer to a question or design problem contains the key phrase, "it depends …" The thing or things upon which "it depends" will likely indicate who needs to be brought into the meeting.

Meetings most frequently involve a subset of the key team members: for example, architect, contractor, and mechanical consultant. Less often, the whole team may need to be reconvened. Nancy Malone of Siegel & Strain Architects in Emeryville, California, says, "I am a fan of grouped follow-up meetings, such as the site team, the energy team, etc." Many "meetings" may take place via conference call, webinar, or even detailed email exchanges.

Establish communication protocols

Before leaving the charrette, decide how subsequent communications will be handled. In addition to assigning an individual to each follow-up or action item, designate a single individual to ride herd on the other team members, to ensure that they complete their research and analysis tasks on time and that the information gleaned is shared with other team members. That responsibility belongs to someone (generally, the architect or team leader) who has a good grasp of the systems interactions that influence overall building performance. This way s/he will be alert to the potential need to involve specific team members as issues arise.

For example, the envelope affects HVAC sizing. Windows affect lighting loads. The lighting design affects cooling loads. Waste heat from one process can be pre-heating for another. And so on. The person assigned to monitor the design development

FACILITATION GUIDELINES

• Speak one at a time.

• Be concise – share the air-time.

• Listen as an ally.

• Say what you are thinking.

• Keep the focus here (stay offline, silence cell phones).

• Queue to speak.

• Follow-on comments are encouraged.

• Put off-topic thoughts in the parking lot (bike rack).

• Carpe diem. Enjoy.

Above courtesy of Doug Brookman, Public Solutions, Baltimore, Maryland

VanMechelen suggests that an idea, once stated in a collaborative meeting, does not belong to the individual but to the group. This avoids anyone taking undue credit, and more importantly, helps eliminate reticence that may cause an individual not to contribute, lest his/her idea prove to be unworkable.[9]

▶ What do we call this person whose job it is to facilitate the integrated design process? So far, a consensus job title has not yet emerged. I'm known as the den mother when I fulfill this role for project teams.

process and alert team members when they need to consult with one another needs to understand these and other relevant relationships among the building components.

What constitutes sufficient communication? When in doubt, it's better to err on the side of too much information than too little – particularly where email is concerned; it's easy to scan and delete (or file) an email that doesn't require your attention, but the sender can rest easy. If you had something to contribute to the resolution of the issue, you would weigh in; if you didn't, no harm was done by including you. It may be helpful to adopt a specific email protocol – e.g., if you're among those in the To: field of an email, you are expected to reply. If you're on the cc: line, responding is optional.

PROJECT MANAGEMENT AIDS

Consider using a project management system to organize and archive project team communications. We use Basecamp (**www.37signals.com**) for this purpose. Although it does have some shortcomings, it is very useful in capturing and saving all emails generated from within the project's Basecamp work space as well as the replies to those emails, even when the replies originate in the respondent's email program. It also provides a central and well-designed repository for files and a number of other helpful, project-oriented features.

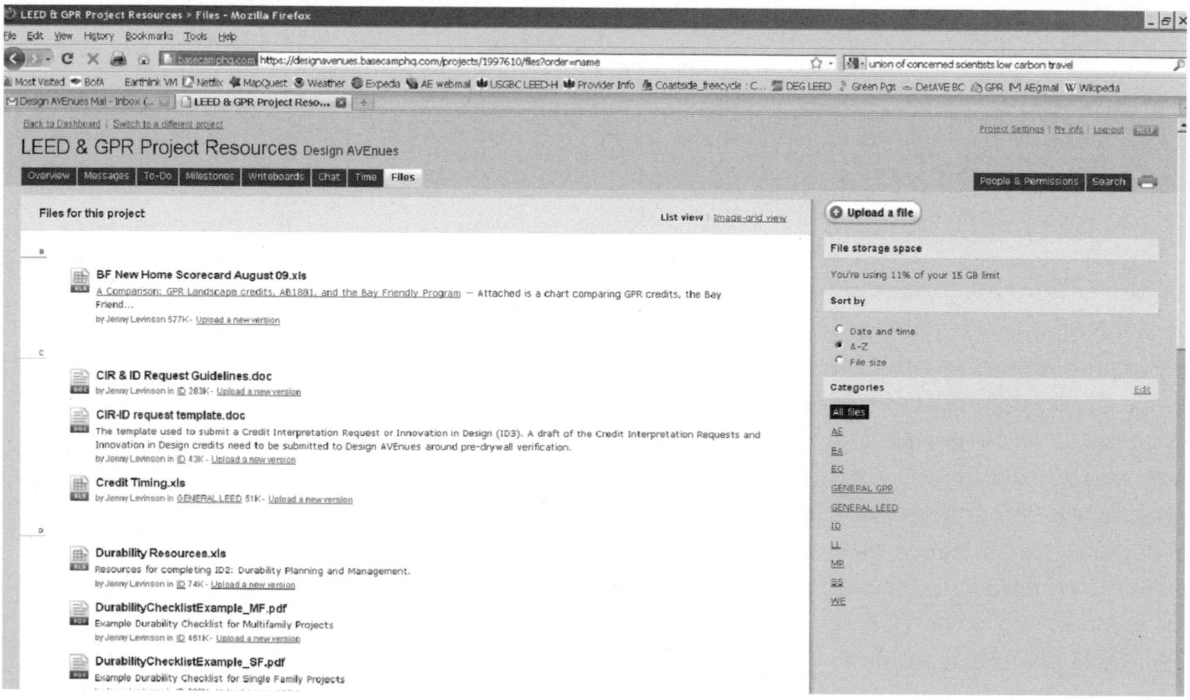

FIGURE 3-4. BASECAMP SAMPLE PAGE

The most important aspect of project communications is *documenting decisions made*. Different project teams have different mechanisms for documenting decisions internally. Ultimately, though, the final repository for all design decisions is the construction document set: drawings, specifications, and/or scopes of work. When project teams are working "outside the box" – as they are when operating in the uncharted territory of designing NZE homes – they've been known to forget to document some of their agreements, sometimes with unfortunate consequences.

A couple of years ago, one of my builder clients called me to ask for advice in dealing with a subcontractor who had failed to supply the agreed-upon low-flow plumbing fixtures. When I asked if this agreement had been included in the sub's contract, the builder paused and then slowly responded, "No …" Notwithstanding all the things that may be new and different about developing energy-free projects, some things remain the same – contracts are the means by which we hold everyone accountable. They are arguably more important than ever in projects that transcend the ordinary.

Thus three things need to be established at the outset of the process:

- A mechanism for logging decisions, readily accessible to all team members and to which all can contribute (this could be a Basecamp "writeboard," a Google Groups document, or another shared resource that includes, at a minimum, the nature of the decision, the date logged, other team members who contributed to the decision, and the name of the person logging it); in architecture firms meeting notes are used for this purpose.

- A point person designated to monitor the log regularly and prompt team members for updates.

- A means of ensuring that all parties are bound by the decisions reached by the team.

At key project milestones – when construction documents are 50 percent complete, 100 percent complete, and/or at other significant points – one or more team members should be charged with checking those documents to ensure that all aspects of the agreed-upon design, including equipment and material specifications, have been incorporated in the construction documents. If the project is pursuing LEED or other ratings/certifications, the responsible parties should be sure those requirements have been addressed, too.

MIND MAPS

Mind maps are an increasingly popular means of generating and recording ideas of individual designers and of collaborating on design projects. Mind-mapping software was used extensively by a team developing a high-performance home project in Portola Valley, California. Team member Mary Davidge, the project's interior designer, attested that the mind-mapping was crucial in helping them optimize many aspects of the design. Among the many innovations that their integrated design process yielded was combining the ground source heat pump ground loops with the structural piers for the home, resulting in significant savings. A sample mind map from their project is shown here.

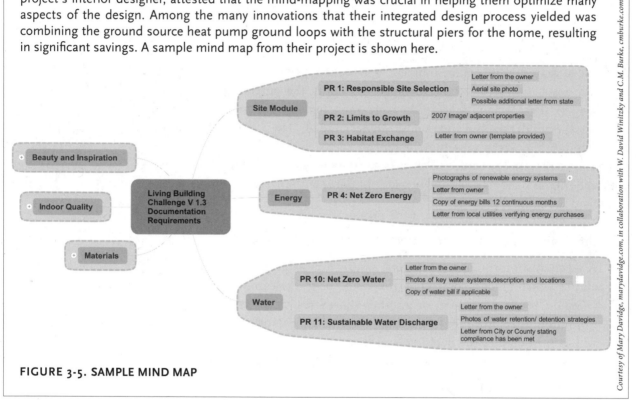

Courtesy of Mary Davidge, marydavidge.com, in collaboration with W. David Winitzky and C.M. Burke, cmburke.com

FIGURE 3-5. SAMPLE MIND MAP

Identify scope of responsibilities and interactions for all parties

Each member of the project team will influence multiple aspects of the design, so besides having a den mother or someone in a comparable role, it is also important to anticipate probable overlaps between disciplines. Before embarking on your integrated design process, develop the list of interactions and parties as completely as possible for your project, based on your set of players. Plan to update the list regularly as the project progresses, because it is likely that you will not fully anticipate all the interactions in advance.

Figure 3-6 shows a few representative overlaps and the parties who should typically be involved in addressing those design and/or construction issues.

You may wish to develop a table like this, using a matrix format similar to the sample agenda shown in Figure 3-3, substituting all the major and minor design decisions for the charrette topic areas, and then indicating the parties who should be involved in those decisions in each row.

Issue	Parties involved
Landscape design/shading	Landscape architect, MEP, energy modeler
Hot water distribution	MEP, owner, architect, builder, energy modeler
Water heating system	MEP, renewables vendor, builder, energy modeler
Ventilation/air quality	MEP, energy modeler, structural, builder, energy modeler
Heating & cooling system(s)	MEP, architect, builder, energy modeler
Materials selection (e.g., cool roofing, paving)	Architect, landscape architect, owner, builder, energy modeler

FIGURE 3-6. TYPICAL DESIGN INTERACTIONS REQUIRING INTEGRATION

Note that in the example above, the builder and energy modeler are almost always involved, as is the architect. They appear in nearly every line of the table because the builder/general contractor will have important input on all aspects of the design as to constructability and cost, as well as on sequencing and availability of materials, equipment, and appropriately skilled labor resources. The energy modeler is involved in the many issues that affect energy performance. The modeler's performance input combined with the contractor's input on cost and constructability will be critical in shaping the decisions about those systems.

Design thrice, measure twice, cut once

All of this may sound orderly and productive – and it can be, truly. However, because design professionals are accustomed to operating in the sequential, hand-off model, it may not unfold in quite such an orderly way, for several reasons:

- Team members may forget that they need to check their decisions with others – habit can overcome good intentions.

- Team members may be resistant to altering their habitual and valued methodologies.

- Time pressures and scheduling challenges may tempt the team to skip meetings.

ENERGY MODELING – WHEN AND WHY?

Model early and often. Modeling should not be reduced to a tailpipe exercise, used just to demonstrate compliance with building or energy codes; it is a powerful tool in identifying opportunities to improve the design's energy performance. First, use it to test the energy implications of basic building forms – short and squat vs. tall and narrow, with or without courtyards, whatever basic configurations are feasible and appropriate.

At each design stage, update the model and test alternatives using parametric analysis, evaluating the effect of one variable at a time on energy performance. Use this information, along with constructability and cost data and the impacts on other aspects of design, to gradually refine those aspects and identify features or strategies that offer the best performance bang for the buck.

Modeling should be done:

- Before the charrette (if any design work has been done already),
- During the charrette,
- To test design options,
- To qualify for tax credits and other incentives,
- To comply with green building programs, and
- To capture the performance as accurately as possible!

- When multiple parties are involved in shaping particular design decisions, the ownership of those decisions may appear murky and so cause discomfort.

- Participants may become impatient with revisiting issues in an iterative process, and frustrated at having decisions they perceive as theirs to make scrutinized by others. This is where having a skilled facilitator (diplomat) on the team can be very helpful. The team may need to be reminded that the purpose of the process is to produce a high-performance home, and that their collective wisdom is needed to achieve that end. The objective of iterating is to ensure, as the design is being developed, that the insights of all the team members are factored in to achieve the best possible performance, with no opportunity overlooked. This is "Measure twice, cut once," applied at the macro level. Perhaps it should be restated, "*Design thrice*, measure twice, cut once." You want the design to be right before the plans ever show up in the carpenter's hands for cutting.

Phase 5. Working through the Design

So just exactly *how* does the integrated design process unfold? What are the steps? An integrated process is to a great extent an outcome of the communications protocol established (and followed with discipline) by the design team. However, I do propose some guidelines for how to approach the design process. While there is not necessarily a single right order in which to develop the design, the steps below are ordered to maximize the opportunities for optimizing the building's energy efficiency.

1. Size

How big does your home need to be? This fundamental decision will have enormous influence on everything that follows and should therefore be considered at the outset. Size is discussed in the next chapter.

2. Behavioral factors

The mantra of many professionals involved in high-performance design is to first consider the basic form factors (to be discussed later), then move on to the building enclosure, then to internal loads, and finally to consider occupant behaviors – i.e., what homeowners and tenants do in their homes that use energy: watching TV, doing laundry, listening to music, computing, etc.

Leaving behavioral factors until last, however, may result in some lost opportunities. Building design can potentially influence some of these energy-using behaviors. For example:

- Providing inviting outdoor spaces can encourage people to spend more time outdoors, reducing reliance on energy for heating and cooling as well as reducing use of power-consuming toys and gadgets during those times.

- Incorporating effective passive cooling strategies – particularly cross-ventilation, thermal "chimney" designs, etc. – can also reduce occupants' use of mechanical cooling.

- Homes not occupied all day may not benefit from some systems. For example, the ramp-up time for a radiant floor heating system may make it inappropriate for a home that is only occupied briefly in the mornings and evenings.

Strategies like these can have a significant influence on building form and are easiest to incorporate in the early stages of design. It's important to consider not just today's behaviors, but how occupants' behaviors and needs (and indeed who the occupants are) may change over time.

Providing occupants with data on their energy use can also be very influential on their behavior. Studies have shown that effective energy consumption feedback alone – independent of other energy-saving measures – can reduce residential energy use by as much as 15 percent.[10] A variety of measurement devices and displays are now on the market, ranging substantially in price and sophistication. A selection of products available at the time of publication is provided near the end of Chapter 5. In some cases it may be simple to incorporate such a monitoring system later in the design process; however, like other features of a building, the sooner the need or desire for it is identified, the more smoothly it will be accommodated.

3. Form factors

As is the case for any highly energy-efficient building design, the first considerations are siting, massing, and orientation. Much has been written about these, and I have included selected titles in Appendix A as well as additional information in Chapter 4. In brief, these factors are important to consider at the outset of the design process, when the basic building forms are determined. After the forms start to gel and more specific aspects of the design start to be developed, it becomes very difficult to revisit decisions related to form, and accordingly more difficult to capitalize on the energy opportunities that can be addressed with form-related decisions.

4. Enclosure elements

Once the building's form has been determined and has been optimized for energy performance, its enclosure elements, or skin – roof, walls, floor, and foundation – also need to be optimized. Buildings, like living organisms, have metabolisms, and the purpose of optimizing the enclosure is to make their metabolisms as efficient as possible. Chapter 4 contains a full discussion of how to minimize enclosure loads. The topics covered include structural systems, insulation, roofing, windows, and air leakage control.

5. System and equipment loads

Once the enclosure loads have been minimized, you're ready to tackle the design of the heating and cooling systems, including ducts (if any), the water heating system, lighting, and appliances. System design should address layout/distribution, equipment efficiency, and "right-sizing" – i.e., ensuring that equipment is neither over- nor undersized for the work it will be doing. Effective design and specification of these systems and equipment will minimize the energy needs of the more-or-less permanent[11] features of the building. Chapter 4, "Minimize what your building needs," discusses most of these issues and touches briefly on lighting. Chapter 5, "Minimize the occupants' energy needs," covers lighting and appliances because they are not built into the home, but are rather plug loads and thus subject to occupant selection (if not the first time, then upon replacement). Chapter 5 also provides information on water use, household gadgets, and monitoring systems.

6. Renewable energy

Besides minimizing all the energy demands of and within the building, you'll need to figure out how to supply the remaining energy needs with renewable energy. Of course photovoltaics – solar electricity – is the most popular option at present, followed by solar water heating. Wind energy is also increasingly popular. Other options also exist: micro-hydro power, fuel cells, hydrogen, etc. Chapter 6 discusses these, offering pros and cons, limitations, cost information, and other variables you'll want to consider based on your unique set of constraints and opportunities: site-specifics related to generating capacity, regulatory issues (noise, aesthetics, solar access), and community concerns.

Does Integrated Design Cost More?

I often encounter some initial resistance to the perceived costs of the integrated design process, and particularly of holding a charrette, most often because my client is understandably reluctant to pay the fees of all the professionals involved for a full day or more, on top of what's already been budgeted.

There is ample empirical evidence that an integrated design process, apart from its other benefits, will in all likelihood result in a *reduction in construction costs*. I'm not aware of any survey or statistical data that supports this. I offer two examples, however, for your consideration.

First, the graph shown in Figure 3-7 illustrates the experience of IBACOS, of Pittsburgh, Pennsylvania, in the DOE's Building America program.[12] They found that when they improved a home design in a step-wise fashion, first tightening the building enclosure, then adding high-performance windows, and then improving equipment efficiency, for example, each step added to the construction cost. However, when they instead adopted

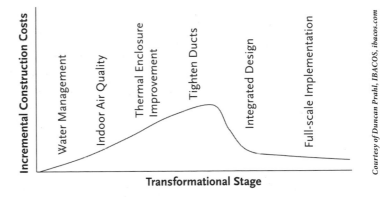

FIGURE 3-7. COST SAVINGS FROM INTEGRATED DESIGN

an integrated design approach, looking at all systems holistically, they found that the overall costs of addressing all the improvements dropped dramatically. The cost increase didn't disappear, because they were creating homes that were no longer the same – the homes were now high-performance rather than garden-variety (merely code-compliant). However, the net increase in cost was much less than it had been when they made improvements one at a time.

The Building Science Consortium, another Building America Team, provided a concrete example of this outcome: improving the insulation levels and thermal performance of windows reduced the heating and/or cooling loads of their homes enough to allow them to put in smaller heating and/or cooling equipment, and the savings from the heating and cooling systems more than paid for the insulation and window improvements.[13]

Scott Shell, an architect with EHDD Architecture in San Francisco who has been involved in many high-performance projects, has this to say about integrated design:

> "Integrated design can reduce construction cost while providing significant sustainable design benefits. On the CSU [California State University] Monterey Bay Library, by comparing a number of integrated structural, mechanical, and architectural schemes, we found that tradeoffs from one discipline more than offset added costs in another, while achieving energy savings of almost 40 percent."[14]

The anecdotal body of experience in the green building community, however, is often not sufficient to overcome the client's cost concerns. This is sometimes – though not always – easily resolved. The opportunity to participate in a project that is setting high performance goals, such as net-zero energy (and potentially LEED Platinum or another comparable "merit badge") is often of great value to design and construction professionals, because this is a growing field and experience of this type can confer significant competitive advantage. And, more often than not, some or all of the project team members may be lacking this experience and will recognize that it will be in their interest to invest some personal time in learning, to better qualify them to participate in such projects.

In such cases, I recommend that the team members be invited to participate in a full-day workshop that will serve as both a continuing education opportunity and a working team meeting. In the charrette, they will learn the principles of high-performance building design, learn the requirements and process elements of any high-performance programs in which the project will be participating, and learn how their work interacts with and influences the work of the other disciplines. The owner should make it clear that attending the charrette – on their own time – is a requirement of participation, an expression of their commitment to the process.

Some professionals might rebel at the notion that they should invest a day or more of their time in this exercise. However, the workshops offer a valuable opportunity for continuing education that the team members will usually appreciate. Most continuing education not only requires committing non-billable hours but also requires paying a fee, and is scheduled at the convenience of the education provider, not of the attendee. So there are several advantages to this arrangement. If you decide to undertake a two-day charrette, it may be possible to split the difference – pay participants for one day and have them participate free of charge the other day.

Of course, if your team members are already seasoned high-performance design professionals, it won't be appropriate to ask them to participate pro bono. Even so, the charrette is a very worthwhile investment – think of it as preventive medicine for a healthy project. If it causes one member of the team to stop and confer with another before making a decision about something that will affect some building system or performance interactions, it will have paid for itself – potentially many times over.

A Footnote about Construction

Achieving net-zero energy isn't just about design; it's inextricably tied to the quality of construction. David Cohan expressed this very succinctly: "A critical area of construction is craftsmanship. Even if the design is followed perfectly, the building will be an energy hog if the quality of construction is poor. For example, windows can be installed so that they are practically airtight or so that they leak like sieves. If the latter is the case, the building will clearly never become a ZEB."[15] Nailing the design is a huge step towards net-zero energy, but construction also requires careful attention.

ENDNOTES

1   Martin Fischer, Stanford Center for Integrated Facility Engineering, personal communication, Fall 2008.

2   http://cife.stanford.edu/Mission/index.html.

3   7Group and William Reed, *The Integrative Design Guide to Green Building: Redefining the Practice of Sustainability* (New Jersey: Wiley, 2009).

4   Projects of both types tend to include a full complement of design professionals and – for entirely different reasons – often have the highest environmental goals: high-end custom projects due to owner commitments and affordable projects due to funding agency mandates.

5   I've worked on single-family and multifamily projects where the general contractor was selected early on, through a competitive process, and then worked actively with the rest of the project team throughout design and cost-estimating.

6   David Cohan, Northwest Energy Efficiency Alliance, "Zero-energy buildings: all the pieces of the puzzle," *Trim Tab,* 03 Quarter 2009.

7   *Charrette* is a French word meaning "cart," and alludes to the earliest days of architecture as a formal discipline taught at the Ecôle des Beaux Arts in Paris. Architecture students, at deadline time, had to deposit their finished projects onto a cart that made the rounds of the studios at a designated hour. The term is now used to mean something quite different, namely, a workshop, or collaborative design or brainstorming session.

8   Greg VanMechelen, VanMechelen Architects, personal communication, September 2009.

9   Greg VanMechelen, VanMechelen Architects, personal communication, September 2009.

10 Sarah Darby, Environmental Change Institute, University of Oxford, "Why, What, When, How, Where and Who? Developing UK Policy on Metering, Billing and Energy Display Devices," *Proceedings of ACEEE Summer Study on Energy Efficiency in Buildings,* Asilomar, CA. August 17-22, 2008.

11 Appliances, of course, are on the "less permanent" end of this spectrum, while heating and cooling equipment are on the "more permanent" end; lighting typically lies somewhere in the middle. All of these systems and equipment items, however, tend to age and be replaced on a shorter cycle than the lifespan of the building as a whole.

12 Building America is a public-private partnership created by the US Department of Energy to foster the creation of the next generation of American housing, incorporating substantial improvements in energy and resource-efficiency, at little or no incremental cost. See www.buildingamerica.gov for further information.

13 Ann Edminster and Betsy Pettit, Building Science Corporation, "Case Studies in Resource-Efficient Residential Building – The Building America Program," http://www.buildingscience.com/documents/reports/RR-9913_Case_Studies_BA_Program.pdf/view?searchterm=edminster (RR-9913).

14 Scott Shell, EHDD Architects, presentation at Greenbuild conference, November 2004.

15 David Cohan, Northwest Energy Efficiency Alliance, "Zero-energy buildings: all the pieces of the puzzle," *Trim Tab,* 03 Quarter 2009.

4

Minimize the Energy Your Building Needs

To minimize a building's energy demands (as distinct from the occupants' energy demands after the home has been built), you can adopt a number of basic strategies. This chapter surveys the spectrum of opportunities for minimizing the building's demands so that none are overlooked as you undertake your NZE design process. Therefore, what follows is a survey of the variables in play, with a brief commentary about each to suggest design avenues that may be open to you in your quest for net-zero energy.

▶ Each topic in this chapter is worthy of a book unto itself, and in fact numerous excellent books have been written on these subjects. Several energy-efficient home design references are listed in Appendix A.

The Basics

Size matters

In all but the mildest of climates, by far the easiest way to minimize the energy demand of your home is to make (or keep) that home as small as possible, relative to the number of people who will live there. Despite the powerful market and broader social forces still at play that whet our appetites for bigger and more elaborate homes, the forces of climate change and peak oil are even more powerful and intransigent, and the writing they are inscribing indelibly on the wall says, **"Small is beautiful."**

In the decades since World War II, the average size of the North American home has steadily increased, while the average household size has steadily decreased. The result: a more than threefold increase in the amount of floor area per person:[1]

- 1950: 292 square feet per person
- 1970: 478 square feet per person (1.6 x 1950)
- 1990: 780 square feet per person (2.7 x 1950)
- 2008: 961 square feet per person (3.3 x 1950)

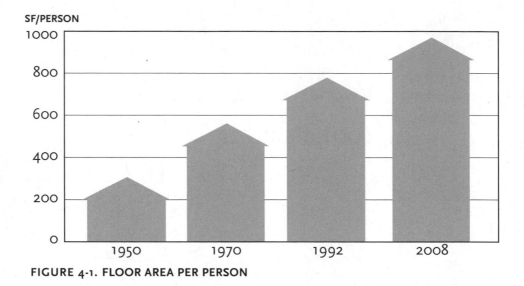

SF/PERSON

FIGURE 4-1. FLOOR AREA PER PERSON

As floor area increases, so do associated per-capita impacts – energy consumption and use of raw materials. Although they increase at a lesser rate than floor area, the overall rates of housing-related energy use and materials use per person have nevertheless climbed consistently over the past half-century. Clearly, with North American housing setting the de facto model standard of living for the rest of the world, it is imperative that we rapidly recalibrate the almighty real estate metric which is the key driver for that standard: square feet.

Interestingly, for the first time in 14 years, the National Association of Home Builders in its 2008 annual housing survey reported a decrease (albeit minor) in the average size of new homes sold over the year before – from 2,479 to 2,459 square feet. [2] (For comparison, the average US home in 1950 was 983 square feet. [3] The average home size in Western Europe is 1,138 square feet.)[4]

Politics and sociology aside, the simple fact remains that a small, energy-efficient home will use less energy than its larger, equally energy-efficient counterpart. Therefore, an energy-free small home will be much easier to create than one that is large. (However, a single-family detached house that is very small (e.g., less than 1,000 square feet) will have a high surface-to-volume ratio, resulting in greater heat loss through the enclosure. Small dwellings with shared surfaces – i.e., multi-family structures – are inherently much more energy-efficient than small detached homes.)

Form factors: the influence of context

The project location has a very large influence on the potentials and strategies of NZE design. Perhaps the overriding location-specific factor is the climate – and microclimate. Climate determines how much heat and cold the building will be subjected to – both the extreme high and low temperatures and the daily and seasonal patterns. A climate with large diurnal (day-to-night) temperature swings dictates a different approach than one that is more consistent. A climate that has extreme heat *and* extreme cold dictates a different solution than a climate that experiences only one of those extremes. A moderate year-round climate is another creature altogether. These factors influence the choice of heating and cooling system, the emphasis on fenestration strategies and/or insulation, the appropriateness of renewable energy applications, and many other aspects of design.

▶ *Fenestration* is the design and placement of windows in a building.

CLIMATE ZONES

In order to aid the design process and in support of energy codes, a number of different North American climate zone systems have been devised.[5] Some of the main ones are listed below.

Building Science Corporation's hygrothermal regions: **www.buildingscience.com/documents/digests/side-bar-hygrothermal-regions/?searchterm=hygrothermal**

US Department of Energy's proposed system of climate zones: **www.energycodes.gov/implement/climatezones_04_faq.stm**

The Federal Building Energy Codes Resource Center's Climate Zone Map of the *2004 Supplement to the International Energy Conservation Code:* **www.resourcecenter.pnl.gov/cocoon/morf/ResourceCenter/article/1420**

The 2009 International Energy Conservation Code: **www.iccsafe.org/e/prodsearch.html?words=3800S09**

The California Energy Commission's 16 California Climate Zones: **www.energy.ca.gov/maps/building_climate_zones.html**

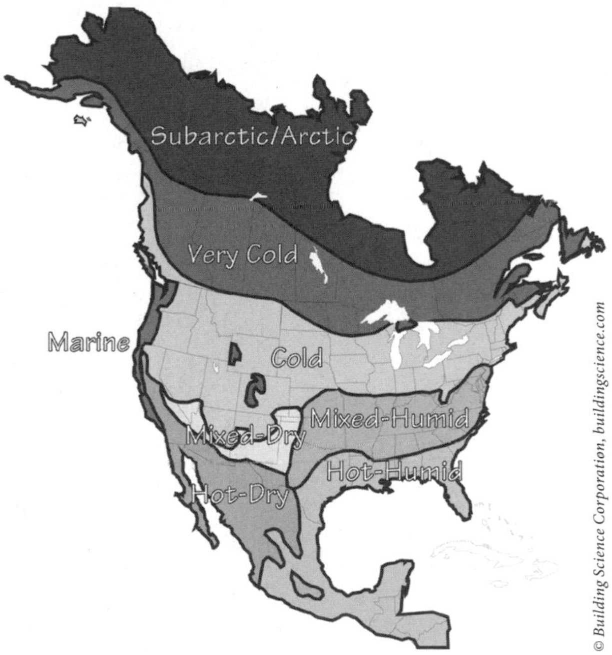

© *Building Science Corporation, buildingscience.com*

FIGURE 4-2.
BUILDING SCIENCE CORPORATION'S HYGROTHERMAL REGIONS

Other aspects of climate that influence energy design are the amount of precipitation, when it occurs and how (in small doses or large), in what form (fog, rain, snow, sleet, etc.) and how long it tends to stick around – each time it happens as well as over how long a season (or seasons). You might not think of precipitation as being a big issue in Phoenix, for example; I certainly didn't before I lived there. It didn't occur to me that rain could be a big deal in the desert. And it isn't … most of the time. But when it rains in the monsoon season, it POURS and pours, and pours some more, and pretty soon the storm drains are overflowing and the water is up past your hubcaps, maybe up to the front stoop of your house. Then it's a very big deal. Another misconception I had about Phoenix was that "it's a dry heat." Again, *mostly* true. But once again, when the monsoons come, it's quite humid *and* very, very hot – a uniquely unpleasant combination. This condition occurs during a relatively brief period each summer, but during that time every year people who are frail, ill, and elderly literally die of the heat. So it is a significant design consideration.

Besides climate, other attributes of place can influence your design in ways similar to climatic factors. For example, nearby natural or human-made features (hills, trees, hedges, buildings, fences, and other structures) can influence the microclimate. They may shade your building site and thereby mediate temperature. They may obstruct (for better or worse) wind and/or views. They also may represent noise sources that influence the enclosure or other aspects of your building design.

The density of the built environment is tremendously influential. In high-density settings, the microclimatic effects of tall buildings are marked. These can include wind tunnel-like effects in streets and other outdoor spaces, dense pools of shade and reduced temperature, and significant limitations to solar access. Although these effects may prove beneficial in some cases, they more typically represent liabilities or constraints.

In more densely-populated locations, you are more likely to be dealing with a tall, thin structure than a low, sprawling one; in addition to all the other influences already noted above, this means the rooftop real estate available to you for solar, wind, skylight, or garden uses is smaller in proportion to the demand than it would be on a more horizontally-oriented building.

Moreover, higher-density projects are typically more constrained as to building orientation. If your residential structure covers a high fraction of your buildable land, the street layout will have a very large influence on the building orientation. Conversely, if you are working with a new, low-density structure on a relatively generous site, you may have the luxury of ignoring the street layout in making building orientation decisions.

A few specific aspects of home energy design to be considered in the context of climate and place are listed below. In general, remodeling or retrofit projects are subject to greater constraints with respect to building form than are new buildings, and high-density projects are more constrained than low-density projects.

Siting

Siting refers to where on the lot the building is placed. It can significantly influence solar access – for passive solar heating, solar hot water, and photovoltaics – as well as access to breezes for passive ventilation cooling. Nearby trees, hedges, and structures (both on- and off-site) may shade the building and/or landscape, which may be either beneficial or detrimental – or both – depending on climate, solar requirements, heating loads, etc.

Massing

Massing roughly describes how the building volume is shaped and distributed. Is the building low or tall, long or short, simple or complex, compact or sprawling? These decisions affect access to sun, shade, natural light, and wind. They also influence energy balance; the lower the surface-to-volume ratio, typically, the lower the rate of heat loss/gain through the building enclosure. Thus – other things being equal – more compact, simple designs are more energy-efficient than more sprawling or complex ones. Massing decisions also will determine how much roof area is available for solar applications.

Orientation

Which way will the building's longest axis be oriented? Which way will most of the windows face? In the northern hemisphere, an east-west orientation is favored for passive solar (optimally energy-efficient) design, to facilitate locating a high proportion of glazing on the building's south side. Besides orientation to the sun, you should consider prevailing wind and storm directions, orientation to neighbors, views, trees, and other landscape features.

▶ See "Doors and Windows" below for a more detailed discussion of window orientation.

Enclosure Design

The enclosure is the boundary between conditioned (heated/cooled) space and unconditioned space and/or the outdoors. The fundamental elements of the enclosure are the walls, roofs, floors, foundations, and openings (doors and windows). I also include here two additional elements: air sealing and shading devices. Air sealing might appropriately be considered a subtopic of walls, roofs, and floors; however, because of its importance in making the building's metabolism as efficient as possible, it deserves to be discussed as a topic unto itself.

Successful NZE enclosure design is grounded in a well-developed understanding of building science, which deals principally with the movement and control of air, heat, and moisture through and within building enclosures. For more information, visit – early and often – **www.buildingscience.com,** a treasure trove of building science resources. I strongly advise the involvement of a capable building scientist on every NZEH project.

WHAT IS BUILDING SCIENCE, AND WHY DOES IT MATTER?

By Peter Yost, Building Green, LLC

Building science is an applied blend of physics, chemistry, and biology. I like to think of the blend this way –

Building is about shelter and creating boundaries between people and the environment. Cells are like buildings. Cells have membranes and even walls that relentlessly observe the laws of physics and chemistry, selectively permitting and excluding passage of all manner of things into and out of the cell, all in an effort to create a secure and comfortable environment. Buildings accomplish the same optimized selective boundaries for light, heat, moisture, and pests (insects, rodents, door-to-door salesmen, and evangelists).

Cells accomplish all this with a minimum amount of energy; not because they want to, but because they have to. Building science is about dovetailing the building enclosure and mechanical systems to optimize the use of energy, just as a cell does.

So, why does building science matter? We can't make our buildings more like cells without applying the science that cells observe. To be truly green our buildings must work as beautifully as they look, must perform as impressively as their product pedigrees. We need to design, construct, operate, and maintain buildings in the same way that nature builds cells – with efficiency, elegance, and unerring deference to the natural laws of physics, chemistry, and biology. A green architect or builder must be a student of science first; great buildings will follow.

What is a Passive House?

Before venturing into the specifics of enclosure design, it will be useful to consider the Passive House (*Passiv Haus*) concept, which originated in Europe in the mid-1990s. There are now tens of thousands of Passive Houses worldwide. Through many conversations with people working on NZEH projects, I have learned that Passive House standards are rapidly being adopted as target performance metrics for NZE homes, even though renewable energy systems are not a prescribed feature of the Passive House approach. In Europe there are both net-zero and energy-positive buildings built to Passive House standards.

Although in the United States there are only a handful of Passive Houses to date, the movement is rapidly gaining a North American following. According to Graham Irwin, a Northern California Passive House designer and proponent, "Passive House is still a nascent movement in the US, but it will gain ground as people begin to strive for what your book suggests – it just makes too much common sense once one sees the math."[6] Irwin's remarks reflect the sentiments of many others with whom I have spoken during the course of my research.

▶ Some US Passive House projects are listed in Appendix B, although none of them yet includes renewable energy.

From the Passive House Institute US (PHIUS) website:

"A Passive House is a very well-insulated, virtually air-tight building that is primarily heated by passive solar gain and by internal gains from people, electrical equipment, etc. Energy losses are minimized. Any remaining heat demand is provided by an extremely small source. Avoidance of heat gain through shading and window orientation also helps to limit any cooling load, which is similarly minimized. An energy recovery ventilator provides a constant, balanced fresh air supply."

Officially certified Passive Houses must verify their compliance with a short list of extremely rigorous performance standards:

- Airtight building shell ≤ 0.6 ACH @ 50 Pascals;

- Annual heating demand ≤ 15 kWh/m^2/year (1.39 kWh/ft^2/year);

- Primary (source) energy demand ≤ 120 kWh/m^2/year (11.15 kWh/ft^2/year); solar-thermal systems may be used to offset the source energy limit, though not heating or cooling loads.

Keys to achieving these standards are high-performance windows, heat- or energy-recovery ventilation systems, and thermal bridge-free construction. The

Passive House metrics are based on a biggest-bang-for-buck approach: minimize the enclosure loads to the point where a large conventional heating system can be eliminated. In short, the Passive House standards embody the key principles to successful NZEH design and offer a concrete set of guidelines for achieving optimum cost-effective energy performance. This is very much akin to the approach described by Bruce Coldham in his *Northeast Sun* article reprinted in Chapter 2 and, as you'll shortly see, consistent with what follows in this chapter.

One of the promising aspects of the Passive House approach is its successful use in Europe not just for single-family homes but for multifamily residences as well as non-residential structures. (The German *Haus* is more akin to "building" than to the English "house.")

Passive House information is available on the following websites:

- **www.passivehouse.us**
- **www.passivhaus.org.uk**
- **www.passiv.de** (which includes English information)
- **www.passivehouseca.org**

► See the lively debate, "Pro/Con: Does Passivhaus Make Sense over Here?" at **www. greenbuildingadvisor. com/blogs/dept/ green-building-blog/ procon-does- passivhaus-make- sense-over-here**

Dietmar Lorenz, of Daniel Smith and Associates in Berkeley, California (architects of the ZETA Communities Lancaster Lofts NZEH project – see Appendix B), offers the following cautions about applying the Passive House model in the United States: "Passive Houses designed in Germany tend to have some cooling loads in the summer, but typically do without mechanical solutions for cooling. They have great insulation and are very airtight, ideal in the winter. But Passive Houses aren't always heavy on thermal mass, and night vent flushing can be limited during central European heat waves (which have become more frequent events)." These passive cooling strategies are often important in US designs for NZE homes.

Lorenz continues, "Also, those super airtight enclosures use recovery ventilation to get enough fresh air exchanges, which does make sense in cold climates. However, in mild climates such as coastal California, there is not enough temperature differential [between indoors and outdoors] to recoup the fan energy (and the embodied energy of equipment, ducting, maintenance). So, while the fundamental principals are pretty universal, the 'import' of the Passive House concept will need a certain amount of adaptation to local climates." A mechanical engineer colleague of mine concurs, noting that mechanical air conditioning is still required in parts of North

America that experience significant humidity and that even with air conditioning, humidity control is often both challenging and critical.

Passive House enthusiasts acknowledge these issues but remain convinced that the concept can be applied successfully in many if not all North American climates. US Passive Houses completed to date are in Massachusetts, Minnesota, Illinois, and California, though the California home has not yet been certified.

Air sealing

Often we heat the inside of our homes during the winter and cool it during the summer. If the heated or cooled air is allowed to escape to the outside, it will be replaced by cold or hot outside air, which then must be heated or cooled. A tight envelope[7] helps to ensure that the highest practicable percentage of the energy used to condition (heat and cool) the building stays inside to do its job, rather than escaping to the outdoors through leaks in the skin.

Considerable controversy surrounds the issue of tight enclosures. Many people believe that a building should "breathe" and that a tight enclosure prevents this. Certainly, a tight enclosure without an adequate ventilation system would be unwise, as would an enclosure design that did not allow for drying, if moisture intrudes. Whether drying occurs to the inside or outside – or both at different times of year – is a topic worthy of additional attention; there are many excellent resources on the subject at **www.buildingscience.com**.

A tight enclosure combined with appropriately designed vapor profiles[9] and a well-designed, efficient ventilation system ensures that the building will "breathe" according to a specific design: air of known quality (i.e., clean and filtered) will be supplied to and exhausted from the building in known quantities, from known sources. The alternative is to have air of unknown quality entering the building in unknown quantities, from unknown sources – that is, via leaks.

Air that leaks into a building also can not be preheated or precooled to minimize the associated energy penalty (cold air entering from the outside in winter will need to be heated; hot air entering in summer needs to be cooled). Air entering via a controlled heat-recovery or energy-recovery ventilation (HRV or ERV)

AIR BARRIER? VAPOR RETARDER?

Air barriers and vapor retarders are different. An air barrier blocks air movement via gaps and cracks in a structure. It is not one or two things but an assemblage of numerous items, and it must be continuous from the footing to the roof. Vapor retarders are intended to stop moisture diffusion, i.e., movement *through* a material rather than around via the gaps (air movement). For decades, the building code has not communicated a clear understanding or directive on how moisture moves through buildings, with resultant confusion about the two terms and their applications. The new versions of the code are addressing this, but the industry still has a significant hurdle to overcome.[8]

MECHANICAL VENTILATION

Mechanical ventilation may not seem directly relevant to reducing building energy loads; in fact, quite the contrary – it requires energy to run a mechanical ventilation system. Why, then, discuss it here? Quite simply, achieving the best practicable level of airtightness is critical to achieving your energy-free goals, and an airtight home requires a permanent, reliable source of fresh outside air for occupant health.

The extent to which a home may rely on passive ventilation (which is most often supplied via open windows) is a function not just of climate, but also of security, noise, and outdoor air quality conditions. Relatively few homes are built in such mild climates, safe and quiet neighborhoods, and clean-air locations that they can rely on open windows 24/7, year-round, for their supply of fresh, clean air. Hence mechanical ventilation should be provided in the vast majority of homes; arguably in all of them. Fortunately, the energy requirements of fresh-air ventilation systems are typically very low.

Your plans for mechanical ventilation should be integral to your space conditioning system design. Some space conditioning systems are designed to provide fresh air; others are not. Those that aren't should not necessarily be ruled out, however; sometimes fresh air can be provided relatively easily and efficiently by other means – e.g., a passive air intake vent coupled with a timer-driven bathroom exhaust fan, as described in Building Science Corporation's "Review of Residential Ventilation Technologies."[10] Another great resource is Martin Holladay's Green Building Advisor blog on mechanical ventilation at **www.greenbuildingadvisor.com/blogs/dept/musings/designing-good-ventilation-system.**

system can be preheated or precooled with exiting air, reducing the heating and cooling loads accordingly. However, it's critical that the motors in the ventilation system do not consume more energy than is being captured, so it's important to use high-efficiency brushless DC (direct current) motors.

Effective air sealing requires a continuous air barrier throughout the enclosure. A continuous air barrier can be created using some or all of the following, alone or in combination, with proper detailing and care in installation:

- Taped and sealed house wrap
- Glued and taped interior drywall
- "Peel'n'stick" or fluid-applied membranes
- Spray foam cavity insulation
- A continuous exterior insulation layer
- Oriented-strand-board sheathing with taped joints

In multifamily structures, air barriers are important both at the building enclosure and between units. Party-wall sealing prevents cigarette smoke and other airborne contaminants or objectionable odors from being transmitted from one unit to the next. It's also important to seal party walls effectively at foundation and attic to minimize energy loss.

The air barrier must be continuous, or it won't function as such. This obviously requires careful attention during construction, but the air barrier's continuity must be assured *in the design phase*, and not left for the contractor to figure out in the field. Particularly critical are transitions at changes of plane (e.g., wall to roof) and door and window openings. Since design professionals historically have paid little attention to air barrier continuity, your design team may not be well-versed in appropriate detailing. Here are several very helpful resources:

- Building Science Corporation's climate-specific *Builder's Guides*, which can be ordered in the bookstore section at **www.buildingscience.com**

- Design details at Green Building Advisor, **www.greenbuildingadvisor.com**

- "Making Air Barriers that Work: Why and How to Tighten Up Buildings," *Environmental Building News*, June 1, 2008 (available at **www.buildinggreen. com**)

Figure 4-3 illustrates a superior example of both thinking through and communicating air sealing details. I am very grateful to Coldham & Hartman Architects for their generosity in sharing this drawing. It is also available as a downloadable PDF at **www.coldhamandhartman.com/completed.php?id=26.**

During construction, maintaining the air barrier's continuity will require that the contractor conscientiously observe all of the relevant design detailing and adhere to a high standard of quality control. All gaps, cracks, and other openings must be completely sealed with appropriate sealing and/or gasketing materials.

How tight is tight enough? As soon as the building enclosure is sufficiently complete to permit testing, you should perform a blower door test to identify any remaining air leakage sources, and then remedy them before proceeding to other stages of construction. In the blower door test, a frame and fabric panel assembly is used to seal an open doorway. The assembly includes a variable-speed fan that pulls air from the house to create a pressure difference between the inside and outside, and devices called manometers for measuring the pressure difference and the air flow created by the fan.

Air flow is generally measured in CFM (cubic feet per minute) and the pressure difference most commonly used for conducting the test is 50 Pascals; accordingly, the test results are reported as CFM_{50}. The CFM_{50} value can be normalized to the size of the house to give CFM_{50} per square foot of floor area.

Other measures of air leakage include air changes per hour at a specified pressure difference, e.g., ACH_{50}, and natural air changes per hour (NACH or ACH_{NAT}). The blower door test measures leakage under limited, controlled (artificial) circumstances, and we are in fact interested in NACH, the house's *actual* leakage under *natural* conditions, i.e., as affected by factors such as wind and temperature differences acting on the house.

▶ **GreenBuilding Advisor** is a comprehensive residential green building resource. See Appendix D for more information and a discounted subscription offer.

▶ To preserve indoor air quality, minimize worker exposure to hazards, and minimize adverse atmospheric impacts, use sealants with the lowest levels of volatile organic compounds (VOCs) that meet other performance specifications. Acceptable "green" levels of VOCs are established by the South Coast Air Quality Management District and may be found at **www.aqmd.gov/prdas/ Coatings/table_of_ standards.htm.**

FIGURE 4-3. AIR BARRIER CONTINUITY DRAWING

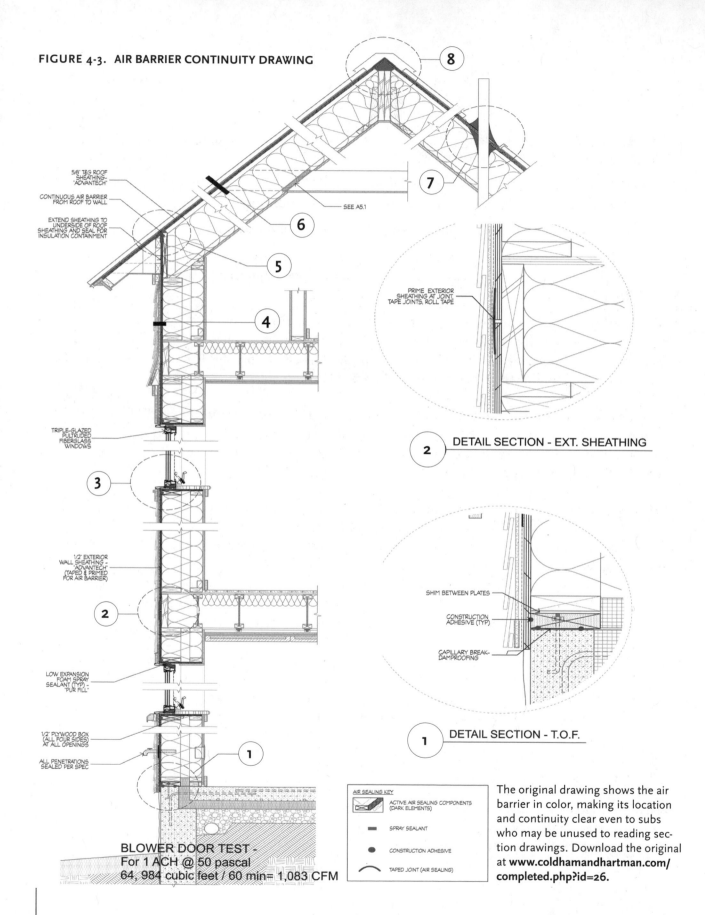

5/8" T&G ROOF SHEATHING - "ADVANTECH"

CONTINUOUS AIR BARRIER FROM ROOF TO WALL

EXTEND SHEATHING TO UNDERSIDE OF ROOF SHEATHING AND SEAL FOR INSULATION CONTAINMENT

SEE A5.1

8

7

6

5

4

3

2

1

TRIPLE-GLAZED PULTRUDED FIBERGLASS WINDOWS

1/2" EXTERIOR WALL SHEATHING - "ADVANTECH" (TAPED & PRIMED FOR AIR BARRIER)

LOW EXPANSION FOAM SPRAY SEALANT (TYP) - "PUR FILL"

1/2" PLYWOOD BOX (ALL FOUR SIDES) AT ALL OPENINGS

ALL PENETRATIONS SEALED PER SPEC

BLOWER DOOR TEST -
For 1 ACH @ 50 pascal
64, 984 cubic feet / 60 min= 1,083 CFM

PRIME EXTERIOR SHEATHING AT JOINT, TAPE JOINTS, ROLL TAPE

2 DETAIL SECTION - EXT. SHEATHING

SHIM BETWEEN PLATES

CONSTRUCTION ADHESIVE (TYP)

CAPILLARY BREAK - DAMPROOFING

1 DETAIL SECTION - T.O.F.

AIR SEALING KEY

▨	ACTIVE AIR SEALING COMPONENTS (DARK ELEMENTS)
▬	SPRAY SEALANT
●	CONSTRUCTION ADHESIVE
⌒	TAPED JOINT (AIR SEALING)

The original drawing shows the air barrier in color, making its location and continuity clear even to subs who may be unused to reading section drawings. Download the original at **www.coldhamandhartman.com/completed.php?id=26.**

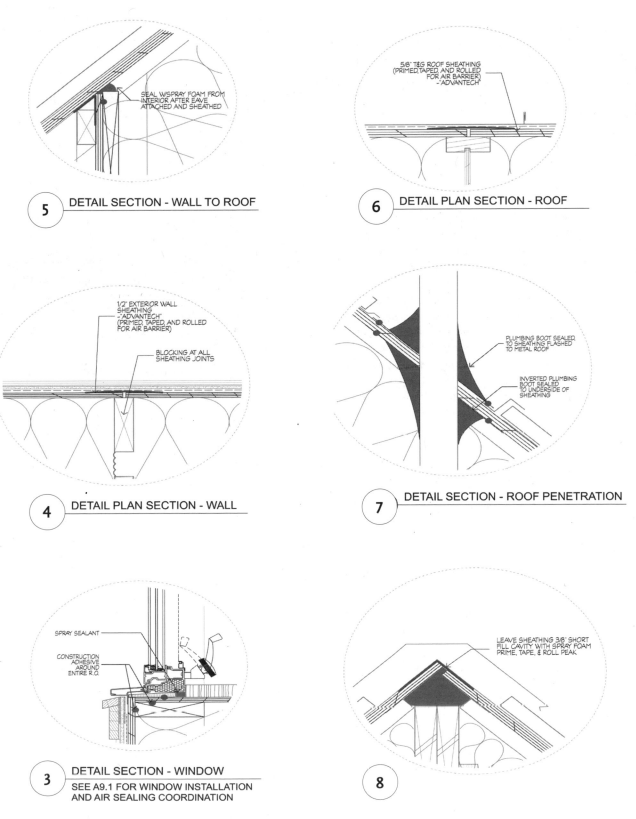

Courtesy of Coldham & Hartman Architects, coldhamandhartman.com

SEAL W/SPRAY FOAM FROM INTERIOR AFTER EAVE ATTACHED AND SHEATHED

5 DETAIL SECTION - WALL TO ROOF

5/8" T&G ROOF SHEATHING (PRIMED, TAPED, AND ROLLED FOR AIR BARRIER) -"ADVANTECH"

6 DETAIL PLAN SECTION - ROOF

1/2" EXTERIOR WALL SHEATHING -"ADVANTECH" (PRIMED, TAPED, AND ROLLED FOR AIR BARRIER)

BLOCKING AT ALL SHEATHING JOINTS

4 DETAIL PLAN SECTION - WALL

PLUMBING BOOT SEALED TO SHEATHING FLASHED TO METAL ROOF

INVERTED PLUMBING BOOT SEALED TO UNDERSIDE OF SHEATHING

7 DETAIL SECTION - ROOF PENETRATION

SPRAY SEALANT

CONSTRUCTION ADHESIVE AROUND ENTIRE R.O.

3 DETAIL SECTION - WINDOW
SEE A9.1 FOR WINDOW INSTALLATION AND AIR SEALING COORDINATION

LEAVE SHEATHING 3/8" SHORT FILL CAVITY WITH SPRAY FOAM PRIME, TAPE, & ROLL PEAK

8

DEFINING AIRTIGHT

Reprinted with permission from **BuildingGreen.com**

If air pressure were equal everywhere, air would not move. Therefore, to measure the air permeance, or leakage, of a barrier between two adjacent spaces, one must assume a pressure difference on either side of the barrier. Using a single common measure for that difference allows air-permeance measurements to be standardized and compared.

In English units, the standard pressure differential for measuring air permeance is 0.3 inches of water, which is equivalent to the pressure differential created by a strong breeze. Almost everyone prefers the equivalent metric of 75 Pascals (Pa), however. To further complicate matters, professionals in the field usually measure air permeance at 50 Pa instead of 75 Pa. To roughly convert a 75-Pa permeance number to a 50-Pa result, divide it by 1.3.

The Air Barrier Association of America (ABAA), founded in 2000 and now a leading authority on air-barrier design and specifications, has defined an air barrier material as having an air permeance of no more than 0.004 cubic feet per minute (cfm) per ft² at 75 Pa. (The metric conversion is 0.02 liters of air per second per m², or 0.02 L/s•m² @ 75 Pa.) This is the permeance of standard drywall.

As air-barrier materials are combined into larger assemblies, the definitions become more forgiving by factors of ten. An air-barrier *assembly* – which is simply any building assembly, such as a wall, designed to block air leakage – should have an air permeance of less than 0.04 cfm/ft² @ 75 Pa (0.2 L/s•m² @ 75 Pa), according to ABAA. When numerous assemblies are combined into an air-barrier system for a whole building, providing a continuous airtight plane, the maximum air leakage for the whole building should be less than 0.4 cfm/ft² @ 75 Pa (2.0 L/s•m² @ 75 Pa). Professionals often abbreviate this metric further, as in 0.4 CFM_{75}. Converted to 50 Pa, that is 0.3 CFM_{50}. A very tight building might test at 0.05 CFM_{50} or less, while a leaky building could test at 1.0 CFM_{50} or higher.

CFM_{50} is converted to ACH_{50} using the following equation:

$$ACH_{50} = \frac{CFM_{50} \text{ x } 60 \text{ min/hr}}{\text{house volume}}$$

One can use the measured leakage value to estimate NACH by applying multipliers to account for factors such as wind speed and the building's height and size. Coldham & Hartman Architects divide ACH_{50} by 17 to approximate NACH for their projects in the Northeast.[11] Other leakage metrics, such as the effective leakage area (ELA) and specific leakage area (SLA), also can be calculated from the measured CFM_{50} value.

As a rule of thumb, 1 CFM_{50} per square foot of floor area (e.g., 6 ACH_{50} for a 2,000-sf home) is considered an average for a reasonably tight building. Houses designed to Passive House standards often are designed to achieve ACH_{50} values in the range of 0.6 to 0.4 (ten times more airtight).

Walls, roofs, and floors

The solid sections of walls, roofs, and floors in residential structures consist of relatively predictable components: insulation, framing, sheathing, and finish materials (siding, etc.). The role of each in the enclosure's energy performance is discussed below.

Insulation: Quantity

The only aspect of insulation that generally gets much attention is quantity, expressed as R-value, or thermal resistance. The larger a material's R-value, the more it resists the movement of heat from one side to the other; the higher the R-value, the better. You may see R-values given for a specific product, for an entire assembly, or in R per inch (which is technically represented as lower-case r).

R-values for a product or an assembly are for a specific thickness – for example, a fiberglass batt valued at R-3 per inch, designed to fit in a 2x4 stud cavity, would be rated R-11; a thicker batt of the same material, to fit a 2x6 cavity, would be rated R-17. Product or assembly values are often rounded to the nearest whole number. Per-inch R-values should be given to tenths, e.g., R-3.9/inch.

Building codes often (but not always) specify minimum R-values for walls, roofs, and floors. The only guidance these values provide is to underscore that anything *less* is illegal; they should not be used to dictate insulation quantities for energy-free homes. This is not to say that you can't achieve an energy-free home with merely code-compliant insulation; you may be able to. However, since insulation is often one of the most cost-effective tools in your energy-efficiency toolbox – that is, a dollar invested in insulation will yield a higher return in reduced energy demand than a dollar invested in another type of energy improvement – you should give serious consideration to increasing insulation well above code minimum.

▶ The discussion of energy modeling in Chapter 3 describes how to use energy modeling to help identify the most cost-effective means of improving energy performance.

Insulation: Quality

Insulation quality is the forgotten stepchild of the building enclosure, likely a casualty of the long-time dominance of batt insulation products. The green and energy-efficient building community has, by and large, abandoned batt insulation as an inferior product. It's not that it can't provide adequate R-value; in fact, the R-values of batt insulation products (usually fiberglass) are often competitive with other types of insulation. The problem is that it's extremely difficult – in some situations virtually impossible – to install batts so that they perform properly.

First, there are two basic ways that insulation is installed: (1) in framing cavities and (2) continuously, usually outside the framing. Batt insulation in framing cavities, in order to do its job properly, has to be in full contact with all six faces of the cavity: top, bottom, outside face, inside face, and the two sides (studs, joists, or rafters). It can't have any significant gaps, dents, troughs, voids, gouges, valleys, or divots. This is challenging enough in an accessible, full-size framing cavity that contains no obstructions. It is nearly impossible in cavities that are narrow, not fully accessible, or contain wiring, electrical boxes, piping, air supply ducts, or other obstacles – in short, a significant fraction of all the framing cavities in a typical building enclosure.

The California Energy Commission, recognizing that this was the case, some time ago incorporated a provision in the state's *Building Energy Efficiency Standards* that de-rated the R-value of batt insulation by 14 percent unless the insulation installation passed a visual inspection by a third party rater (more on this later). This inspection, known as the Quality Insulation Installation (QII), has had a well-known effect on California's home construction industry: if the insulation subcontractor is informed that the project will be subject to a QII, s/he will increase the cost of the job by 30 to 100 percent. This carries a twofold message: 1) doing a really high-quality job with batts is very time-consuming; and 2) if you hadn't told me my work would be inspected, I would have done a lousy job!

Long story short: consider other types of insulation. What are the options?

- Blown-in cellulose (recycled newspaper)

- Blown-in fiberglass (sometimes called blown-in batt system or BIBS)

- AirKrete (proprietary mineral-based cementitious material)

- Spray polyurethane foam, open-cell (low-density) or closed-cell (medium- or high-density)

I'm often asked about bio-based (renewable) or recycled-content insulation: isn't it better (more environmentally friendly) than products that *don't* contain bio-based ingredients or recycled content? It depends. All performance characteristics being equal, yes, it's great to choose an insulation product, or any kind of product, that contains such materials. However, rarely are all other characteristics equal, and when it comes to insulation, *how well it insulates* (provides thermal protection) is the paramount consideration. Short of toxicity concerns, insulating performance should be the governing attribute.

Architect Dan Smith of Daniel Smith and Associates has observed that fire resistance should also be considered, commenting, "NZE projects tend to use unusual and intense wall insulations which are not typically rated assemblies."[12] In fact, unusual assemblies may be the norm in NZEH projects, in order to create enclosures that are as thermally robust as possible. Green Building Advisor includes many above-code insulation details such as the rim joist detail at **www.green buildingadvisor.com/cad/detail/inset-band-joist-mudsill.**

Figure 4-4 summarizes the pros and cons of several different cavity insulation types. A detailed discussion is provided in "Insulation: Thermal Performance is Just the Beginning," *Environmental Building News,* January 1, 2005.[13] Another useful reference is available at **www.energysavers.gov/your_home/insulation_ airsealing/index.cfm/mytopic=11510.**

Characteristic	Blown-in cellulose	Blown-in fiberglass	AirKrete	Open-cell spray polyurethane foam	Closed-cell spray polyurethane foam
R-value (R/inch)	3.0 – 3.7	2.2 – 4.0	3.9	3.4 – 4.5	6.2 – 6.9
Air-sealing	Negligible	Negligible	Negligible	Good	Excellent
Filling	Good - fills cavities well	Good - fills cavities well	Excellent – foaming substance fills cavities very well	Excellent – expands to fill extremely well	Excellent – expands to fill extremely well
Moisture and mold resistance	Not good – degrades, provides organic foor for mold	Good – inorganic material	Good – inorganic material	Not good – degrades	Excellent
Extraction/ ecosystem impacts	Made from recycled newspapers; no outstanding concerns	Made primarily from silica sand (plentiful mineral)	Made from magnesium oxide from seawater, calcium (plentiful minerals), some aluminum (which is energy-intensive)	Made from fossil fuels, water as blowing agent, halogenated flame retardants (may be persistent bioaccumulative toxicant)	Made from fossil fuels, non-ozone-depleting blowing agent, halogenated flame retardants (may be persistent bioaccumulative toxicant)
Occupant health issues	No known issues	Some (but not all) brands may contain formaldehyde (a carcinogen) binder	No known issues	Toxic during installation, requires airing out building before occupancy	Toxic during installation, requires airing out building before occupancy

FIGURE 4-4. CAVITY INSULATION COMPARISON

WHAT IS A HERS RATING?

The Home Energy Rating System is used by HERS raters to evaluate the energy performance of homes. A HERS rating consists of energy modeling (see Appendix A for a list of software programs and URLs), on-site verifications including a thermal bypass inspection, and diagnostic testing of mechanical equipment. The diagnostic testing typically includes a blower door test, a duct leakage (also called duct blaster) test, various additional tests of the ventilation system, combustion safety checks, and other similar activities.

A HERS rating assesses the home's energy performance relative to a minimally energy code-compliant home in the same location, and of the same size and configuration. The rating produces a HERS Index, a number that represents the percent of energy demand of the home as compared to the minimally code-compliant home.

The code-compliant home's HERS rating would be 100; a home that used half as much energy would have a HERS rating of 50. A net-zero energy project would achieve a HERS rating of zero. A net-energy-producing home would have a HERS rating in the negative range.

A HERS rating is an excellent aid to achieving a high-performing home. Of particular significance is the thermal bypass inspection (in California, sometimes treated as synonymous with the quality insulation installation – see Appendix A for several resources dealing with these topics). The thermal bypass inspection is designed to ensure the quality of the air sealing and insulation installation.

Builders who are not experienced with the thermal bypass inspection rarely pass it the first time. This means several things:

- The standard approach to air-sealing and insulating buildings is not high-quality;
- You can not expect a high-quality job without prior training and experience;
- Unless expectations for quality are communicated clearly at the outset of the job, there is high potential for conflict between builder and insulation subcontractor and/or between owner and builder.

A number of resources are available to help set the expectations – i.e., educate the builder and the insulation sub ahead of time. A few of these are listed in Appendix A.

In California, energy modeling software used for code compliance does not yet factor in onsite renewable power generation, and the California HERS approach is therefore somewhat different. Appendix A lists several California-specific resources.

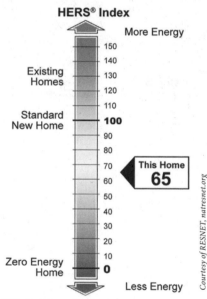

HERS® Index

More Energy

150
140
Existing Homes — 130
120
110
Standard New Home — **100**
90
80
This Home **65** — 70
60
50
40
30
20
10
Zero Energy Home — **0**

Less Energy

Courtesy of RESNET, natresnet.org

FIGURE 4-5. HERS INDEX

Framing

The primary structure of most residential buildings is framed with either wood or steel. The vast majority of low-rise homes are wood-framed; steel is common in mid-rise and almost ubiquitous in high-rise residential structures. The framing members are most commonly spaced at 16 inches on center (o.c.), with insulation between them. Heat follows the path of least resistance through a structure; therefore, since both wood and steel have lower thermal resistance (higher conductance) than insulation, the framing is the thermal weak link in the enclosure.

There are two ways to reduce the thermal conductance of the structure: reducing the framing factor, or fraction of the enclosure surface area occupied by framing members; and/or covering the outside of the building with continuous insulation.

The framing factor can be reduced by adopting practices known collectively as optimum value engineering or advanced framing. These include increasing the spacing of structural members to (usually 24 inches o.c.), using two-stud instead of three-stud corners, sizing headers over openings for the actual loads, and eliminating superfluous framing members such as headers in non-bearing walls, jack and cripple studs, and the like. Informational resources on advanced framing include the following:

- Green Building Advisor advanced framing details, **www. greenbuilding advisor.com/cad/advanced-framing**

- "Information Sheet for All Climates: Common Advanced Framing Details," Building Science Corporation, **www.buildingscience.com/documents/ information-sheets/2-framing/information-sheet-common-advanced-framing- details/**

- *Builder's Guide to [Type] Climate*, Joseph Lstiburek, Building Science Press, 2004-6, **www.buildingsciencepress.com/Builders-Guides-C1.aspx**

- *Efficient Wood Use in Residential Construction: A Practical Guide to Saving Wood, Money, and Forests*, A. Edminster and S. Yassa, Natural Resources Defense Council, 1998

- *Cost-Effective Home Building*, 1994, National Association of Home Builders Research Center

Continuous insulation is also quite beneficial, providing an improvement in assembly performance disproportionate to its R-value. This is because the continuous layer of insulation significantly reduces the thermal bridging[14] between the interior and exterior. In one single-family home modeled in our office, we found

▶ Polystyrene, either extruded (XPS) or expanded (EPS), is often used for continuous insulation in buildings. However, environmental concerns about polystyrene caused *Environmental Building News* recently to question whether it should be used in a green building. *EBN*'s August 2009 article on the subject provides a detailed discussion of the issues and the alternatives to polystyrene.[15]

that adding a layer of continuous insulation to the walls produced an improvement in energy performance roughly comparable to adding twice the R-value of the continuous insulation to the wall cavity. For example, a layer of R-4 continuous insulation with R-11 cavity insulation produced a result very close to R-19 cavity insulation with no continuous insulation. In addition to the improvement in thermal performance, continuous insulation also can aid in reducing condensation due to thermal bridging and its consequent problems.

Sheathing

Residential buildings, particularly in areas prone to earthquakes or high winds, are often sheathed with plywood or oriented-strand-board (OSB), continuously applied to the outside surface of the framing. This connection creates a thermal bridge and limits the effectiveness of cavity insulation is limited; heat can still travel from the outside skin of the building through the framing to the interior. Strategies to minimize the thermal bridging associated with sheathing include structural alternatives to sheathing such as diagonal bracing (which is quite rare these days, but was once commonplace); limiting sheathing to structurally-necessary locations; and using a layer of continuous insulation over the sheathing, as described above.

Finish materials

Finish materials may influence building energy performance in several ways:

- The color/reflectivity of interior surfaces affects the lighting power density (Watts per square foot of floor area) needed to achieve an appropriate level of lighting for indoor tasks; lighting in turn – in many climates – translates into cooling loads. (See the excellent discussion of these relationships in *Integrative Design*.[16])

- The color/reflectivity of exterior surfaces can affect the amount of solar radiation absorbed and subsequently converted to heat inside the building; in hot climates, "cool roofs" can be particularly important, as noted by Danny Parker: "At the Florida Solar Energy Center (FSEC) ... we have found cooling energy savings from white reflective roofing in residential buildings on the order of 20% over darker, less-reflective roofing." FSEC's research also shows that increasing the reflectivity of walls can reduce cooling loads by as much as 9 to 11 percent.[17]

COOL ROOFING

Contributed by Lisa Gartland, **www.pstvnrg.com**

Did you know that most roofs reach summer peak temperatures of 150 to 190 degrees Fahrenheit? Traditional roofing materials – like asphalt shingles, concrete tiles, metals roofs, and built-up roofing systems – absorb 80 to 95 percent of the sun's energy. The resulting excessive roof temperatures create many problems for homeowners and communities, including:

- Increased cooling energy use and higher utility bills;

- Higher peak electricity demand, raised electricity production costs, and a potentially overburdened power grid;

- Reduced indoor comfort;

- Increased air pollution due to the intensification of the "heat island effect";

- Accelerated deterioration of roofing materials, increased roof maintenance costs, and high levels of roofing waste sent to landfills.

These problems can be alleviated with cool roofing – highly reflective and emissive roofing materials that stay up to 60 degrees cooler than traditional materials during peak summer weather.

Cool roofing has two properties. First, high solar reflectance keeps a material from absorbing the sun's heat. The highest reflectances, 70 to 85 percent, are found in the brightest white materials. Colored materials have also been developed to reflect the infrared energy, or heat, from the sun. The solar reflectance of these spectrally selective materials ranges from 25 to 65 percent, and these materials are often identical to their hotter, traditional counterparts.

Second, high thermal emittance allows a material to radiate away any heat it has absorbed. The vast majority of roofing materials already have thermal emittance of 80 percent or higher. But bare metal roofs and metallic coatings tend to have much lower thermal emittance, ranging between 20 and 60 percent, depending on their surface finish, and levels of wear, oxidation, and dirt. Thankfully, metal roof products are often finished with spectrally selective coatings to raise both their solar reflectance and thermal emittance.

Cool roofing has been in use since the 1970s, and research confirming its benefits began to mount in the 1990s. Thousands of cool products are now available. The coolest materials – bright white coatings and single-ply materials – are used on low-slope (essentially flat) roofs of most commercial buildings and some houses. Cool colored materials – like spectrally selective tiles, shingles, and metal roofing – help the sloped roofs of houses stay cool without sacrificing appearances. Cool colored roofs are the fastest growing product in the roofing market, with producers and installers scrambling to manufacture and distribute the most effective materials.

The independent Cool Roof Rating Council has an online, searchable database of roof materials, **www.coolroofs.org,** where they publish the solar reflectance and thermal emittance of thousands of roof products. You can use their list to find the right cool product for your roof. See also the following websites:

- US Environmental Protection Agency **www.epa.gov/HeatIsland/mitigation/coolroofs.htm**

- Lawrence Berkeley National Laboratory, Heat Island Group **heatisland.lbl.gov/Cool Roofs**

For more valuable information about cool roofing and heat island mitigation, see Lisa Gartland's book, Heat Islands, Understanding and Managing Heat in Urban Areas. *Earthscan, London, UK, May 2008.*

- Gypsum wallboard and hard-surface flooring such as concrete, stone, or tile provide thermal mass (defined as the capacity of a material to store heat), which can help to modulate interior temperatures. Thermal mass strategies are particularly beneficial in climates that have significant day-to-night temperature differences: during the daytime, the thermal mass absorbs heat, which is then re-radiated into cooler interior spaces at night. A double layer of sheetrock is used by some passive solar design proponents and may provide an energy benefit; however, there is little hard evidence to support this, particularly in well-insulated buildings.[18]

- Earthen and lime plasters are widely reported to assist in moderating interior environments by adsorbing moisture vapor from the air and then releasing it back in dry periods, reducing discomfort associated with humidity extremes and so potentially reducing cooling loads. The hard science on this remains somewhat elusive, but the anecdotal evidence from a range of climate zones is far too strong and consistent to ignore.[19]

- Masonry wall finishes, particularly in existing buildings, are quite thermally massive and conductive. Without climate-appropriate design and construction detailing, they can be a significant thermal (and durability) problem. Building Science Corporation's *Builder's Guide* series is an excellent resource for designing wall systems. The guides are listed in Appendix A.

► Thermally massive wall systems can also be effective components of passive energy design strategies in specific climates. See the discussion of thermal mass later in this chapter.

Foundations

Foundations (slabs, stem walls, retaining walls, etc.) have an important role in a structure's energy performance. Typically made of solid concrete or concrete block, both of which are quite thermally conductive, foundations should be well-insulated to limit the flow of heat and cold between the structure and the ground. And yet, particularly in milder climates, foundation insulation has been sorely neglected. Be sure to include appropriate foundation insulation. One method thought to be particularly effective in cold climates is a shallow frost-protected foundation. Green Building Advisor states, "A frost-protected shallow foundation allows foundations as shallow as 16 in. (0.4 meters) in the most severe American climates. Insulation, strategically placed around the foundation, raises the frost depth around a building. Since the late 1970s in Scandinavia, more than 1 million homes have used this technique successfully. This type of foundation reduces concrete use and excavation."[20]

► Excellent details for foundation insulation can be found at **www. greenbuildingadvisor. com** as well as in Building Science Corporation's climate-specific Builder's Guides, available at **www. buildingsciencepress. com.**

There are also a number of proprietary insulated foundation systems such as Superior Walls (**www.superiorwalls.com**) and PolySteel Forms (**www.polysteel.com**).

PolySteel is one of a family of products called insulated concrete forms (ICFs). The principal benefit of ICFs is to produce a much better-insulated concrete wall system than a conventional one, and in several instances it has also been shown to reduce considerably the use of materials.[21]

Doors and windows

Windows and exterior doors comprise a significant fraction of the building enclosure. Of the two, windows represent considerably more surface area and therefore are more significant from an energy perspective than doors, although doors should by no means be neglected.

Doors

When selecting doors, consider the principal material (wood, glass, steel, fiberglass?) and its thermal conductance; the amount of glass (if any) and its thermal characteristics (see the discussion of windows below); and the quality of weatherstripping.

How much glass?

The amount of window (and skylight) area in a home is referred to as window-to-floor area ratio (WFA). WFA is generally larger in moderate climates, single-family homes and high-end homes, and lower in severe climates, multifamily homes and lower-cost homes. In homes with large amounts of glazing, window selection may play an even greater role than insulation in the overall thermal performance of the building enclosure, particularly when the orientation of the windows is sub-optimal (not primarily south-facing).

Where?

Window placement is important. Glazing on the building's south face allows the sun to enter during the winter, when sun angles are low, while allowing direct mid-day sunlight to be blocked by overhangs or other horizontal shading devices such as awnings during the summer, when the sun is high in the sky.

It is generally desirable to minimize glazing on the east (sunrise) façade and particularly the west (sunset) façade, where sun angles are low year-round, making it more difficult to incorporate shading strategies that don't also obstruct views.

▶ See "Overhangs and other shading devices" for more information about shading east- and west-facing windows.

In the northern hemisphere, windows on the building's north face will not provide significant solar heat gain in the winter, when the sun rises and sets farther

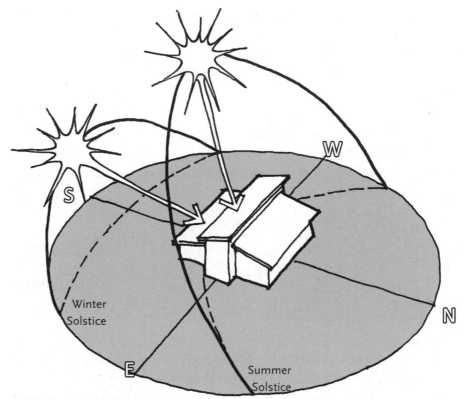

FIGURE 4-6. SOLAR GEOMETRY

to the south than it does in summer. Therefore, windows here should be limited as much as practicable without sacrificing daylight to interior spaces.

Skylights are often more a liability than an asset. Because they are completely exposed at all hours, year-round, they allow uncontrolled radiation both when it's desirable and when it's not – solar heat gain throughout the day (increasing cooling loads) and radiant heat loss to the night sky (increasing heating loads). They should therefore be used judiciously. Skylights are least problematic in heating-dominated climates.

Tubular skylights (sometimes called solar tubes) can be an excellent option for closets, hallways, interior baths, and other spaces that will benefit from daylight which would otherwise be difficult to provide. They typically have specially designed caps, reflective shafts, and diffusers to maximize light penetration while limiting thermal losses by minimizing the surface area exposed to the sky. They can provide daylight in much more constrained spaces than skylights would

Courtesy of Sun-Tek, sun-tek.com

**FIGURE 4-7.
TUBULAR SKYLIGHT**

require, and often without structural reinforcement. The interior opening can also be offset somewhat from the roof location. Several types of tubular skylights are reviewed at **www.greenbuildingadvisor.com**.

Performance variables

Besides the amount of glazing in the home, and where it is located, there are five key window variables that influence energy performance: U-value, solar heat gain coefficient, air leakage, visible transmittance, and quality construction. They are discussed below. Only the first two typically get any attention – and even then, not enough.

U-value or U-factor is the inverse of R-value, and as this suggests, lower values are better. U-values range between 1 and 0. Values for residential dual-paned windows are commonly between U-.25 (R-4) and U-.5 (R-2), with some values both lower and higher. Single-paned, aluminum-framed windows – common in existing homes – typically have values around U-1 (R-1). U-value *should* reflect the performance of an individual window unit, accounting for the combined effects of the frame and the glazing.[22] Different unit sizes and/or operation types (e.g., casement or double-hung) typically have somewhat different U-values even if they are otherwise constructed similarly. In our modeling, we have found U-value to be consistently one of the biggest influences on overall building energy performance.

Energy efficiency proponents advocate using R-value for windows instead of U-value, because R-value is more familiar as well as more intuitive: a higher number equals higher performance.

Solar heat gain coefficient (SHGC) is the fraction of solar radiation that enters the building via the window (contributing to internal heat gain). SHGC values range between 0 and 1; lower SHGC values equal lower heat gain, desirable in cooling-dominated climates. Higher SHGC values may be desirable in heating-dominated climates, especially for windows that contribute to passive solar heating. Passive solar design strategies often use different SHGC values for different window orientations. Modeling should be used to test the effect of different values, which can vary widely based on climate and glazing orientation, ranging from relatively minor to quite substantial.

▶ Recent introductions from Serious Windows (**www.seriouswindows. com**) have full-frame U-values ranging from .29 to .09 (R-3.4 to R-11.1), the highest now available from US manufacturers. ENERGY STAR requires a maximum U-value of 0.35 (R-2.9) in northern zones, 0.40 (R-2.5) in north central and south central zones, and 0.55 (R-1.8) in southern zones. Many green building experts believe that ENERGY STAR should reduce its required U-values (i.e., improve minimum thermal performance).

Air leakage (AL) is a measure of how much air moves through the window assembly, expressed in cubic feet of air per square foot of window area. Just as less leakage is desirable for the building enclosure as a whole, lower window air leakage values are preferred. While air leakage testing is not mandated and few US window manufacturers include this value in consumer information, many products are tested to ensure that AL is .3 or less, the upper limit set by the *International Energy Conservation Code*, which is in effect in many states. Although many windows test well below this value, results are given in tenths (i.e., a test value of 0.17 would be given a rating of 0.2) and the best possible rating by the National Fenestration Rating Council (NFRC) is 0.1. However, principally due to the increasing interest in the Passive House movement, which emphasizes tightly constructed windows, more buyers are starting to ask for air leakage numbers. Published values I found, which represent new uninstalled units, ranged from a low of .003 cfm/sq. ft., for an individual Canadian tilt-and-turn model, to the allowable maximum of .3 cfm/sq. ft.

Dariush Arasteh, a window expert at Lawrence Berkeley National Laboratory, cautions against placing too much emphasis on air leakage, advising buyers to look for a quality window which will maintain its infiltration seal over time, make sure that windows are installed properly and well-sealed against the framing, and concentrate on lower U-factors and the right SHGC for the orientation and microclimate. "The energy difference between windows with air leakage .05 (typical of many quality North American products with compression seals) versus .003 is about the difference between a .250 U-factor and a .255 U-factor, and this difference is well within the uncertainty of U-value reporting. Fixed windows have negligible air-infiltration rates; casements and awnings, which have compression seals, generally have low infiltration rates for operable windows; and sliders generally have the highest AL rates."[23] Tilt-and-turn units typically have the lowest AL values among operable windows; double-hung windows are slightly more airtight than horizontal sliders but not as good as casements and awnings.[24]

Visible transmittance (VT or T-vis) is the fraction of light that passes through the glass; values range between 0 (none) and 1 (100 percent). Tinted glass generally has a lower VT than clear glass. VT is important because low values can increase the need for artificial light.

Quality construction is not rated or quantified. However, windows that are better-built and made of more dimensionally stable materials will provide better energy performance and durability over time, because they will be less prone to expand, contract, and deform, all of which degrade airtightness, due to use. Price is one rela-

▶ **Is energy all that matters about windows? What about the frame material?** Much like insulation, the overriding "green" consideration for windows is energy performance. However, the prevailing sentiment in the green building community tends to be anti-vinyl, despite the relatively good thermal performance of vinyl frames. This is due to the weight of ecosystem and human health concerns associated with the vinyl production lifecycle. Thus nearly any other material is preferable. I'm a fan of fiberglass and clad windows, because of their superior durability.

tively good indicator of quality, as is detailing. If you are not familiar with window construction, ask your architect or builder to help evaluate the quality of construction.

To optimize your windows' overall energy performance, you will need to factor in all of the relevant characteristics. In general, the best strategy is to develop a good shading design (see below) to protect your windows from excess solar heat gain. Then specify windows with low U-values and high SHGC (good for passive winter heat gain); this combination of variables always has good (high) visible transmittance.

Note that off-the-shelf residential windows commonly sold as "high performance" may have a good (low) U-value but also have a low (*not* good) VT, which would compromise your daylighting and so increase lighting energy loads. This is not an inescapable relationship, however – a good U-value does not automatically mean you'll have to sacrifice VT. Since off-the-shelf window glazing may not meet your needs, you may need to do more due diligence with your window supplier. Or you may be better served by choosing a garden-variety window that is Low-E (low-emissivity – not to be confused with Low-E², which is spectrally selective), which is likely to have a fairly good U-value and a high SHGC and therefore decent VT.

Unique design circumstances may occasionally result in a situation where you need to trade off different glazing performance variables – choosing between one that is good and another not-so-good. Evaluating the overall effect on energy performance and other factors, including architectural objectives, can be very challenging. In some instances you may even want to consult a specialized daylighting design firm, of which there are only a few in this country.

NFRC RATINGS

The National Fenestration Rating Council (NFRC, **www.nfrc.org**) has established a labeling system used for most residential windows produced in North America. NFRC labels show U-factor, SHGC, and VT. At the manufacturer's discretion they may also display air leakage and/or condensation resistance[25] (although these latter two values are rarely provided).

Non-residential windows do not typically have NFRC ratings, yet they may be used in residential projects, and the performance variables are important for energy modeling. U-value and SHGC can be determined via computer simulation of window performance, using a software program called WINDOW (not to be confused with Microsoft Windows products) – see **www.windows.lbl.gov/software/window/window.html** for more information.

FIGURE 4-8. NFRC RATING LABEL

**FIGURE 4-9.
HELIODON SHADING
STUDY FOR
TAH.MAH.LAH.[26]**

*Noon at June 21 (top)
and noon at
December 21 (bottom)*

Shading

Shading, whether provided by overhangs or other devices, vegetation, or adjoining structures, can have a substantial impact on energy performance. Shading devices can also influence visual comfort by assisting with glare control. An understanding of solar geometry is important to determining the most appropriate shading strategies for a given building and climate.

Computer energy simulation and computer or physical sun shading modeling give us tools for developing shading strategies. Energy modeling provides information about the hours during which cooling and heating are required. Sun shading modeling shows when windows are exposed to direct sunlight, and how much. This information can be used to determine optimum sizes and positioning of shading devices. Windows should be unshaded during the heating season, when the sun's warmth can help reduce heating loads; and windows should be substantially shaded during the hottest times of year, particularly if active (mechanical) cooling will be needed.

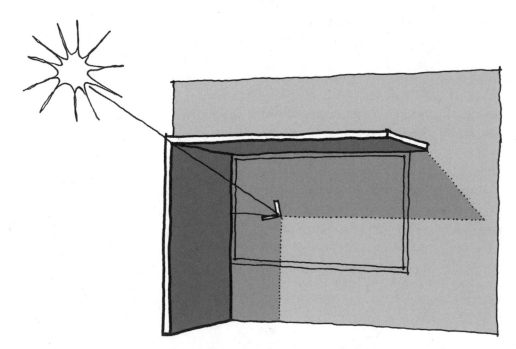

FIGURE 4-10. SHADING DEVICES (FIN-OVERHANG COMBINATION)

Overhangs and awnings, which shade from above, are most effective on south-facing walls, where they protect against direct sun intrusion when the sun is high in the sky on summer days. Vertically-oriented shading devices, such as shutters or fins, are more effective on east- and west-facing walls. In locations where other shading options do not work, trellises may be provided with designs optimized for shading.

Assemblies and layering

Acquiring an understanding of the enclosure elements and how they affect the building's energy performance is critically important, but it's not the whole story, even for the enclosure.

Building professionals and non-professionals alike too often think about bits of the building in isolation rather than about their role in the greater whole. The *enclosure* consists not just of those components I've discussed up to this point in the chapter, but very importantly, those components appear within the building

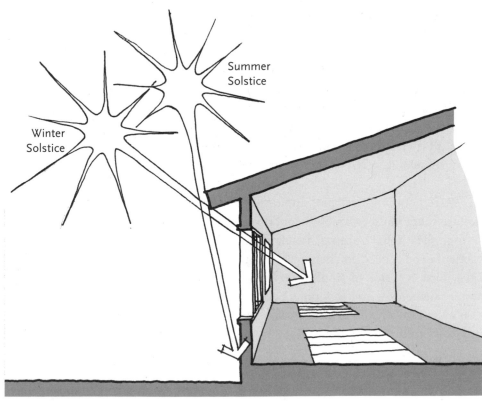

FIGURE 4-10. CONTINUED (OVERHANG)

in *assemblies*: a wall assembly, a roof assembly, a foundation assembly, and often a floor assembly in addition to the foundation assembly.

Creating an assembly that embodies the key attributes of energy-free design requires careful consideration. First off, in all probability you'll need to achieve R-values quite a bit higher than you have in past projects. You'll have to figure out how to do that, as it's unlikely that the assemblies you've been accustomed to will deliver the needed level of thermal performance. This means you and your team will need to get creative and cook up some new assembly designs. New assembly designs are likely to require new details.

For example, suppose you decide that in order to achieve the insulation values you need, you're going to have to do a double-stud wall. This means a much thicker wall section than normal, which in turn means your usual window and door installation details are going to need reworking.

Coldham & Hartman Architects have given a great deal of thought to the pros and cons of different NZEH assemblies. Bruce Coldham's article on this topic is scheduled for publication in *Fine Homebuilding* in December 2009.

Similarly, the business-as-usual approach to air sealing (which is to say, virtually no attention to it) isn't going to be adequate in the least. You're going to need to think through and then clearly communicate how all the air sealing will be done. Please refer back to and closely study the air sealing drawing from Coldham & Hartman Architects in Figure 4-3. (Emulation being the most sincere form of flattery, they will be enormously flattered if you will adapt their details for your own projects.)[27]

As you're noodling over new and different assembly designs, throw this in your noodle soup: those assemblies contain not just the basic elements (e.g., for walls: siding, sheathing, framing, insulation, drywall, and paint); not just the new elements you'll need for better energy performance (e.g., double studs or vertical I-joists in place of single studs); they also contain a host of other building system elements – wiring, piping, phone and cable, anchor bolts, you name it. Your new assembly is going to have to accommodate all these things, too, and all their implications for air sealing.

Stewart Brand, in *How Buildings Learn,* drew our attention to how building systems are layered and admonished us to factor that into our designing. The most permanent aspects of the building (generally the structure, including foundation) might be layered deep within the building, since they are rarely altered. Less permanent aspects, which are more frequently altered, should be more accessible, and less entangled, in order to facilitate the eventual alterations they are likely to experience.[28]

Now more than ever, since we have come to recognize that the rate of technological change we experience is ever-quickening, we should factor the inevitability of change into our assembly designs, rendering those elements most prone to later modification *very* readily accessible indeed.

In the Unity House project, Tedd Benson of Bensonwood did just that, with input from Kent Larson of MIT. The home includes several innovative features aimed at disentangling systems that were likely to experience later alterations. More information about this project and the underlying principles, referred to as "open building," is available at **www.unity.edu/NewsEvents/News/UnityHouseGlobe1008.aspx**.

Comfort Strategies and Systems

The discussion that follows should not be confused with professional, project- or location-specific design advice. Rather, it is offered to illustrate a range of solutions and circumstances in which they may be appropriate. I strongly encourage all project teams to consult with a qualified, energy-savvy mechanical engineer who has experience in designing highly efficient residential HVAC systems.

The need for heating is nearly universal; there are few (if any) homes in North America that do not need *some* heating, for *some* part of the year. A hypothetical exception might be a residence designed to meet the Passive House standard in a Southern US location, such as Florida, where there are few heating degree-days. In such a case, all heating needs conceivably might be met by heat generated by "internal loads" – i.e., the occupants, appliances, lighting, electronics, and so forth. Most North

HEATING DEGREE-DAYS

Early in the twentieth century, engineers developed the concept of heating degree-days (HDD) as a useful index of heating fuel requirements. They found that when the daily mean temperature (calculated by adding the day's maximum and minimum temperatures and dividing the total by 2) is below 65 degrees Fahrenheit, most buildings require heat to maintain a 70-degree indoor temperature. Each degree of mean temperature below 65 degrees is counted as 1 heating degree-day. Conversely, cooling degree-days (CDD) are used to determine air-conditioning requirements. (Excerpted from *The Old Farmer's Almanac*, **www.almanac.com**.) Contemporary engineers sometimes use different base temperatures, depending on their design assumptions or aims, e.g., 50 degrees Fahrenheit instead of 65 for determining heating degree-days.[29]

A variety of resources are available for determining the number of HDD/CDD for your climate. Here are a few:

• **www.weatherdatadepot.com/dd.asp** (US only)
• **www.degreedays.net/**
• **cdo.ncdc.noaa.gov/cgi-bin/climatenormals/ climatenormals.pl?directive=prod_elect2&prodtype= CLIM8102&subrnum=**

American homes are heated with natural gas, fuel oil, or propane; many with heat pumps or electricity; and some with electricity, coal, or firewood.

Mechanical cooling is increasingly common. In 1973, 49 percent of single-family US homes had air-conditioning; by 2008 that figure had increased to 89 percent. In climates with 2,000 or more cooling degree-days, air-conditioning is included in nearly all new homes. (US climates range from zero to nearly 5,000 CDD.[30]) Although air-conditioning is now the most common type of cooling system, other types include evaporative cooling, heat pump cooling, and radiant cooling. All of these systems are electric.

▶ I use the terms "mechanical" and "active" interchangeably to describe heating and cooling strategies, distinguishing them from passive strategies. Passive strategies make direct use of natural forces (sun, wind, etc.) for heating or cooling, with little or no reliance on mechanical equipment.

Often, though not always, the choice of heating system is influenced by the presence or absence of an active (mechanical) cooling system. However, because of its near-universality, I discuss heating below before moving on to a discussion of cooling. Incidentally, the "need" for cooling is even more culturally determined than that for heating. It is based to a significant degree on expectations unique to time and place, which are themselves a product of societal norms. For instance, once air conditioning became widely available and relatively inexpensive, people's perceptions about what constituted a comfortable environment changed significantly, as did their leisure pursuits. Instead of settling down on the front porch with a fan and a tall glass of something cool to drink, people began to spend more time indoors watching television in their air-conditioned living rooms. Whether this will ultimately be viewed as progress in the historical context of an energy-free future is debatable.

Factors that influence the energy efficiency of a space conditioning system include the efficiency of the equipment, the distribution system, whether or not the system is sized properly for the home, and the quality of installation.

Equipment efficiency. The LEED[31] for Homes Rating System categorizes heating and cooling equipment efficiency[32] as shown in Figure 4-11.

Distribution system. If the home is heated with air, the layout and sizing of the ducts are important. If the home is heated with water, sizing and layout of the piping are less significant. Duct systems are discussed under "Forced air" below.

System sizing. Even efficient equipment, if it is oversized or undersized, can do a poor job at space heating and/or cooling. Oversizing equipment is widespread due to a prevailing belief that an oversized system is a safeguard against other potential

Heating equipment type	Good is ≥	Better is ≥	Best is ≥
Furnaces (gas, oil, or propane)			
Heating - IECC climate zones 1–3	80 AFUE	90 AFUE	92 AFUE
Heating - IECC climate zones 4–8	90 AFUE	92 AFUE	94 AFUE
Boilers (gas, oil, or propane)			
Heating - IECC climate zones 1–3	80 AFUE	85 AFUE	87 AFUE
Heating - IECC climate zones 4–8	85 AFUE	87 AFUE	90 AFUE
Air-source heat pumps			
Heating - All IECC climate zones	8.2 HSPF	8.6 HSPF	9.0 HSPF
Cooling - IECC climate zones 1–3	14 SEER	15 SEER	16 SEER
Cooling - IECC climate zones 4–8	13 SEER	14 SEER	15 SEER
Ground-source heat pumps, open loop, all IECC CZ			
Heating	3.6 COP	4.0 COP	4.3 COP
Cooling	16.2 EER	17.8 EER	19.4 EER
Ground-source heat pumps, closed loop, all IECC CZ			
Heating	3.3 COP	3.6 COP	4.0 COP
Cooling	14.1 EER	15.5 EER	17 EER
Ground-source heat pumps, direct expansion, all IECC CZ			
Heating	3.5 COP	3.9 COP	4.2 COP
Cooling	15 EER	16.5 EER	18 EER

LEGEND
AFUE = annual fuel utilization efficiency
COP = coefficient of performance   EER = energy efficiency ratio
HSPF = heating seasonal performance factor   SEER = seasonal energy efficiency ratio

FIGURE 4-11. RELATIVE ENERGY PERFORMANCE OF SPACE CONDITIONING EQUIPMENT

shortcomings in the space conditioning system's design. The *Air Conditioning Contractors of America (ACCA) Manual J – Residential Load Calculation* is widely recommended for use in sizing space conditioning equipment. Equipment sizing is commonly left to HVAC contractors, who often use rules of thumb, informal advice received during on-the-job training, or habits developed over years of practice. This is likely to result in systems that are oversized for your energy-free home (such an energy-efficient home probably will defy all past experience of your HVAC contractor). An oversized air conditioner can lead to humidity control problems – it won't run long enough to remove sufficient moisture from the air. Other benefits of "right-sizing" include minimizing comfort problems, minimizing short-cycling, and maximizing run time in forced air systems, so that heated air has time to be distributed and mix in the conditioned space. Therefore, you should insist that your mechanical system designer – preferably a qualified mechanical engineer – use *ACCA Manual J* or a comparable scientific method for system sizing.

Some heating options make sense only if you will be cooling via the same system. Some of them make sense only if you are *not* actively cooling. In any case, you will need to consider heating and cooling system options as a package to determine the most efficient approach to space conditioning.

Installation quality. A high-quality installation includes proper attention to unobstructed air flow, appropriate refrigerant charge, correct control settings, and similar issues. As David Cohan observed, "There is a huge body of research showing that new buildings rarely function as designed [but] only a small fraction of all buildings have a meaningful level of commissioning [quality control] performed." Having your system inspected by a qualified third party, such as a HERS rater is a worthwhile investment (see the sidebar about HERS earlier in this chapter).

Heating

There are a number of different heating strategies. Several are described below, starting with those that require little or no power (passive strategies) and progressing to active options. The system that will be most efficient for a given building depends on several factors and must be determined by a qualified design professional.

No heating

Parts of the US South and Southwest have such low heating loads (e.g., 1,083 heating degree-days in Phoenix, Arizona or 162 in Miami, Florida – base 65 degrees F) that it is arguable whether active heating systems should even be needed, if the homes were designed and built properly. In fact, if homes in these climates were designed to Passive House standards, conventional heating systems would be grotesquely oversized for the homes' heating needs. Even in climates with high numbers of HDD, conventional systems have been shown to be substantially oversized for Passive House heating needs. For example, the Fairview I House in Urbana, Illinois (6,359 HDD), designed by architect Katrin Klingenberg, used five 500W electric-resistance baseboard heaters because all conventional furnaces were too large by far for the home's heating demand.[33]

The US *International Residential Code* requirement for heating is performance-based: "When the winter design temperature … is below 60 deg F (16 deg C), every dwelling unit shall be provided with heating facilities … The installation of …

► Heating and cooling systems always should be considered together, starting with whether active cooling will be provided – its presence or absence will influence subsequent space conditioning system design decisions.

portable space heaters shall not be used to achieve compliance."[34] According to building official Lynn Underwood (Norfolk, Virginia), this code doesn't explicitly require the inclusion of active heating systems, but local officials often insist on fixed electric or fuel gas equipment, although wood stoves and even passive solar heating systems meet this requirement in some areas. It is unusual for projects to be approved without active heating systems.[35] However, the reality is that there are climates in which energy-free homes might not really need them, with effective design and construction.

Passive solar

Passive solar heating employs the principles of massing, orientation, glazing, and thermal mass, all of which have been discussed previously in this chapter. A brief summary of the applicability of each of these principles to passive heating follows:

- **Massing.** Compact building forms help to minimize surface-to-volume ratios and in turn minimize heat loss through the building enclosure.

- **Orientation.** Orienting buildings with the long axis roughly east-west, and most of the glazing facing within 15 degrees of the equator (due south, in the Northern Hemisphere) generally offers the best opportunity to maximize solar gain in the heating season.

- **Glazing.** Optimizing window placement, size, U-value, and SHGC for the climate and exposure (façade orientation) is key to maximizing solar heat gain when it is beneficial and minimizing it when it is a liability. Shading design strategies can be equally important.

- **Thermal mass.** Interior thermal mass, designed in concert with the glazing so as to receive direct sunlight, can absorb incident solar radiation during the day to provide night-time warmth. Note that thermal mass also can provide cooling benefits, as described later in this chapter.

Radiant (hydronic)

Radiant or hydronic heating is provided by running hot water through radiators and/or through pipes or cross-linked polyethylene (PEX) tubing in or under floors. The water is heated by a conventional water heater or a boiler, either alone or in combination with a solar water heating system (see Chapter 6 for a discussion of solar hot water systems). The efficiency of the water heater or boiler is a key factor in the heating system's overall efficiency. Boiler efficiency was shown in Figure 4-11.

In-floor radiant heating is done in several ways:

- "Staple-up" systems, which are the dominant solution for retrofitting;

- "Warm-board" systems, in which the tubing is inset in grooves precut in the subfloor;

- Embedded within either a structural concrete slab or a thin topping slab of concrete or gypcrete.

Courtesy of Energy Earth LLC, energy-earth.com

Courtesy of Warmboard®, warmboard.com

FIGURE 4-12. STAPLE-UP AND WARM-BOARD SYSTEMS

Your choice of in-floor systems versus radiators to deliver radiant heat will be influenced by two principal factors:

- **Cost and construction considerations.** Cost, as always, will be influenced by project specifics. Particularly in retrofits, in-floor systems may be difficult and expensive to install because of access issues, the cost relative to other alternatives, etc. When we did an extensive energy retrofit of our home several years ago, we replaced the old, inefficient furnace and forced-air system with radiant heating. We used a combination of in-floor heating on the first story, over a crawl space that was not insulated at the time and therefore nicely accessible (yes, insulation immediately followed), and wall radiators in the second story, where installing in-floor radiant heating would have been horribly disruptive and expensive.

- **Responsiveness.** Wall radiators are very responsive – they produce heat quickly with an increase in thermostat setting, and equally promptly cease providing it when the thermostat is turned down. In-floor systems are much less responsive, because they first heat the floor's thermal mass by conduction; the warm floor then radiates heat into the room. Thus responses to thermostat settings are much slower. This can be problematic in climates that experience significant short-term temperature swings. The floor material and the presence or absence of carpets or rugs also affect the extent of delay between a change in thermostat setting and a change of heat output from the floor. I recommend consulting a mechanical engineer experienced in radiant system design to be sure that your heating system and flooring choices are compatible with your needs for system responsiveness.

Radiators come in two basic varieties: baseboard and wall. Both are shown in Figure 4-13.

Wall radiators are perhaps the most common type of radiator, and newer, more attractive designs have replaced the old-fashioned, clanking metal contraptions many of us lived with in apartment houses of yore (and many still do). They now come in a wide range of sizes and proportions, from long and low to tall and skinny, rendering them suitable for many different locations. Manufacturers continue to advocate that they be placed against exterior walls to benefit from the convective action that a cool wall surface fosters; however, in an energy-free home or one designed to a Passive House standard – that is, a home whose exterior walls are not cold on the interior surface – this may no longer be such a significant consideration. John Weale of Rumsey Engineers in Oakland, California notes, "Very good windows are still poor insulators; triple element windows are around R-8 in practice, so windows still are a concern, albeit to a lesser extent than in the olden days of R-1 windows, or even with today's good R-3 windows." Thus radiators may be most effectively placed below windows.

▶ Well-insulated enclosures (including windows) eliminate the drive to place heating outlets, whether radiators or supply grilles, at exterior walls. This change can significantly reduce the length of supply runs (piping or ducting), saving money, too.

(left and center) Courtesy of Peter Yost; (right) Ann Edminster

FIGURE 4-13. BASEBOARD AND WALL RADIATORS

Specialized wall radiators include radiant-heated towel racks for bathrooms, which do double duty, both warming the room and preheating towels – a delightful luxury. Baseboard radiators have been around for a long time without substantial modification. They are relatively inexpensive, but tend to be unsightly (at least I find them so) and may require a significant run of wall to provide adequate heating capacity, which can significantly limit furniture placement.

Electric resistance

Electric-resistance heaters tend to be the pariah of the world of energy efficiency, largely because of the inefficiencies inherent in electrical grid transmission – on average, two-thirds or more of the energy content of the fuel used for electrical production is lost between the energy source and the plug. Another strike against electric heating in heating-dominated climates is that electric-resistance heating may contribute to peak load. In California, for example, electric resistance heating carries a stiff penalty in energy modeling; a home using electric resistance heating must incorporate significant energy improvements merely to meet the code-required level of energy performance, let alone surpass it.

Nevertheless, in some circumstances electric heat makes sense. For instance, in the Fairview I Passive House mentioned above, Klingenberg selected electric-resistance baseboard heat because it offered the minimal heating capacity she required at very low first cost, and avoided the need for wall penetrations that would have been needed had she chosen gas heating. Other low-energy homes are purported to use sealed combustion gas space heaters in lieu of electric-resistance heaters. These may be more somewhat costly up front, but cost less to operate.

Electric-resistance options include ceiling panel radiators. One such product is shown in Figure 4-14. These are unusual and may be best-suited to "task" heating. Similar to task lighting, they provide heat to a specific location that is relatively limited in size – e.g., over a desk where someone sits for a substantial portion of the day, or above a bed or dining table. These panels were specified for one retrofit application where the homeowner anticipated a substantial remodel some years later and therefore did not want to invest a lot in improving the building envelope, but did want to improve both comfort and energy performance. Rather than replace her

Courtesy of Solid State Heating Corporation, sshcinc.com (Enerjoy)

FIGURE 4-14. CEILING PANEL RADIATOR

antiquated gas furnace and its duct system, which she rarely used due to its inefficiency, she selected ceiling panel radiators for her bedroom and dining/work area, for use only during times she occupied each space. Because the panels provide direct "line-of-sight" heat from the panel to room occupants rather than heating the air or the mass of the building, they provide adequate thermal comfort at relatively low energy cost, despite being electric-resistance units. Of course, while this may be a good choice for a leaky building, ideally an energy-free project will include a good job of air sealing.

Forced air

Forced air systems circulate air, heated by a furnace or heat pump, through ducts to each room in a home. The most common means of heating air for forced air systems in North American is a gas warm-air furnace. Furnaces are now available with AFUE levels up to 98 percent, and with modulating and staged firing rates that allow a good match between heat output and heat load. Some units permit zoned installations, allowing occupants to control temperature of rooms individually. There are also models with brushless DC motors, which can reduce electrical energy consumption substantially compared to conventional models.

In addition to equipment efficiency and appropriate sizing, the third important factor in the efficiency of a forced air system is the distribution system – the location, design, and construction of the ducts. If the ducts are installed inside the conditioned space, there is little energy penalty associated with duct leakage; however, leaks can lead to uneven heating and cooling of the space. Duct runs should be as short and straight as possible, minimizing the number and angle of bends, and should be sized properly for the spaces they will serve. Done properly, minimizing duct lengths minimizes both first cost and operating cost.

Also, as noted above in the section on radiant heating, a well-built enclosure may make it possible to greatly shorten duct runs, as they may not need to be located at the exterior walls.

Ideally, ducts should be installed in conditioned (heated and/or cooled) space. *ACCA Manual D – Residential Duct Systems* is widely recommended for reference in designing forced air distribution duct systems. The duct system design should of course be considered along with the overall architecture, structural, and enclosure design, and not be an afterthought, which can lead to very convoluted duct layouts. Too frequently, the design team fails to give adequate guidance, so that the HVAC contractor has to figure out how to move the air through the home during construction, often with distinctly sub-optimal results. Examples include the installation of dropped soffits where they were not planned, large holes being cut through structural framing members in inappropriate locations, and ducts being severely flattened or crimped because they had to be routed through tight spaces (with corresponding loss of comfort due to reduced delivery of heated/cooled air).

Courtesy of ShurTech Brands, shurtech.com

**FIGURE 4-15.
UL 181-COMPLIANT
DUCT TAPE**

Duct installation is equally important. Particularly if ducts are not installed in conditioned space, air leakage should be minimized by sealing the ducts well with mastic or duct tape that conforms to UL (Underwriters Laboratories) standard 181, as shown in Figure 4-15 (note the UL stamp on the tape itself). Duct losses can account for more than 30 percent of energy consumption for space conditioning, especially if the ducts are in an unconditioned space such as an attic.[36] The best assurance of a quality installation job is to have it inspected by a third party, such as a HERS rater.

Heat pumps

Heat pumps can provide cooling as well as heating, and there are three general types of heat pumps: air-source, mini-split, and ground-source. Each type is described below. Ducted central and duct-free systems are rated using SEER for cooling and HSPF for heating, as shown in Figure 4-11. A central ducted air-source heat pump must have a SEER of 13 or better and HSPF of 7.7 or better, per DOE minimum efficiency regulations.

► The acronyms used here are explained in Figure 4-11.

Ground-source and room units are rated using COP in heating mode and EER in cooling mode. EER and COP are typically measures of steady-state efficiency, whereas HSPF and SEER are measures of cyclic efficiency.

Air-source heat pumps. An air-source heat pump works like an air-conditioning system, forcing the transfer of heat by pumping a loop of refrigerant through a vapor-compression cycle – when the refrigerant is compressed, it heats up; when it expands, it cools off. The heat pump normally includes a system that allows the direction of heat flow to be reversed, so that the heat pump can be used for both heating and cooling. A heat pump can capture heat from a cool area and transfer it to a warm area, against the natural direction of flow, or it can enhance the natural flow of heat from a warm area to a cool one.

Although they run on electricity, heat pumps are significantly more efficient than conventional electric heaters. Their efficiency, COP, is the amount of heat delivered by the heat pump relative to the amount of energy required to run it. COP values range from around 2 to 4 – that is, a heat pump can deliver up to four times as much energy as it uses in its operation. Although this might seem counterintuitive, it is possible because heat pumps move heat rather than converting it from fuel.

Mini splits. According to the US Department of Energy, "Ductless, mini-split-system heat pumps ('mini splits') make good retrofit add-ons to houses with 'non-ducted' heating systems ... They can also be a good choice for room additions, where extending or installing distribution ductwork is not feasible."[37] They may also be a good choice for homes with small cooling loads.

Advantages of mini splits include small size and flexibility. They allow for zoning – that is, heating and cooling individual rooms, and some systems can support as many as four units (for four zones or rooms). Each zone has its own thermostat, allowing use only when occupants are present and thereby reducing energy usage and operating cost. Also, mini splits have no ducts, simplifying installation and avoiding associated energy loss. The primary disadvantage of mini splits is their cost, which DOE states is about 30 percent higher than central air conditioning systems (not including ductwork) and twice as much as window units of similar capacity. Depending on design specifics, potential energy savings from zoned cooling usage, and the expense of installing ductwork, mini splits may be worthwhile investigating.

Ground-source heat pumps. A ground-source heat pump (GSHP), sometimes referred to as a geothermal system, employs the earth's stable temperature below the surface to temper either air or water used in space-conditioning systems, preheating or precooking the air before it is further heated or cooled by space-conditioning equipment.

In a typical installation, deep holes are bored into the ground under or near the home; pipes are inserted in the holes and then a special conductive concrete mix is poured around the pipes, thermally connecting them to the surrounding earth. Water is run through the pipes where, depending on the season, it is either heated or cooled to the temperature of the earth. The water then circulates to a heat pump where energy is transferred between the water in the ground loop and either air or water in the home's space conditioning system. In an alternative installation, pipe loops are laid horizontally in a large 6- to 8-foot-deep trench (below the frost line).

Locations with roughly balanced heating and cooling loads are favored for GSHP systems because, through the course of the heating season, removing heating energy from the earth gradually cools off the surrounding earth, diminishing its effectiveness at preheating; when the season and direction of heat movement change, heat is removed from the home and rewarms the surrounding earth over time, restoring its heating capacity for the subsequent heating season. In a heating- or cooling-dominated climate, the earth's precooling or preheating capacity will be compromised after years of "lopsided" operation.[38]

GSHP systems are costly to build. They are most frequently found to be economically attractive in areas with significant heating *and* cooling loads; climates dominated by only heating or cooling generally have lower utility bills, so it takes longer to recoup the cost of installation.

Ren Anderson at NREL offers these cautions regarding GSHPs: "GSHPs can be good performers, but the performance of a GSHP strongly depends on the quality of the system design and the quality of the installation. Total GSHP system performance will be reduced if ground loops are undersized, if the pumps used to move the water through ground loops are oversized, or if soil thermal conductivity is low. Also, GSHP manufacturers are not required to include the actual energy that is used to operate the ground loop as part of their equipment performance ratings. As a result, energy ratings for GSHPs cannot be directly compared with energy ratings for air source heat pumps or air conditioners."[39]

At the Salah Residence in Portola Valley, California, the GSHP ground loops were integrated with the foundation piers, greatly reducing the cost attributable to the ground loops per se. This type of innovative approach may offer considerable savings.[40]

Magic boxes

In Europe, many new Passive Houses are being heated with "magic boxes" – compact packaged units that provide space heating and water heating. Although such equipment is not yet available in the United States, enthusiasts are hoping to see their introduction soon. One such unit, the Viessmann Vitodens 343-F Compact Energy Tower, a gas-fired condensing boiler with integral solar cylinder, solar control unit and Solar-Divicon, is shown in Figure 4-16.[41]

Courtesy of Viessmann Manufacturing Company Inc.

FIGURE 4-16. MAGIC BOX

Fireplaces

Fireplaces, pellet stoves, and other combustion devices, while seeming old-fashioned, may sometimes be an appropriate choice of heating system, particularly in the absence of any need for air conditioning and/or where heating loads are relatively low, and when they are used with a renewable fuel.

Courtesy of Tulikivi Corporation, tulikivi.com

Some fireplaces are designed for remarkably efficient operation. These include site-built Rumford fireplaces and masonry heaters such as the Tulikivi unit shown in Figure 4-17. Two fundamental principles underlie these combustion devices: complete combustion and thermal mass. A small amount of fuel (usually wood) is burned in a chamber designed for optimum combustion, so that as much as possible of the fuel is converted to useful energy, and the resulting heat is absorbed by the mass of the fireplace as the combustion gases travel through the exhaust system and out the chimney. The stored heat is then re-radiated into the home over an extended period. Fireplace designs must provide make-up air for combustion to safeguard indoor air quality.

**FIGURE 4-17.
TULIKIVI FIREPLACE**

According to Tulikivi, one burn can heat a good-sized living space for 18 hours or more, with peak output 3 to 5 hours after the burn is started and tapering off gradually. One of their smaller units can heat a space as large as 750 square feet with as little as 22 pounds of wood; larger units can heat spaces up to 1,080 and 1,400 square feet with as little as 44 or 70 pounds of wood, respectively.[42] However, even the most efficient wood stoves and fireplaces purportedly emit significantly greater nitrous oxide emissions than a standard gas furnace and are less efficient.

► Choose fireplaces that meet clean-air standards, both for the sake of the occupants and for broader environmental reasons. See the *LEED for Homes Rating System*, EQ2, Combustion Venting, or the EPA's Indoor Air Plus Construction Specifications, Item 5.2, for selection guidelines.[43]

A key to the successful use of masonry heating fireplaces is their central placement within the living space – if the unit is placed against an exterior wall, much of its heat will be radiated to the outdoors rather than to the home's interior, significantly reducing its effectiveness.

Cooling

A range of residential cooling strategies is described below, starting with those that require little or no power (passive strategies) and progressing to more power-intensive (active) options. However, as with heating, which of the active options will be most efficient depends on a number of variables and must be determined by a qualified design professional.

No cooling

There are a few locations in North America – for instance, along the Northern California coast, where I live – that have cooling loads so low that mechanical cooling is rarely installed in residential buildings and, in fact, little attention is paid even to passive cooling strategies. In these locations, the usual complement of doors and windows is generally believed to provide enough air movement for warm-weather comfort except during a very few days of the year.

Even in such mild-climate locations, however, some homes may be challenged by occasional excessive heat gain. This can be a particular issue for urban or multifamily residences, due to limited window area, difficulty in providing adequate cross-ventilation, and/or the undesirability of keeping windows open for reasons of security, noise, or air pollution. Energy modeling can yield valuable information about the number of hours the building will be subject to uncomfortably high interior temperatures. These data should be used to evaluate the desirability of incorporating explicit passive and/or active cooling strategies.

▶ The American Society of Heating, Refrigerating, and Air-conditioning Engineers, in its outdoor air ventilation standard (ASHRAE 62.2), exempts climates with fewer than 4,500 infiltration degree-days (approximately the sum of HDD + CDD) from mechanical ventilation requirements. This is a commonly accepted definition of a mild climate.

Thermal mass

The most passive of all cooling strategies is the use of thermal mass, the capacity of a body to store heat. The ability of thermally massive materials to retain heat creates a thermal flywheel effect – that is, the mass will absorb heat when its surroundings are hotter than the mass, and release heat later, after its surroundings have cooled. Thus thermal mass within a building has the effect of dampening interior temperature swings relative to exterior temperatures.

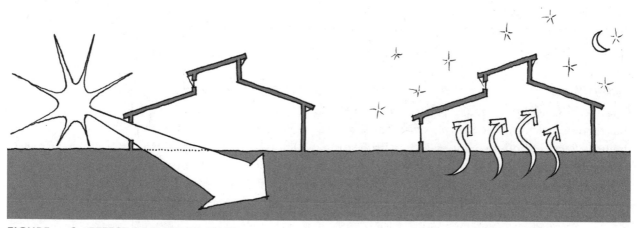

FIGURE 4-18. EFFECT OF THERMAL MASS

Thermal mass can be heated directly, by the sun striking it, or indirectly, by contact with warm air. Of the two mechanisms, direct solar gain is by far the most effective.

The higher a material's thermal mass, the more heat it will hold and the longer it will take to release that heat; thus the more significantly it will modulate interior temperature. Materials with relatively high thermal mass include rammed earth, brick, concrete, ceramic tile, gypsum board, and water; materials with lower thermal mass include wood, air, and insulation materials.

Thermal mass may be employed for passive cooling in a variety of ways. The use of gypsum board and hard-surface flooring, such as tile, to provide thermal mass was described earlier in this chapter. Thermal mass wall systems, such as solid concrete, insulating concrete forms (ICFs), rammed earth, and adobe can also be used effectively for passive cooling (and night-time heating) in certain climates. Thermal mass in excess may prove to be a liability, however. For example, a solid concrete or rammed earth structure in a climate that does not cool down substantially on summer nights may be a disaster – the walls will absorb and continually re-radiate heat into the interior, contributing significantly to discomfort and

▶ Be sure to get competent design assistance before deciding to incorporate large amounts of thermal mass, such as rammed earth walls.

therefore to cooling loads. In a climate with prolonged periods of winter cloud cover, the mass may not experience enough solar radiation to warm it up, but instead will absorb heat from objects (including people) in the interior over extended periods, thereby increasing heating loads. Thermal mass located within the insulated envelope is a far more effective flywheel than a solid mass wall, and less likely to be a thermal liability.

Indigenous structures in the tropics and subtropics, such as the Thai house shown in Figure 4-19, reflect intelligent responses to local climate conditions; they minimize thermal mass and are designed to facilitate air circulation around and through all building surfaces.

FIGURE 4-19. TRADITIONAL THAI HOUSE

© Shariffc | Dreamstime.com

Thermal mass was used extensively by solar building design pioneers in the 1970s. One of the most popular approaches, referred to as a Trombe wall, consisted of water or another thermal mass embedded in a wall behind a panel of glass, exposed to direct sun. By and large, however, Trombe walls have fallen from favor. This is because they provide benefit within only a rather narrow set of circumstances and require specialized expertise to design.[44]

In general, a modest amount of thermal mass will be beneficial in many climates. It may be provided in the form of thicker-than-usual gypsum wallboard, tile flooring, or solid concrete floors (a good match with radiant heating) – properly insulated, of course! Water is also a very good thermal mass medium; for example, the water in the tank for a radiant heating system can be used for thermal mass storage. The degree to which thermal mass will provide an energy benefit can best be determined through energy modeling, although modeling programs vary in their ability to successfully simulate the effects of thermal mass. Ask your design team members, particularly your architect and/or energy consultant, if they have experience with thermal mass and whether the software will accurately predict the effect of the mass. If not, you will need to rely on your team's experience or have modeling done in another program, one that better captures mass effects.

▶ See Appendix A for a list of energy modeling programs.

Passive ventilation

Passive ventilation provides cooling effects by displacing warm air with cooler air – known as stack effect – and to a lesser degree through the sensation of air movement (wind). John Weale notes, "The stack effect is very reliable. If any wind is available, it is usually more powerful than the stack effect in low-rise structures. However, it is very difficult to count on the wind, or even predict where it comes from, hence we focus on stack effect over the more powerful but unreliable wind-catching approaches."[45]

Passive ventilation cooling consists of strategically locating windows and other openings to capitalize on localized wind patterns and/or naturally-occurring pressure differentials within and around a building. A principal passive ventilation mechanism is stack effect– the tendency of warm air to rise. Stack effect can be used to good effect by placing openings high in a building, such as at the top of a stairwell or solar chimney, in clerestories, etc. As hot air rises and exits, the negative pressure created by the exhausting air draws in cooler air from openings lower in the building.

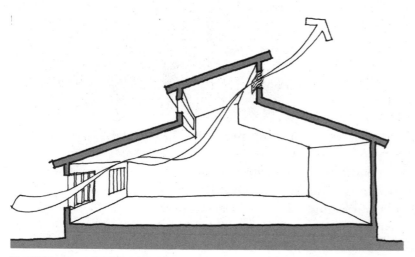

FIGURE 4-20. STACK EFFECT

Stack effect and pressure differentials will vary in their effectiveness at cooling a home based on a number of variables:

- The difference in height between openings

- The horizontal distance between openings

- The number and sizes of openings

- The relative placement and distribution of openings within the home and/or within rooms

- The type of window operation (casement, double-hung, awning, hopper, etc.)

- Climatic variables such as diurnal temperature swing

- Microclimatic and building conditions such as sunlight and shading

- How effectively the openings are regulated (opened and closed); their operation can be either manual or automated (sensor-based)

Passive ventilation design is not a precise science but an art informed by experience, intuition, and observation. Although ventilation strategies can be tested with models in specialized wind-tunnel facilities, such facilities are quite uncommon, usually found only at universities and building research institutions. Guidance from a design professional experienced with passive design is the best alternative.

Fans

Fans offer an active ventilation cooling strategy relying on air movement, sometimes with consequent changes in air temperature. There are several types of fans designed for air movement: paddle fans, window fans, and whole-house fans.

**FIGURE 4-21.
WINDWARD III FAN**

Courtesy of Danny Parker, Florida Solar Energy Center, fsec.ucf.edu

Paddle fans function primarily by creating the sensation of air movement against the skin, which can add several degrees to the high end of the personal comfort range – for example, at 60 percent relative humidity, 85 instead of 78 degrees will feel comfortable.[46] However, most paddle fans are relatively inefficient – so much so that the energy used to run them may exceed the energy savings associated with reduced air-conditioning demand. The notable exception is The Windward, developed by Danny Parker of the Florida Solar Energy Center in 1997. Parker, in conversing with his father-in-law, a pilot, observed that the paddles on conventional fans were always flat, in contrast to airplane propeller blades, which are shaped specifically for aerodynamics – that is, to move air effectively. He applied this principle in designing The Windward, which uses roughly 40 percent less energy than conventional fans. The Windward is available at Home Depot stores throughout the US.[47]

Window fans are portable electric fans that are usually placed in double- or single-hung windows for the summer season, pushing air into a single room. Like paddle fans, they function primarily by creating the cooling sensation of air movement, and are not particularly efficient. However, where cooling loads are minimal, they may be an appropriate strategy. Used at night to draw cooler outside air into the house, they may also assist in modulating interior temperature by cooling the room's thermal mass to night-time temperatures, which is very effective in some climates.

Whole-house fans, typically installed in attics, operate as a single central exhaust to pull warm air out of the entire house at night, replacing it with cooler outside air. The powered cousins of passive ventilation, whole-house fans similarly require windows to be open to admit the cooler night air. Used properly, they can pre-cool the interior mass and thereby delay the need for air conditioning the following day.

Like conventional whole-house fans, the NightBreeze® ventilation system, developed by Davis Energy Group,[48] circulates cool, filtered, outside air through the home at night, precooling the interior mass for the following day. However, it is an automated, "smart" system – it decides when and how to operate based on conditions both outdoors and in the home – and does not require windows to be opened. During the summer, if the house is warm and the outside temperature is cool, the NightBreeze system automatically brings outside air into the house through a damper and ventilation duct. (NightBreeze also can be used to circulate heat from the water heater or furnace while periodically introducing fresh air for ventilation.) This system is designed for climates with low humidity.

Evaporative cooling

Evaporative coolers – often called swamp coolers – are self-contained units usually placed in the lower portion of double-hung windows in homes, or similar through-wall units in hotels. Evaporative coolers provide cooling by moving hot air past water. A fan pulls air through water-soaked pads in the cooler and on into the home. As the outdoor air passes through the water-soaked pads, the water absorbs heat from the hot air stream, both reducing its temperature and humidifying the air. So-called direct evaporative coolers tend to work effectively only in conditions with low relative humidity, such as desert climates. As humidity increases, they lose effectiveness. In contrast, indirect evaporative cooling is used to improve the efficiency of a conventional air conditioner by precooling the entering air stream. One disadvantage to evaporative coolers is that they can use a lot of water.

Air conditioning

Air conditioners, designed to control both temperature and humidity, operate using an evaporator and a condenser. Liquid refrigerant vaporizes in the evaporator section and absorbs heat from the metal in the evaporator coil. The coil then becomes cold and removes heat from warm air blown through the coil and into the home. The vaporized refrigerant carries the heat it collected from the indoor air to a compressor, where the refrigerant vapor is compressed and sent to the condenser. In the condenser, the refrigerant then condenses back to a liquid, releasing its latent heat of vaporization and heating the condenser coil. The condenser coil has a higher temperature than the air moving through it, so the heat flows from the coil to the air outside the home.

Air conditioners vary in efficiency, ranging in SEER from 10 to 24; higher numbers reflect higher efficiency ratings. Garden-variety air conditioners currently found in production homes and home improvement retail stores are usually rated SEER 13, which is the US Department of Energy minimum standard; older units often have lower ratings. SEER ratings of 14 and above are generally considered good. Depending on climate and other factors (such as the current federal tax credit for SEER 16+), SEER 16 often offers the best bang for the buck. Units rated SEER 18 and higher sometimes may not be cost-effective in comparison with photovoltaics – that is, you may be able to add more PV generating capacity at a price that is lower than upgrading to a higher SEER rating.[49] LEED for Homes rankings of SEER ratings are shown in Figure 4-11.

Another factor in air conditioner efficiency is the motor used to circulate air in the home: a brushless DC fan motor, because it consumes less energy, emits less heat and therefore maximizes cooling efficiency. And if you live in a humid area, you also will want to look for a unit that allows you to control humidity settings as well as temperature settings. This is an important comfort feature and can also help reduce risks associated with humidity-related mold problems.

Heat pumps

Heat pumps, which provide both cooling and heating, are covered above in the section on heating systems.

Radiant cooling

Radiant cooling is relatively unusual, and typically – though not always – done in conjunction with radiant heating. Cool water is circulated through surfaces in the home in small-diameter piping or PEX tubing, cooling the building surfaces, which then radiate "coolth" to other parts of the building and the occupants. (In reality, you – the warm body – radiate heat *to* the cool surfaces, but what you experience is the cold radiating at you.)

Radiant cooling is more frequently placed in ceilings than in floors, to work in concert with rather than in opposition to the propensity for heat to rise and cold to fall. However, when a single system provides both radiant heating and radiant cooling, it is usually done in the floors.

Radiant cooling is tricky. According to radiant cooling expert Peter Rumsey, "Radiant cooling works best with inorganic surfaces, such as tiles and concrete. This is due to the slightly higher humidity ratio that will develop near the cooling surface. Water temperatures in radiant cooling need to be in the 60 to 65 deg F range instead of the typical chilled water temperature of 45 deg F or colder. Air going into the building should be dehumidified in order to prevent condensation on the cooling surface. If designed properly, radiant cooling can provide superior comfort, low energy use, and better indoor quality compared to standard all-air-based HVAC systems."[50]

John Weale adds, "A radiant system also requires a source of cooled water, which is rarely provided in residential buildings. It can be generated evaporatively, or by small compressor systems similar to those used in window air conditioners or refrigerators, but it is not a common residential approach."[51] This is certainly true. However, in at least one NZEH project, Tah.Mah.Lah. (see Appendix B), a ground-source heat pump is being used in conjunction with a radiant in-floor cooling system.

Prioritizing Elements

Now, what do you do with all this information? There are a lot of decisions to be made, and I've given you relatively little prescriptive guidance for making them. As discussed in previous chapters, it's critical that the decisions be made in an integrated process – one that ensures the input of all the team members who have relevant expertise. There are simply too many variables to offer one-size-fits-all advice. Rather, solutions have to be tailored to the project and location specifics.

It's crucial that energy modeling be used to inform your decisions. In order to illustrate the variable significance of a range of building performance characteristics based on building type and climate, in our office we ran a number of Micropas simulations on two different buildings, a suburban detached single-family home and an urban zero-lot line single-family home, shown in Figure 4-22.

Courtesy of Prakash Chandran (suburban); Ann Edminster (urban)

FIGURE 4-22. MODELED HOMES (SUBURBAN, LEFT; URBAN, RIGHT)

Both are located in the San Francisco Bay Area; we modeled them in San Francisco (2,700 HDD, 100 CDD), Palm Desert (800 HDD, 4,200 CDD), and South Lake Tahoe (7,800 HDD, 40 CDD) to test the influence of different building characteristics in these three very different climates.

In each climate, we tested a range of values for each of the following seven parameters:

- Orientation (rotating through 360 degrees in 45-degree increments)
- Wall insulation (values from R-13 to R-43[52])
- Roof insulation (values from R-19 to R-74)
- Window area (as-built, 20 percent more, and 20 percent less)
- Window U-values (best and worst values – U-.09 and U-.87 respectively)
- Window SHGC (best and worst values – 0.2 and 0.7 respectively)
- HVAC equipment (gas furnaces, heat pumps, and combined hydronic with a range of efficiency values)

The modeling outcomes were stated in terms of the percentage change in source energy for the proposed design compared to the standard (i.e., minimally code-compliant) design. Then we looked at how much the changes in each parameter influenced the overall building energy use, based on the range of values we had used. In other words, how much did changing the value of the parameter (e.g., roof insulation R-value) affect building performance?

For example, we modeled each building in eight different orientations and looked at the change in performance for each model. When we modeled the Urban home in San Francisco, we found that energy performance ranged from 29.6 percent to 32.3 percent better than the standard design – an influence range of only 2.7 percent. The same home modeled in Palm Desert, however, produced energy performance values ranging from 23.4 percent to 48.2 percent *worse* than the standard design – an influence range of 24.8 percent. This climate-based differential can be attributed to the home having glazing on only two facades, and the base case glazing SHGC not being optimized for cooling; in San Francisco's mild climate, the effect of this is much less important than it would be in the heavily cooling-dominated climate of Palm Desert.

By contrast, the Suburban home produced a much narrower influence range for changes in orientation in all three climates (5.7 percent in San Francisco, 8.0 percent in Palm Desert, 3.9 percent in South Lake Tahoe). Since there is glazing relatively evenly distributed among all four façades and the location has virtually no cooling load, this very different outcome makes sense.

Figure 4-23 shows the influence range for each parameter we modeled, and its ranking, with 1 being the parameter that had greatest influence on overall building performance in each scenario and 7 being the parameter that had the least influence.

While recognizing that this modeling reflects a very limited, non-representative exercise, without applicability to any specific project, a few of our more notable findings, and their implications, are listed below.

> **Finding 1:** In all but one scenario, window U-value had the greatest influence range (#1 ranking), with values from 22.6 percent to 54.8 percent. **Implication:** Low U-value windows are likely to provide excellent performance benefits in many projects. Note that neither of these projects has a particularly high WFA ratio; in projects with higher WFAs, U-value will be even more important.

| Influence of parameter | San Francisco | | | | Palm Desert | | | | South Lake Tahoe | | | |
| | Suburban | | Urban | | Suburban | | Urban | | Suburban | | Urban | |
	Range	Ranking	Range	Ranking	Range	Ranking	Range	Ranking	Range	Ranking	Range	Ranking
Home orientation	5.7	5	2.7	7	8.0	4	24.8	5	3.9	6	4.1	6
HVAC	11.4	4	13.0	3	2.8	7	15.5	6	15.8	4	20.7	2
Roof insulation	4.3	6	3.0	6	5.5	6	8.6	7	5.2	5	4.4	5
Wall insulation	19.0	2	14.0	2	19.5	3	25.0	4	24.2	3	19.1	3
Window SHGC	18.1	3	6.5	4	19.9	2	87.0	1	36.3	2	0.3	7
Window U-values	35.4	1	48.4	1	22.6	1	44.2	2	48.6	1	54.8	1
Window area	1.9	7	6.0	5	6.7	5	27.9	3	2.0	7	9.1	4

FIGURE 4-23. RANGE OF INFLUENCE OF DIFFERENT BUILDING PARAMETERS BY CLIMATE ZONE

Finding 2: Window SHGC produced the biggest spread in influence range, with values from 0.3 percent to 87 percent. Its influence is generally high, however, ranked #1, #2, or #3 in four of six scenarios. **Implication:** SHGC is likely to be quite influential on performance and – no surprise to anyone who is passive solar-savvy – it is highly climate- and orientation-specific. It therefore should be analyzed carefully to optimize glazing performance.

Finding 3: Roof insulation had much less influence than I expected, given the emphasis generally placed on it; values ranged from 3.0 percent to 8.6 percent, rankings in the bottom three. **Implication:** My cautious observation here is that both of the homes modeled were two-story, and one-story homes would be likely to show more influence from changes in roof insulation. It also should be noted that the minimum level of roof insulation modeled was R-19, and since the law of diminishing returns dictates that the effect of each added point in R-value has less impact, this should not be interpreted to suggest that less roof insulation would represent a good economy. Not so.

Finding 4: Wall insulation, by contrast, is relatively high in influence, with rankings of #2 or #3 in all but one scenario, and influence range values between 14 percent and 25 percent. **Implication:** Bumping up values in wall insulation deserves careful consideration, with particular attention to the inclusion of continuous insulation, which – as mentioned earlier – has roughly twice the impact of a comparable R-value added to the wall cavity.

You'll need to do your own modeling to uncover the unique effects of the different characteristics on your design and to establish your own design (and investment) priorities. Also keep in mind that while energy modeling is a very valuable guide, the benefits of the most innovative approaches may not be fully captured in a model, so a critical evaluation of results by the most experienced NZEH designer you can find can be invaluable for the final design optimizations.

Hot Water

Four factors affect energy use associated with hot water:

- Water heating equipment efficiency (how much of the input energy is converted into useful energy);

- The design of the hot water delivery system (to minimize energy lost as water travels through the system);

- Drain water heat recovery (to recapture and reuse energy stored in warm water exiting the system); and

- Patterns of use (which, as in so many other systems, can either increase or decrease water and energy demands, independent of system design).

Selection of plumbing fixtures and appliances is also important, as it affects both hot and cold water use; this topic is covered in Chapter 5.

Water heating equipment

Water heaters vary in their efficiency in converting the input energy (typically gas or electricity) to heat. That efficiency is most frequently expressed as an energy factor (EF) and less commonly, for combined water and space heaters, as combined annual efficiency (CAE). According to the LEED for Homes Rating System, water heater efficiency is categorized[53] as shown in Figure 4-24; higher EF and CAE values correspond to better performance. Energy-free homes often include solar hot water, discussed separately in Chapter 6, along with a highly efficient storage or tankless water heater.

Water heater type	Good	Better	Best
Gas	EF 0.53-0.79	EF ≥ 0.8 for storage water heater or CAE ≥ 0.8 for combination water + space heater	
Electric	EF ≥ 0.89 (80 gal) EF ≥ 0.92 (50 gal) EF ≥ 0.93 (40 gal)	EF ≥ 0.99 for tankless heater	EF ≥ 2.0 for heat pump
Solar (backup system with preheat tank)		Provides ≥ 40% of annual load	Provides ≥ 60% of annual load

EF = energy factor   CAE = combined annual efficiency

FIGURE 4-24. RELATIVE ENERGY PERFORMANCE OF WATER HEATERS

Note that the test for water heating efficiency assumes that the water heater is within conditioned space; if it is not (e.g., if it is located in the garage), then energy losses (for storage tank models in particular) are greater than assumed in the rating.

For all-electric NZE homes in California, water heating may represent a challenge. The most efficient electric water heaters available use heat pumps. However, architect Dan Smith notes that, while promising, these appliances are new and unusual; slow-recovery models may require electric-resistance backup heat, which can diminish the overall system performance. Further, the energy models used for code compliance in California are blind to onsite energy production, so electricity use is generally weighted more than three times higher than gas in simulations (reflecting site-to-source multipliers as discussed in Chapter 1). The effect is to penalize electric heat pumps, even when they're run by onsite renewable energy systems.[54]

Tankless or storage? There is a popular misconception that tankless water heaters are more efficient than storage (tank) water heaters. I believe this arises from confusion between how the water is heated and how it is delivered; when a water heater of either type is located close to the point of use, energy losses associated with delivery are minimized (more about this below). Perhaps because tankless units are often installed close to the point of use, they have been perceived as efficient, per se. However, the proximity of the heater to the tap is altogether independent of the efficiency of the water heater itself. Both equipment and delivery system should be optimized for best overall performance.

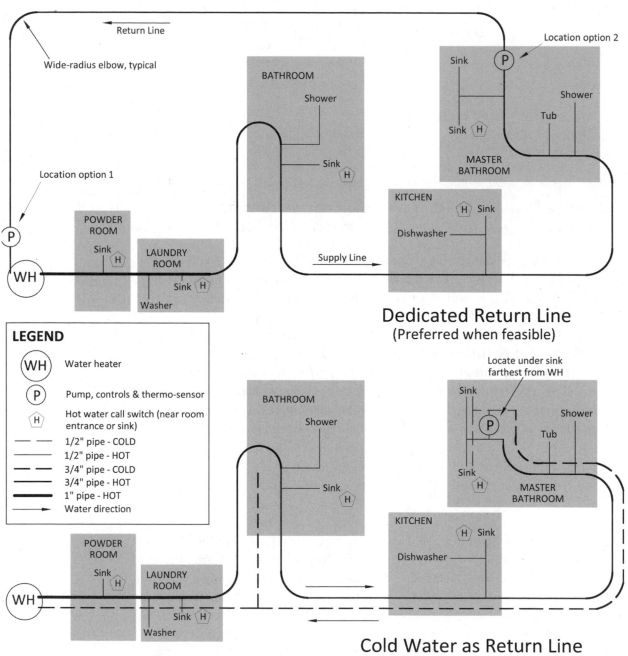

Return Line

Wide-radius elbow, typical

Location option 2

Location option 1

BATHROOM

Shower

Sink (H)

Sink

Sink (H)

Shower

Tub

MASTER BATHROOM

POWDER ROOM

Sink (H)

LAUNDRY ROOM

Sink (H)

Washer

KITCHEN

(H) Sink

Dishwasher

Supply Line

WH

P

Dedicated Return Line
(Preferred when feasible)

LEGEND

(WH)   Water heater

(P)   Pump, controls & thermo-sensor

(H)   Hot water call switch (near room entrance or sink)

– – –   1/2" pipe - COLD

———   1/2" pipe - HOT

– – –   3/4" pipe - COLD

———   3/4" pipe - HOT

———   1" pipe - HOT

———▶   Water direction

Locate under sink farthest from WH

BATHROOM

Shower

Sink (H)

Sink

Sink (H)

Shower

Tub

MASTER BATHROOM

POWDER ROOM

Sink (H)

LAUNDRY ROOM

Sink (H)

Washer

KITCHEN

(H) Sink

Dishwasher

WH

P

Cold Water as Return Line
(When dedicated return is not feasible)

Concept courtesy of Gary Klein, Affiliated International Management, LLC; drawn by Jenny Levinson

FIGURE 4-25. STRUCTURED (RECIRCULATING) PLUMBING LAYOUTS

Hot water delivery

The heated water needs to be delivered to the various points of use in the home. Some energy is lost en route; how much energy is lost is a function of the distance traveled via hot water pipes, how well-insulated those pipes are, and the range of ambient temperatures the pipes are exposed to along the way. Thus an efficient delivery system will minimize travel distance (and pipe volume), maximize insulation, and keep as much of the piping as possible within conditioned space.

The best solution is to design the home with a compact, centralized plumbing core, locating the water heater as close as possible to the hot water fixtures – the bathrooms, kitchen sink, and clothes washer (though it's better not to use hot water for washing clothes). In some homes, one or more of the points of use may be remote from the water heater while others are nearer. In such cases it may make sense to have more than one water heater, for example, a storage unit that serves most of the home and a small tankless unit to serve a single remote hot water use location. Water heating expert Gary Klein offers, "The type of water heater is somewhat dependent on the intermittency of use … think remote powder room or remote guest bathroom, neither of which gets used very often. A small electric tankless would make sense for the powder room. An on-demand pump would probably make more sense for the guest bathroom, unless the distance was very great."[55]

Although every effort should be made to achieve a compact layout, if it is not feasible an *on-demand* recirculating system can help minimize energy use by pumping hot water to points of use only when it is actually needed. Two such systems are shown in Figure 4-25. Many custom homes have recirculating systems, but these typically recirculate the hot water 24/7, with energy losses through the walls of the pipes as the hot water travels the loop, as well as from unnecessary pump use. Sometimes timers are used to pump hot water through the system only at designated times; these are also less than ideal, however, since they will run whether someone is there to use the hot water or not – for instance, while the family is away on vacation.

An efficient on-demand system is activated by pushbuttons, which should be located near each point of use (e.g., next to sinks and/or in the master bedroom). The system should be electronically controlled so that the pump will be activated only when the water drops below the minimum delivery temperature. If it is at or above that temperature, the pushbutton will have no effect. If it is below the preset temperature, it will pump hot water from the water heater, pushing cold water

► **GreenBuilding Advisor.com** includes many helpful plumbing resources and a glossary of building industry, energy efficiency, and green building terms that should be of particular use to anyone new to the field.

through the loop and back to the water heater; after a brief interval, hot water will be available throughout the loop. As occupants learn how long it takes for hot water to be delivered, they can wait the few seconds after pressing the button before turning on the tap. This avoids wasting the water that otherwise would be allowed to run down the drain before the hot water arrives.

Klein notes, "For those who want less interaction with their hot water delivery, there are dedicated motion sensors that will send a signal to the pump when their beam is crossed. These specialized motion sensors have directed beams and lock-outs that prevent continuous triggering, thereby minimizing the energy consequences of this type of convenience."[56] Even so, this strategy will entail greater energy use than the pushbutton method, as the sensors can't detect whether hot water is needed – the person crossing the beam may be fetching an aspirin, getting a drink of water, or arriving to take a shower.

Note that a recirculating system can't be used with home-run plumbing (a water distribution system in which individual plumbing lines extend from a central manifold to each plumbing fixture or water-using appliance).

Courtesy of Larry Weingarten, waterheaterrescue.com

FIGURE 4-26.
DRAIN WATER HEAT RECOVERY

Drain water heat recovery

While there is little conclusive information about the magnitude of energy savings that can be achieved through drain water heat recovery, it is nevertheless a technology worth investigating for use in energy-free homes. In simplest form, the system consists of a feeder pipe for the water heater coiled tightly around the drain water line; as heated water exits the house via the drainpipe, heat is transferred to the incoming cold water. More information on this technology is available at **www.greenbuildingadvisor.com/green-basics/drain-water-heat-recovery** (detailed information available only to subscribers). The Canada Mortgage and Housing Corporation (CMHC) has published a free report, *Drain-water Heat Recovery Performance Testing at CCHT* (December 2007); search for "drain water heat recovery" at **www.cmhc-schl.gc.ca/en/inpr/search/search_001.cfm**. CMHC also has an online energy savings calculator for drain water heat recovery at **www.ceatech.ca/calculator**.

Drain water heat recovery installations require some vertical drain line height, prohibiting their use in slab-on-grade applications or in single story homes with shallow crawl spaces.

The ZETA Communities Lancaster project in Oakland, California (**www.zetacommunities.com**), has installed a drain water heat recovery system. Preliminary testing indicates that water heating use reductions may be lower than numbers in published literature; however, further study is planned.

Hot water use

Most of us in the United States have become accustomed to hot water on demand, yet in some climates cold water is adequate for hand-washing and clothes-washing nearly year-round, and in others it is adequate during many months. Even hot water used for showering can be minimized by turning water off while soaping up, then back on for rinsing off. This strategy is facilitated by choosing showerheads with built-in temporary shutoffs (shown in Figure 5-9), called navy valves.

However, Gary Klein cautions against using navy valves with typical gas tankless water heaters. "Every time you turn off the tap, a gas tankless water heater turns off and then goes through a cool-down cycle of 60 to 90 seconds (just about time to finish soaping up). When you turn the tap back on, it goes through a ramp-up cycle of 10 to 15 seconds, during which cold water is entering the hot water distribution system. This creates the problem called the cold water sandwich. The Navien model with a small upstream tank (before the burner) would eliminate this problem. So would a downstream buffer tank or tube on the typical gas tankless."[57]

The fixture's flow rate also has an influence on hot water uses. However, even low-flow fixtures will use less water (both hot and cold) if turned on part-way rather than full-blast. Choose faucets that allow flow to be regulated easily – some operate more smoothly than others – and that make it easy to select hot-only or cold-only operation. And, although I haven't come across any studies on this, I also suspect that two-handle lavatory faucets may be a better choice than one-handle models by forcing users to make a conscious choice of cold versus hot (although left-handers and some other users may habitually reach for the hot valve first).

▶ Low-flow plumbing fixtures are discussed in Chapter 5.

Multifamily considerations

This section was contributed by multifamily energy consultant and Green Building Alameda County Program Manager Heather Larson, of Berkeley, California.

Water heating tends to be a dominant energy use in multifamily buildings, partly because the exterior surface area of the individual dwelling units is less than that of single-family homes, with less associated heat transfer through those exterior surfaces. The result is that hot water is a larger fraction of the total energy use.

In multifamily buildings with individual water heaters for each unit, the issues and strategies of distribution system design and efficiencies are similar to single-family homes. However, it is common for multifamily buildings to have central water heaters (boilers) with a large distribution system and recirculation loop. Boilers are typically gas appliances with efficiency stated as AFUE, as shown in Figure 4-11. Some boilers are manufactured using a super-high-efficiency condensing technology (AFUE 92 to 98). Comparably efficient "indirect" units, which are essentially oversized tankless water heaters, are also available. Atmospheric technology boilers are slightly less efficient (AFUE 82 to 90).

Tank-type boilers can be combined with solar preheat systems for significant energy savings. Distribution system strategies such as extra insulation, recirculation controls, and high-efficiency recirculation pumps also represent opportunities for savings.

Boilers raise some additional issues. While it is cheaper to install one or two very efficient boilers for 100 dwelling units than it is to install 100 really efficient individual water heaters, there are major regulatory barriers to individually metering hot water usage from a central boiler. Hence occupants of buildings with central systems are typically not billed for water. Because it is bundled in with their rent, they receive no price signal and thus have no incentive to conserve hot water. The obstacles to submetering hot water use from central systems need to be removed to further energy efficiency and conservation in multifamily housing.

Endnotes

1   National Association of Home Builders, Housing Facts, Figures and Trends, March 2006, http://www.soflo.org/report/NAHBhousingfactsMarch2006.pdf; and U.S. Census Bureau, Housing and Household Economic Statistics Division, Table HH-6: Average Population Per Household and Family: 1940 to Present, http://www.census.gov/population/www/ socdemo/hh-fam.html, and National Association of Home Builders, Construction Statistics, Median and Average Square Feet of Floor Area in New One-Family Houses Sold by Location, June 2009, http://www.nahb.org/fileUpload_details.aspx?contentID=80051.

2   National Association of Home Builders, Construction Statistics, Median and Average Square Feet of Floor Area in New One-Family Houses Sold by Location, June 2009, http://www.nahb.org/fileUpload_details.aspx?contentID=80051.

3   National Association of Home Builders, Housing Facts, Figures and Trends, March 2006, http://www.soflo.org/report/NAHBhousingfactsMarch2006.pdf.

4   Federcasa & Ministry of Infrastructure of the Italian Republic, Average Housing Statistics in the European Union 2005/2006, page 54, http://www.federcasa.it/news/housing_ statistics/Report_housing_statistics_2005_2006.pdf. This document reports floor area by country for years ranging from 2000 to 2006; the average for all western European countries (as defined by http://www.nationmaster.com/encyclopedia/Western-Europe) is 1,138 square feet.

5   Climate classifications systems are discussed e.g. in "Climate Classification for Building Energy Codes and Standards," by Robert S. Briggs et al., Pacific Northwest National Laboratory, March 26, 2002, http://www.energycodes.gov/implement/pdfs/climate_ paper_review_draft_rev.pdf.

6   Graham Irwin, Zero Impact Architecture, Personal communication, September 2009.

7   The terms "envelope" and "enclosure" are used more or less interchangeably in the building industry; "envelope" is more common, but experts favor "enclosure" because it is more descriptive and accurate. "Skin" is also used to mean essentially the same thing.

8   Paraphrased, with apologies, from Coldham & Hartman Architects, Lesson 3, "The Zero Energy Home - What, How, and If," Boston Architectural College course, Summer 2009.

9   The "vapor profile" is the relative vapor-permeability of the different components of the assembly, and their placement in the assembly to assure appropriate drying potential.

10 BuildingScience.com, Review of Residential Ventilation Technologies, pages 8-9, http:// www.buildingscience.com/documents/reports/rr-0502-review-of-residential-ventilation- technologies/view?searchterm=review%20of%20residential%20ventilation.

11 "The Zero Energy Home: What, How, and If," Boston Architectural College, Summer 2009, taught by Andrew Webster and Thomas Hartman, Coldham & Hartman Architects.

12 Dan Smith, Daniel Smith and Associates, Personal communication, September 2009.

13 Environmental Buildng News, "Insulation : Thermal Performance is Just the Beginning," Jan 2005, http://www.buildinggreen.com/auth/article.cfm/2005/1/1/Insulation-Thermal- Performance-is-Just-the-Beginning/.

14 Thermal bridging refers to the propensity for heat to travel via the path of least resistance –
in stick-framed walls, via the framing members, which have lower thermal resistance than
the cavity insulation between them.

15 Environmental Building News, "Polystyrene Insulation: Does It Belong in a Green Building,"
August 2009, http://www.buildinggreen.com/auth/article.cfm/2009/7/30/Polystyrene-
Insulation-Does-It-Belong-in-a-Green-Building/.

16 Reed, et al.

17 Danny Parker, Florida Solar Energy Center, "Reflective Walls," Home Energy,
May-June 2009.

18 Ren Anderson, National Renewable Energy Laboratory, Personal communication,
August 2009.

19 Bruce King, Ecological Building Network and author, *Buildings of Earth and Straw*, among
others, Personal communication, August 2009.

20 Green Building Advisor, "Use a Frost Protected Shallow Foundation," http://www.
greenbuildingadvisor.com/strategies/use-frost-protected-shallow-foundation.

21 The LEED for Homes Materials and Resources Technical Advisory Subcommittee, which
I chair, has ruled favorably on several requests for credit for ICF systems, based on the
demonstrated material savings.

22 Promotional literature for windows sometimes misleadingly presents center-of-glass
U-values, so be sure to check that the U-values you're working with are for the full-frame
windows.

23 Dariush Arasteh, Lawrence Berkeley National Laboratory, personal communication,
September 2009.

24 David Paulus, PhD., P.E., "U-factor, SHGC, CR, VT, Air Infiltration – What does this stuff
mean?",www.wascowindows.com/Documents/U-factor.pdf.

25 Condensation resistance indicates a product's ability to resist the formation of
condensation on its interior surface. It is expressed as a number between 0 and 100;
the higher the number, the better the product is at resisting condensation formation

26 Tah.Mah.Lah. is a native Ohlone word meaning mountain lion. It is the name of a private
residence, under construction in the fall of 2009, in Portola Valley, California. Case study
resources are included in Appendix B.

27 Coldham & Hartman Architects, Personal communication, August 2009.

28 Stewart Brand, *How Buildings Learn: What Happens After They're Built*, Penguin, 1995.

29 Kohta Ueno, Building Science Corporation, Personal communication, August 2009.

30 US Census Bureau, Manufacturing, Mining and Construction Statistics, www.census.gov/
const/www/charindex.html#multibldg; and National Climate Data Center; and Energy
Information Agency, Department of Energy, www.eia.doe.gov/emeu/recs/recs2005/c&e/
detailed_tables2005c&e.html.

31 LEED is the U.S. Green Building Council's Leadership in Energy and Environmental Design
green building rating system. See www.usgbc.org/leed or Appendix C for more information.

32 "Good" systems earn 1 point, "better" options earn 2 points, and "best" earn 3 points.

33 Katrin Klingenberg, Mike Kernagis, and Mary James, *Homes for a Changing Climate: Passive Houses in the U.S.,* Low Carbon Productions, 2008.

34 *International Residential Code,* 2006, Section R303.8.

35 Lynn Underwood, City of Norfolk, VA, personal communication, August 2009.

36 DOE Energy Efficiency and Renewable Energy website, http://www.energysavers.gov/ your_home/space_heating_cooling/index.cfm/mytopic=12630.

37 U.S. Department of Energy, Ductless Mini-Split Heat Pumps, http://www.energysavers. gov/your_home/space_heating_cooling/index.cfm/mytopic=12630

38 Rumsey, Rumsey Engineers, personal communication, August 2009.

39 Ren Anderson, National Renewable Energy Laboratory, personal communication, September 2009.

40 Presentation by George Salah and Mary Davidge at Living Future 2009, Portland, OR.

41 Viessmann, Vitodens 343-F, http://www.viessmann.com/com/en/products/Gas-fired_ condensing_boilers/vitodens_343.html.

42 Tulikivi, http://www.tulikivi.com/www/kotien.nsf/WWWTakka/Fireplace%20 Size!OpenDocument&id=TE6; and Tulikivi product brochure, available for download at above link, pp. 58-59.

43 The LEED for Homes Rating System can be downloaded free at www.usgbc.org/leed/ homes. The EPA's Indoor Air Plus Construction Specifications can be downloaded free at http://www.epa.gov/indoorairplus/pdfs/construction_specifications.pdf.

44 John Reynolds, FAIA, "Thermal Mass Makes Winter Warm," *Solar Today,* January-February 2009.

45 John Weale, Rumsey Engineers, personal communication, September 2009.

46 Fuller Moore, *Environmental Control Systems: Heating Cooling Lighting,* McGraw-Hill, Inc., 1993.

47 Paul Shark, "From Helios to Our House," *Mechanical Engineering,* 2001, http://www. memagazine.org/backissues/membersonly/aug01/features/helios/helios.html; and Danny Parker, personal communication, November 2008.

48 Davis Energy Group, Night Breeze, http://www.davisenergy.com/technologies/ nightbreeze.php

49 Ren Anderson, National Renewable Energy Laboratory, personal communication, August 2009.

50 Peter Rumsey, Rumsey Engineers, Personal communication, August 2009.

51 John Weale, Rumsey Engineers, Personal communication, September 2009.

52 This is simplified for the purposes of this discussion. The "real" value is U-0.023 for the wall assembly, factoring in the percentage of framing and all other layers. The insulation consists of a layer of R-14 continuous insulation and R-40.5 cavity insulation (foam plastic insulation, R-3.6/inch in 2x12 cavity).

53 "Good" systems earn 1 point, "better" options earn 2 points, and "best" earn 3 points.

54 Dan Smith, Daniel Smith and Associates Architects, personal communication, September 2009.

55 Gary Klein, Affiliated International Management, personal communication, September 2009.

56 Gary Klein, Affiliated International Management, personal communication, September 2009.

57 Gary Klein, Affiliated International Management, personal communication, September 2009.

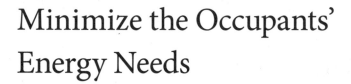

5 Minimize the Occupants' Energy Needs

Once you have minimized the energy needs inherent in the design of your home, you'll need to develop strategies to minimize the energy use of its occupants. We do a host of things in our homes that use energy; we operate:

- Heating and cooling systems

- Major appliances

- Lighting fixtures and lamps

- Water fixtures and features

- A spectacular array of electronics, tools, and gadgets

The line between what the *building* needs for energy and what the *occupants* need is admittedly blurry; once occupancy begins, the distinction becomes somewhat academic. I'm drawing the line between these two categories – and chapters – to distinguish features of the building that are more or less built-in, permanent, and/or fixed from those that the occupants can modify relatively easily, along with issues relating to their lifestyles. Chapter 4 addresses the former, while this chapter focuses on the latter, offering advice both about selecting energy-efficient items and about operating them.

Courtesy of EPA

FIGURE 5-1. ENERGY STAR LABEL

Major Appliances

All major appliances draw energy, but some are more significant to the home energy equation than others. The following appliances are typically the most significant from an energy perspective:

- Refrigerators
- Dishwashers
- Clothes washers and dryers
- Televisions (not necessarily individually, but as a household total)

► **ACEEE.org** provides regularly updated, in-depth guidance on selection and use of efficient appliances. Other performance characteristics are evaluated regularly and comprehensively by Consumer Reports **www. ConsumerReports.org**.

The most basic energy-efficiency qualification for these appliances is an ENERGY STAR label. ENERGY STAR-labeled appliances have met federal standards for energy efficiency that are 20 percent better than models that are not so labeled. The ENERGY STAR label, however, should be considered no more than an indicator of the least acceptable level of energy performance, probably not in itself a high enough level for energy-free homes. The Consortium for Energy Efficiency (CEE) publishes listings – updated monthly – of "super-efficient" (defined as the upper end of the ENERGY STAR efficiency spectrum) appliances at **www.cee1.org/resid/ seha/refrig/refrig-main.php3.** They group ratings into Tiers 1, 2, and 3, the most efficient models being Tier 3.

A new effort to help consumers locate the most energy-efficient products, TopTen, has been operating in Europe for a few years and will be launching in the United States in early 2010. See **www.toptenusa.org** for more information about the most energy efficient appliances and electronic products.

► Check with your local power and water utility offices to find out whether your efficient appliances qualify for rebates.

In general, the performance of appliances whose job is mostly to provide heat is dominated by how much heat is called for, and specifics of the appliance's design are less significant. In this category are cooktops, ranges, ovens, and clothes dryers. How much energy they consume is primarily a function of how much heat they are called upon to provide – the more (and wetter) the clothes that are run through the clothes dryer, the more energy it will use; the more you cook, the more energy you will use. There is a notable exception, however, among cooking appliances – induction cooktops.

Induction cooktops

Electric induction cooking is becoming increasingly popular for several reasons, among them the fact that cooking energy is transferred directly from the cooking element to what you're cooking without heating up the range top. This is an attractive safety feature, and also means that more of the energy the appliance supplies does useful work instead of literally going up in flames (and fumes). Induction cooktops are of particular interest in energy-free homes because of the logic of choosing an all-electric home – i.e., one that uses no fossil fuels.

Research done by Lawrence Berkeley National Laboratory finds that cooking with magnetic induction is 84 percent efficient, as compared to conventional electric ranges at 74 percent efficiency and gas ranges at 40 percent efficiency (or half that for pilot-light models).[1] Induction cooktops also offer more settings than traditional cooktops and have sensors that automatically adjust for the pot size. There are no open flames or fumes, and if the unit is on and no pot is present, the surface remains cool.

The National Association of Home Builders Research Center's **Toolbase.org** says, "With magnetic induction, the pot, not the stove is essentially doing the cooking, so … the time required to heat the pot's contents is reduced, providing additional energy savings. Units are available in traditional sizes … [but cost] three to four times more than an electric cooktop."[2] Magnetic induction requires using iron or steel cookware – if a magnet will stick, it will work (stainless steel will not always hold a magnet). This rules out aluminum, glass, and copper pots.

According to **ConsumerReports.org**, "Induction cooktops are the fastest-heating cooktops we've ever tested … Besides breaking our speed record for bringing 6 quarts of water to a near boil, the induction cooktops we tested simmered sauce flawlessly and remained relatively cool because most of the heat generated by induction goes into the pan, not the surrounding kitchen. The cooler cooktop minimizes burnt-on spills. Induction elements can also shut off automatically when the pot is removed, even if you don't turn them off. This reduces the chance of cooking fires, which are a leading cause of house fires." A further benefit is less contribution from cooking to cooling loads.

However, induction cooktops may pose some small risk for pacemaker patients. The details are provided in *Europace* journal online.[3]

▶ ACEEE offers excellent guidance about cooking efficiency in its online Consumer Guide to Home Energy Savings, at **www.aceee. org/consumerguide/ cooking.htm.**

▶ Read Alex Wilson's "Efficient Cooking" article at **www. greenbuildingadvisor. com/blogs/dept/ energy-solutions/ efficient-cooking.**

Courtesy of Kuppersbusch, kuppersbuschusa.com

FIGURE 5-2. KUPPERSBUSCH INDUCTION COOKTOP WITH WOK

Refrigerators

The EPA advises, "If you still have a fridge from the 1980s, replace it with an ENERGY STAR qualified model and save over $100 each year on your utility bills. Replace a fridge from the 1970s and save nearly $200 each year!"[4] The ENERGY STAR website (**www.energystar.gov**) provides listings of qualified models and other useful resources, including a simple calculator that will help you estimate potential savings.

Selection

- **Choose a top-mounted or bottom-mounted freezer instead of a side-by-side model.** Side-by-side refrigerator/freezers use more energy than similarly sized top-freezer models, even if both carry the ENERGY STAR label, because the two categories are held to different standards (side-by-sides are allowed to use 10 to 30 percent more energy). To compare energy performance across types, look for the measured kWh/year, which is available on the ENERGY STAR website, the yellow EnergyGuide label on the refrigerator itself, and manufacturers' websites.

- **Avoid micro-fridges.** The energy consumption per cubic foot is far greater than that of a standard fridge.[5]

- **Avoid icemakers** and through-the-door ice dispensers, if possible; they increase energy use.

- **Keep it small.** Refrigerators under 25 cubic feet use significantly less energy than larger models (and help keep pack-ratting to a minimum). However, if you need more refrigerator space, it is generally much more efficient to operate one big refrigerator than two smaller ones.

Use

- Check the door seals periodically to ensure they are tight.

- Keep the refrigerator compartment between 36°F and 38°F and the freezer compartment between 0°F and 5°F. Warmer settings use less energy.

- Locate the refrigerator out of direct sunlight and away from other heat sources, such as the oven, range, or dishwasher.

- If there is a power-saver switch, turn it on unless you have noticeable condensation.

- Defrost whenever there is a noticeable ice buildup.

- Let foods cool before putting them in the fridge.

- Avoid keeping the refrigerator door open any longer than necessary.

- Keep both the fridge and the freezer full (even if it's just with containers of water).

Dishwashers

Dishwasher efficiency is indicated by energy factor (EF), which measures the number of cycles that can be run with 1 kWh of electricity. (Unlike clothes washer efficiency ratings, dishwasher EF does not take into account water use.) CEE classifies dishwashers in two tiers. Tier 1 dishwashers have an EF of at least 0.72, use no more than 5 gallons of water per cycle, and use less than 307 kWh/year; Tier 2 models have an EF of 0.75 or better, use no more than 4.25 gallons per cycle, and use less than 295 kWh/year. See listings at **www.cee1.org/resid/seha/dishw/dw-prod.pdf.**

Selection
- **Low water use.** To find the most water-efficient models, check the manufacturers' literature or your local water utility. Some ENERGY STAR models use half as much water as others, saving hundreds of gallons of water each year.

- **Wash cycles.** The more wash cycle options you have, the better. Some (not all) highly-efficient dishwasher models use a "soil sensor" to automatically adjust water use.

- **No-heat dry option.** Look for a model with a no-heat drying feature, which circulates room air through the dishwasher rather than using an electric heating element for drying.

Use
- **Use it.** Hand washing rarely beats the performance of late-model dishwashers.

- **Scrape, don't rinse.** Don't pre-rinse – most dishwashers made within the last decade do a great job, even on heavily soiled dishes. If you must rinse, use cold water. (Peter Yost of BuildingGreen reports, however, that a manufacturer's rep told him he could reduce cycle time as well as detergent use by cold-water rinsing by hand; standard cycle lengths and detergent amounts are based on worst-case scenarios, i.e., dishes not scraped or rinsed and then left until food hardens on them.)

- **Load properly.** Completely fill the racks to optimize water and energy use, but allow proper water circulation for adequate cleaning.

- **Run only when full.** The dishwasher uses the same amount of water regardless of what's inside, so don't run your dishwasher until it's full. If there's a long wait between loads, use the rinse and hold feature, which uses 1 to 2 gallons of water. (Compare to Pete's hand-rinsing method described above.)

- **Use energy-saving cycles.** Select the cycle that requires the least amount of energy for the job. Use the no-heat drying feature if your dishwasher has one.

- **Turn down the water heater.** Most newer US-made dishwashers have built-in heaters to boost water temperature, so you can turn down your water heater thermostat to 120°F.

▶ Alex Wilson of BuildingGreen comments, "If your electric rates are really high and you heat water with inexpensive natural gas, solar, or wood, it sometimes makes sense to keep the water heater set higher so that the electric-resistance booster heater doesn't have to come on (though there is some anecdotal evidence that dishwasher booster heaters tend to come on whether or not they're needed)."[6]

Clothes washers and dryers

Clothes washers represent a threefold opportunity for energy savings. Some models are designed to use less energy than others, some use water more efficiently, and some do a better job at removing water from clothes, thereby reducing drying energy (assuming you dry your laundry in a clothes dryer rather than hanging them on a clothesline). The metric used to indicate energy efficiency is modified energy factor (MEF), which accounts for dryer energy and associated water heating energy. The federal standard for MEF is 1.26; the minimum for ENERGY STAR is therefore 1.51. water factor (WF), the second important metric, indicates the number of gallons needed for each cubic foot of laundry; the minimum WF listed for ENERGY STAR models as of July 2009 was 3.1.

The LEED for Homes Rating System awards ½ point for ENERGY STAR-labeled clothes washers and an additional point (1 ½ points total) for clothes washers with MEF 8 2.0 and WF < 5.5. These are considered both water-efficient and energy-efficient.

Selection

Buy the clothes washer with the **highest MEF** and **lowest WF** you can, considering your budget, capacity needs, and the other factors described below:

- **Front- vs. top-loaders.** Most front-loading (horizontal-axis) washers are more efficient and clean better than top-loading (vertical-axis) models. They also tend to have a higher spin speed and therefore remove more water, thereby saving drying energy, too.

- **Water controls.** Look for a model that automatically adjusts the water level according to the load size. All front loaders have this feature. Otherwise, choose a machine that lets you select lower water levels for smaller loads.

- **Cycle options.** Water temperatures have a dramatic impact on energy use, so choose a washer that has a range of wash and rinse temperature options.

Selection of clothes dryers relies on different factors. There is currently no ENERGY STAR labeling program for dryers. The ENERGY STAR website explains that this is because a DOE study found that energy use among clothes dryers in the US market does not vary significantly among models. Also for this reason, the Federal Trade Commission does not require clothes dryers to carry a yellow EnergyGuide label. Over the next few years, DOE expects to reconsider the current federal energy standards for clothes dryers, and it's possible that an ENERGY STAR label for clothes dryers will emerge.[7]

In the meantime, if your dryer is in good working order and includes a moisture-sensing auto-off switch, you may do well to keep it. A moisture sensor is an important feature, as it will turn the dryer off when the laundry is dry, avoiding excess energy use. If your dryer does not have this feature, you may wish to replace it, or avoid using the dryer in favor of line-drying.

Use

- **Optimize load size.** Don't under- or overload either your washer or dryer. (Underloading washers is common.) In general, it's better to run one large load than two smaller ones.

- **Use lower temperatures.** Whenever possible, use cold water for wash and rinse cycles in the clothes washer. (Note that some detergents work better than others in cold water.) Using cold-water rinse cycles almost always makes sense, and a cold-water wash cycle should also be selected if it does an adequate job of cleaning. Use a lower temperature in the dryer, too. Although this may be counterintuitive, Chris Calwell of Ecos Consulting advises, "We've found that reducing the drying temperature and lengthening the drying period tends to reduce energy use (as well as lengthening the lifetime of your clothes)."[8]

- **Use the dryer's moisture sensing feature.** If your dryer has an auto-dry setting, use it. It will save energy as compared to the timed option.

- **Minimize dryer use.** Air-dry whenever possible. When you can't, reduce power needs by drying similar fabrics together, drying multiple loads in quick succession to take advantage of residual heat, and cleaning the filter after each load.

- **Consider a heat pump or condensing clothes dryer.** More commonly available in Europe than in the United States, these models save energy by recovering some of the heat from the dryer exhaust to preheat air entering the dryer. By reducing the amount of conditioned air the dryer vents to the outdoors, non-venting models can also help reduce the amount of energy used by your air conditioner or furnace.

HANG CLOTHES TO DRY

Using a clothesline is the most energy-efficient option out there! I've found that even partially air-drying clothes can significantly reduce dryer run-time. In my damp climate, if the laundry isn't dry by dusk, there's no point keeping it out overnight, so I toss it in the dryer and it's done in a few minutes. It would be more energy-efficient to bring it in for the night and re-hang it in the morning, but I'm seldom that virtuous, much as I aspire to be.

I've rarely seen clotheslines in multifamily projects, but where space permits, they should be accommodated – on rooftops, perhaps?

Dryer cabinets are an alternative to clotheslines, although they're uncommon in the United States. Some homes may have space in attics or basements that can be used for hanging laundry.

FIGURE 5-3. CLOTHESLINES, NORTH AMERICAN & EUROPEAN

Lighting

Just as the sun is the highest-priority source of heat, so it is the highest-priority source of light! And not just for energy, but also for health. A good lighting design, therefore, starts even before choosing fixtures, by locating windows and skylights to provide sufficient daylight for as many household tasks as possible. Later, as you occupy the space, or in remodeling projects, carefully consider how furniture can be placed to capitalize on available daylight. Light-colored finishes on walls and ceilings also make optimal use of daylight and therefore minimize reliance on artificial lighting.

According to the ENERGY STAR website, lighting accounts for about 20 percent of electric usage in the average US home. Choice of lighting is therefore important to reducing the overall energy demand. There are two general types of lighting: installed fixtures (also called *luminaires*) and portable table lamps and standing lamps. In many older homes, including those built *en masse* in the housing rush after World War II, the number of installed fixtures tends to be relatively low and the reliance on plug-in lamps accordingly high. This is also generally the case in affordable housing projects. In contrast, many newer homes feature an exceedingly high number of installed fixtures, with recessed can lights the hands-down favorite, especially in production home models – probably because they are relatively inexpensive and also unobtrusive, and are therefore unlikely to be an aesthetic issue for home buyers.

The installation of more fixtures is a mixed blessing. On the down side, often far more fixtures are installed than are truly needed for adequate lighting levels, leading to inordinately high lighting energy loads. On the plus side, if home lighting is well-designed so that installed fixtures address most of the occupants' daily lighting needs and do so energy-efficiently, this can minimize the energy needed for supplemental (plug-in) lighting and for lighting overall.

▶ What most of us call light bulbs, the lighting industry refers to as *lamps*, and what we know as lamps or light fixtures the industry calls *luminaires*.

As with appliances, the ENERGY STAR label appears on qualifying fixtures and lamps (of both kinds). For years, ENERGY STAR fluorescent fixtures arguably have represented the highest available standard for overall residential lighting performance, because requirements for labeling included both energy efficiency and other performance standards.

There are two principal types of residential lighting that are energy-efficient, or *high-efficacy*: fluorescent and light-emitting diode (LED). Both provide lighting levels comparable to incandescents for one-third to one-quarter the amount of energy, while also offering a longer life span. Lighting efficiency is most often expressed as *luminous efficacy*, the units of which are lumens of light delivered per Watt of electricity.

EFFICACY (lumens/Watt)

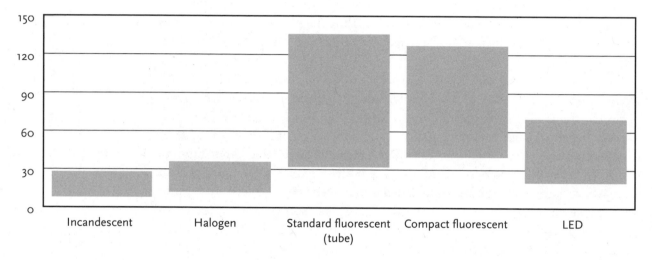

LIFESPAN ('000 hours)

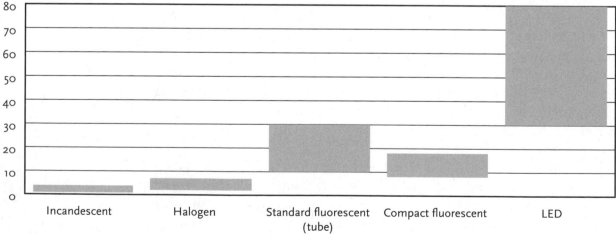

FIGURE 5-4. LIGHTING EFFICACIES AND LIFESPANS[9]

Fixtures

Although LED fixtures became eligible for ENERGY STAR labeling in late 2008, relatively few ENERGY STAR-labeled LED fixtures were available as of the summer of 2009. In any event there is some controversy surrounding the validity of this label as applied to LED fixtures, because the labeling standard currently in effect considers only the efficacy of the LED light source and not efficacy for the *luminaire,* which accounts for the light leaving the fixture as a whole. However, DOE is working to change that.[10]

In principle, LEDs offer a great deal of promise for improving lighting energy performance. According to **BuildingGreen.com,** "LEDs … have been improving in light quality and efficacy … at a rapid pace. The highest-efficacy LEDs today produce about 50 lumens per watt, more than twice the efficacy of incandescent and halogen lamps. Although fluorescent lamps have higher efficacy than today's LEDs, the ability to more precisely focus LED light output can enable LED luminaires to outperform fluorescents in certain applications. LEDs also have a very long life (30,000 to 50,000 hours) and they are the only common non-incandescent light source that does not rely on mercury vapor."[11] LEDs have their own unique design considerations, however. The primary concern expressed about them is that they produce a very bright, cold (bluish) light. Their focused output also makes them less suitable for some general illumination purposes.

> ### LIGHTING DESIGN GUIDE: THE COLOR OF LIGHT
>
> Color temperature and color rendition are two lighting characteristics that affect lighting aeshetics. Fluorescent lamps are available in different color temperatures. A color temperature of 3000 to 3500 deg K will be more similar to an incandescent than a higher value. If your lighting designer, architect, or interior designer is not well-versed in these topics, you may wish to consult the Lighting Design Lab's *2009 Green Home Lighting Guide* at **www.lightingdesignlab.com/articles/2009%20Green%20Home%20Lighting%20Guide%20web.pdf** – which has lots of other useful information, too!
>
> Other helpful lighting resources are available at Pacific Gas & Electric's Pacific Energy Center, **www.pge.com/mybusiness/edusafety/training/pec/toolbox/ltg/.**

Figure 5-5, excerpted from the ENERGY STAR website, compares fluorescent and LED lighting.

Notwithstanding the attractiveness of the energy benefits and longevity of fluorescent and LED lighting, designing low-energy residential lighting systems remains a challenge. This is so for several reasons:

- Many people have strong feelings and preferences about lighting aesthetics.

- Fluorescent lighting has a bad reputation for its history of poor color rendition and buzzing (problems which have been largely rectified).

- Few places in the United States are subject to lighting energy-efficiency standards that exceed the requirements of the *International Residential Code, 2009 edition* (California being the notable exception).

	Fluorescent	LED
Energy use	75% less energy than incandescent fixtures	At least 75% less energy than incandescent fixtures, getting more efficient all the time
Cost	Typically more expensive than incandescent fixtures ($)	Typically more expensive than fluorescent fixtures ($$)
Lifetime	≈9 years (based on 3 hours of use/day)	22+ years (based on 3 hours of use/day)
Warranty	2-year warranty	3-year warranty
Fixture types	Available in many decorative styles	Currently available in select fixture types including recessed cans, under cabinet lights, & porch lights
Replacement bulbs	Special "pin-based" bulbs available for replacement	LEDs are part of the fixture, typically not replaceable
On/Off time	Typically less than 1 second to turn on and up to 3 minutes to reach 80% brightness	Instant on
Recycling	Contain a small amount of mercury and should be recycled	Contain electronic parts and should be recycled (like computers or cell phones)

FIGURE 5-5. ENERGY STAR FIXTURES: FLUORESCENT VERSUS LED

- As a result, the lighting industry has been slow to innovate and provide energy-efficient options in a wide range of styles and models (pendant, sconce, etc.).

- Relatively few home lighting systems are designed by energy-savvy designers.

When we did an extensive energy retrofit of our home in 2005-6, I wanted to replace most of the home's lighting with ENERGY STAR fixtures. California had just updated its lighting efficiency standards, so I went to the showrooms optimistic about finding what I wanted. I was sorely disappointed. I saw little improvement in selection from my shopping experience ten years earlier, when I had designed a second story for our home. I could find ENERGY STAR fixtures, yes, but if I found a pendant I liked, I could not find a companion sconce or couldn't get the finish I wanted. Even when I broadened my criteria to consider *any* fluorescent fixture (at that time LEDs were few and far between, and out of our budget range) I had little to choose from. Architect colleagues report similar, more recent experiences.

I ended up selecting nearly all conventional, screw-based fixtures, into which I put compact fluorescent lamps (CFLs). Although CFLs are not favored by some in the energy-efficiency world because they can be replaced easily with incandescent lamps, I reasoned that we would be in the home for the long haul, and being responsible occupants, would continue to replace the lamps with CFLs. We have done so, and I have had no reason to be disappointed with this strategy, although I remain frustrated with the industry's failure to provide more design options.

I discovered along the way, however, that a number of manufacturers will customize fixtures, converting them from incandescents to pin-based fluorescents for an up-charge ranging from approximately $30 to $70 per fixture. I ultimately decided this didn't make economic sense for us.

CFLs have come a long way from when they were first introduced. They have become smaller, they come in several colors (soft white, natural white, daylight), and a number of different lamp styles are available, as shown in Figure 5-6 below. There is a great deal of useful information on ENERGY STAR lighting at **www. energystar.gov** (under PRODUCTS, click on LIGHTING), including a guide to the different types of CFLs and where each can be used.

Bill Burke at the Pacific Energy Center in San Francisco advises that the best CFLs (i.e., ones that last and retain their brightness longest) are those rated for use in enclosed fixtures; some others "die" well before the end of their theoretical service life, possibly due to heat build-up within the fixtures.[12]

Tube fluorescents offer more options now, too. The standard tubes of the past were T12s, 1-½ inches (12 eighths of an inch) in diameter. Newer tubes are available in T8 (1 inch) and T5 (⅝-inch), in a range of lengths and wattages. Hera SlimLite T5s, for example, range from 10 inches (7W) to 59 inches (35W) and can be linked together in many configurations. We used them for cove lighting and under our kitchen cabinets.

For all fluorescent lighting, be sure to choose fixtures with electronic ballasts, which offer much better performance than magnetic ballasts.

▶ A number of the fixtures I chose had amber glass shades, which create a lovely, warm glow and render any issue about the color of the light provided by the CFLs completely moot.

Courtesy of Regents of the University of California, Davis Campus, California Lighting Technology Center, cltc.ucdavis.edu

FIGURE 5-6. COMPACT FLUORESCENT LAMPS

▶ **About mercury –** Fluorescent lamps contain contain small amounts of mercury, a toxic substance. However, coal-burning power plants are the principal source of mercury emissions in the US, and CFLs actually reduce mercury emissions. **ENERGYSTAR.gov** notes that a 13W CFL, because it saves 376 kWh over its lifetime, avoids 4.2 mg of mercury emissions if the bulb goes to a landfill, 4.5 mg if it's recycled. Check with your local waste company for recycling or safe disposal options. If you break one, see cleanup instructions at **http:// energystar.custhelp. com/cgi-bin/energystar. cfg/php/enduser/std_ adp.php?p_faqid=2655.**

▶ **Avoid halogen torchieres!** They are very inefficient (and therefore expensive to use) and burn dangerously hot. Their manufacture was banned as of 2006. Buy an ENERGY STAR replacement.

Table and standing lamps

Unfortunately, there are relatively few high-efficacy portable lamps. The best option with many such lamps is to use CFLs (described above) instead of incandescent bulbs. Halogen lamps are a specialized type of incandescent. Slightly more efficient than standard incandescents, halogen lights sometimes may be a more effective choice than fluorescents where high light quality or precise light focusing is required.

The California Lighting Technology Center, at the University of California – Davis, has many projects underway to improve lighting efficiency. Working with Full Spectrum Solutions, the Center has developed one very successful fluorescent table lamp, The Berkeley Lamp II, which can be purchased online at **www. berkeleylamp.com**. One appealing feature of the Berkeley is a plug in its base which allows another electrical item – a laptop, for example – to be plugged in there instead of on the floor.

Courtesy of Regents of the University of California, Davis Campus, California Lighting Technology Center, cltc.ucdavis.edu

FIGURE 5-7. THE BERKELEY LAMP II

Controls

Even the most efficient lighting will burn excess energy if it's left on when it isn't needed. Although some people can be relied on to turn off unnecessary lights faithfully, if you are designing for less conscientious or for unknown occupants, you may want to install occupancy sensors that will turn lights off after a predetermined time interval during which no motion is sensed in the room. Timers and/or dimmers also may help to minimize lighting energy use. (Also see the discussion on automation later in this chapter.)

Dimming incandescent and halogen lights extends lamp life while saving energy. However, if you plan to install dimmers on fixtures that use CFLs, be sure to install CFLs that are rated for use with dimmers; not all of them are. Unless your CFL specifically states that it is rated for use with a dimmer, it can burn out very quickly, even if the dimmer is kept at full power.[14]

Using your lights

After you've done your best to maximize the efficiency of your lighting choices, it's up to you or your building occupants to use them as energy-consciously as possible. Avoid using general room lighting for critical visual tasks, as this will require keeping light levels high in a much larger space than that in which the work will be done. Instead, use "task lighting" – lighting focused specifically on the work area. And of course, turn off lights when they're not needed – especially if you don't have sensors.

OUTDOOR LIGHTING

Efficient outdoor lighting options include ENERGY STAR fixtures, as well as solar walkway and patio lights, which are widely available and easily installed by anyone. The solar lights are not tied to the household electric system, but instead run on miniature photovoltaic arrays which are either integral to the fixtures or mounted separately nearby. Architect Greg VanMechelen observes, "This saves a LOT of money up front from not having to hard-wire; it's also very safe."[13] Motion sensors can also help save energy by eliminating the need to leave entry or driveway lights turned on for after-dark arrivals. Sensors may not work well with some fluorescents, however.

In addition to ENERGY STAR, look for outdoor fixtures that are certified by the International Dark-Sky Association **(IDA, www.darksky.org)** to save energy as well as minimize light pollution. If you install fixtures that will be left on all night (though you should avoid doing this, if possible) be sure to choose fixtures that turn off automatically in daylight.

According to the IDA, nighttime light pollution is increasingly a matter for concern, because of its adverse impacts on human health and on the environment. To give just one instance, newly-hatched sea turtles find their way to the sea by navigating toward its bright, flat surface; light pollution can cause them to go astray, leading to increased mortality rates. And of course, light pollution wastes energy – IDA estimates that more than $10 billion is wasted annually on unnecessary lighting.

Water Use

► In California, nearly one-fifth of electrical energy statewide is consumed by devices and systems for moving water.

Moving water around takes a significant amount of energy, so the less water we use, the more energy we save. What water we do use can be moved around more or less efficiently. Chapter 4 discussed efficient water heating and hot water distribution because these are built-in aspects of the home.

What follows is an overview of our major home-based water-using activities – in bathrooms, kitchens, gardens, and sometimes in spas or pools – and the opportunities to minimize the associated water and energy demands. (Laundry appliances, the other major home water use, were discussed above.)

Bathrooms

We use water in bathroom sinks (lavatories), toilets, tubs, and showers. Here's how BuildingGreen, EPA, and LEED for Homes rank these fixtures. Tub fillers are not rated because tub water usage is not known to be influenced by flow rate.

Fixture type	LEED for homes "high efficiency" (1 point)	LEED for homes "very high efficiency" (2 points)	BuildingGreen's GreenSpec listing threshold	EPA WaterSense labeling requiremenet
Toilets[15]	≤1.3 gpf	≤1.1 gpf	≤1.28 gpf	≤1.28 gpf
Lavatory faucets	≤2.0 gpm	≤1.5 gpm	≤1.5 gpm	≤1.5 gpm
Showerheads	≤2.0 gpm	≤1.75 gpm	≤1.75 gpm	≤2.0 gpm (draft specification)

gpm = gallons per minute   gpf = gallons per flush

FIGURE 5-8. PLUMBING FIXTURE EFFICIENCY RATINGS

Water-efficient plumbing fixture listings are available at **www.bewaterwise.com** and at **www.buildinggreen.com** with other green product rating information. Some considerations for selecting these fixtures follow.

- **Toilets.** Anecdotally, the all-star contender for overall quality and performance in (and even outside) the green building arena is Toto. Most Toto dual-flush toilets are rated at 0.9 gpf for the "#1" flush and 1.6 gpf for the "#2" flush, which yields an average rate of 1.13 gpf. The rounding rules adopted for LEED for Homes, contrary to standard mathematics, require rounding to the nearest hundredth, so the program doesn't recognize most Toto models as "very high efficiency." The exception is the Aquia III, which rounds to 1.101 gpf and therefore does qualify. LEED points notwithstanding, Toto has my vote.[16] There are also new pressure-assisted toilets that use about 1 gpm and which tend to be quieter than their predecessors.

- **Lavatory faucets.** Lavatory faucets are the easiest fixtures to find with low flow rates and satisfactory performance. Most people don't seem to be overly particular about lavatory faucets with flow rates as low as 0.5 gpm, although the lower the flow rate, the longer it will take for hot water to reach the faucet. Some tankless water heaters also need flow rates over 0.5 gpm to deliver hot water. Faucet water use may be further reduced by incorporating sensors (such as those commonly found in airports, hotels, etc.) that turn the faucet on when you put your hands under them, and off when you remove your hands. The added expense may not justify them, but depending on use patterns they may be worth considering.

- **Showerheads.** Showerheads are somewhat more challenging, because the shower experience is a highly personal one, and showerhead water delivery is unique and influenced by a variety of design factors, not simply the rate of flow or even water pressure, necessarily. The hydraulic engineering of showerheads is complex, and a spray that satisfies one person may not satisfy another. Early low-flow showerheads delivered water in tiny droplets that cooled off quickly, but newer low-flow showerheads have larger droplets that retain heat much better. The best way to select a showerhead is to buy it and try it out. Ideally, have several people try it, especially if the showerheads you are going to install will be used by a number of different people. You may also want to consider showerheads that have a temporary shut-off (the navy valve, described in Chapter 4), used to stop the flow briefly while you're soaping up.

FIGURE 5-9.
SHOWERHEAD
WITH TEMPORARY
SHUT-OFF
(NAVY VALVE)

Courtesy of Niagara Conservation, niagaraconservation.com

- **Flow restrictors.** Flow restrictors can be used to reduce the flow in lavatory faucets as well as showerheads. Dave Edwards of EarthBound Homes in Northern California reports using flow restrictors from NRG Savers LLC (**www.savingnrg.com/prodwater.htm**) in showerheads in all of his projects, with no occupant complaints. However, he cautions that if flow restrictors are used with tankless water heaters, the flow rate/temperature rise may need to be adjusted to a lower setting to avoid having the water heater shut itself off.[17]

Kitchens

Water used for cooking comes from kitchen faucets. LEED for Homes does not include a requirement for kitchen faucets, presumably based on the assumption – which may or may not be correct – that the amount of water used in the kitchen is influenced more by other factors (the volume needed to fill spaghetti pots, for example) than by flow rate. **BuildingGreen.com**'s Alex Wilson says, "Foot- and knee-control and special shut-off devices are what separate 'greener' kitchen faucets."[18] Pedal controls by T&S Brass and Bronze Works are listed at **GreenBuildingAdvisor.com**, which observes, "Water savings are significant but difficult to quantify."[19]

The other major cooking-related water use comes from washing dishes; if not from the kitchen faucet, it's delivered via the dishwasher. See the discussion of dishwashers earlier in this chapter.

Gardens

Home garden irrigation water use is driven by several factors:

- The size of the garden
- The relative thirstiness of the plants
- The relative indulgence of the gardener
- Garden maintenance regimes
- The efficiency of the irrigation system

Size. Simplistically speaking, the smaller the garden, the less water it will require. But here's a case where, depending on where you draw the boundary around your living system, it may be a bit more complex than that. If a larger garden allows you to grow some or all of your food, that could well reduce big-picture water use (and other energy use) attributable to your household. How many times does a head of lettuce get misted at your local supermarket? How many times does it get washed before it ends up in your salad bowl?

Plants. Some plants need more water to thrive than others do. Choose landscape plants that are native, drought-tolerant, and/or climate-adapted to minimize their needs for water as well as for synthetic chemicals (fertilizers, pesticides, and herbicides) to achieve healthy growth. All those chemicals have associated energy and water demands, too!

▶ How does your diet affect water use? Writer Thomas Kostigen calls the amount of water needed for the production of any product from start to finish "virtual water," and cites the virtual water footprint of a cup of coffee as 37 gallons (gulp!). For a pound of wheat, it's 155 gallons, and for a pound of meat, it's somewhere between 750 and 1,500 gallons.[20] See **www.waterfootprint.org** for a wealth of information on water use and impacts worldwide. (You'll find, perhaps unsurprisingly, that the United States has the highest domestic per-capita water use footprint and the highest industrial water use footprint of any country on Planet Earth.)[21]

Gardener. Your plants need tough love. Plants are living things and can become habituated to either more generous or more frugal allotments of water (and nutrients – ideally, compost). If you coddle them by watering lavishly, they will "need" that greater amount of water to stay happy; on the other hand, if you are a mite stingier, they will learn to get by.

Maintenance. More than 20 years ago, when I moved into my present home, the lot (just under ¼ acre) was badly overgrown with weeds, and so I decided I had better become a gardener. I attended classes at the San Francisco Botanical Garden, and the instructors always advised mulching. Mulch, mulch, more mulch. I believed them, but mulch was never high on my list of things I wanted to spend money on. So I never took mulching seriously until a few years ago, when an arborist moved in across the street. Voilá – a constant supply of wood-chip mulch. Once I started using it, I was astounded at what a dramatic difference it made in retaining water in the soil, soil workability, my ability to pull weeds, and weed suppression. Now I'm a real believer. Mulch is the single best thing you can do to reduce water loss to evaporation!

TASTY APPLES

In 2004, organic farmer Dan Lehrer's apple orchards in Sebastopol, California, went dry: no more irrigation. The drastic measure was not intended as an experiment; it was an economic necessity. His irrigation system had broken down and the repairs were just too expensive.

Before the taps closed, Dan's trees had been used to 24/7 drip irrigation throughout the area's five-month dry season. Their response? They didn't stop producing fruit. With Mother Nature's intrinsic wisdom, they simply conserved. They yielded apples that were smaller, but also crisper and more flavorful.

Other benefits of the imposed drought included longer shelf life, major savings on Lehrer's water bills, and greatly reduced drain on his well and the public water system. Five years later, Lehrer and his Red Rome Beauties aren't going back to their thirsty ways. Why not? "The quality is way better," Lehrer says.[22]

Irrigation system. Drip irrigation delivers water directly to plants or the soil rather than spraying it into the air, providing water much more efficiently than sprinkler systems. This makes drip a better choice than hand-watering. Drip systems can be activated either manually or with a timer. Timers are convenient, but basic models are also "dumb" – that is, they will deliver water whether the conditions warrant it or not, so even if the delivery method is inherently efficient, the system itself, overall, may not be. The best solution to this is a "smart controller" – a timer that includes an evapotranspiration (ET) sensor. ET sensors either detect ambient conditions (temperature, humidity, wind) or acquire satellite weather data and turn on the irrigation system only if water is actually needed. See **www.bewaterwise.com** for more detailed information on efficient irrigation systems and components.

▶ See the *Sustainable Sites Initiative Guidelines and Performance Benchmarks* (at **www.sustainablesites.org**) for detailed advice on water- and resource-efficient landscape and irrigation system design.

Pools and spas

Of course, the best way to save water on pools and spas is to not have them. If you're going to have them, though, there are many things you can do to minimize your pool's energy use and overall environmental impact.

Pools use energy in two ways, both of which present opportunities to save energy: pumping water for filtration, and heating the water. One of the easiest and most important ways to use less energy is to keep the pool covered with an insulated cover when it's not in use. This also reduces water loss through evaporation. Other ways to save energy include buying energy-efficient heaters and pumps, using a solar thermal system for water heating, and using photovoltaics or a ground source heat pump to power the filter pump.

There are also more integrated and complex methods for reducing a pool's energy use. A lower pool temperature will reduce energy needed for heating and also for filtration, as bacteria and other contaminants thrive in warmer water. Pool water should be "turned over" and run through a filtration system a few times a day depending on the type and size of the pool, but this process can use large amounts of energy. If the filtration system is somewhat oversized, less pumping will be needed to filter the same amount of water.

The principal issues with pools, besides energy use, are water use, per se, and the use of chemicals to keep the pool clean. Fortunately, there are great opportunities to reduce water and chemical use. Use captured rainwater to fill the pool and top it off as needed. The best solution is a natural pool – one that is designed using principles of biomimicry ("an ancient concept recently returning to scientific thought that examines nature, its models, systems, processes, and elements – and emulates or takes inspiration from them to solve human problems sustainably"[23]). A natural pool uses a biological filtration system of aquatic plants, eliminating the need for chlorine or salt water (which produces chlorine).

Mick Hilleary, a US expert in the design and construction of natural pools, has designed such a pool for Tah.Mah.Lah. (see case study resources in Appendix B). For more detailed guidance from Hilleary on minimizing environmental impacts associated with pools and spas, see **www.totalhabitat.com**.

Using less

Once you have selected all your fixtures and systems for the lowest possible water use, how you use them becomes important. As with any other part of your home or your lifestyle, you can be wise and efficient in your use, or careless and wasteful.

- Operate clothes washers and dishwashers for optimum efficiency, as described earlier;

- Take shorter showers and use the shut-off, if you have one, while you soap up;

- Use a flow rate no greater than you need for any given task, and don't run the water any longer than necessary; and

- Capture in a bucket the cold water that comes out of the shower before the hot. It is good for watering house plants, rinsing dishes, etc.

▶ For more water-saving tips, see:

www.watersaverguide. com

www.wateruseitwisely. com/100-ways-to-conserve/index.php

www.watersavingtips. org/saving.html

www.americanwater. com/49ways.htm

Household Gadgets

Besides the major appliances and lighting, the myriad other things we plug into the wall – so-called plug loads – represent an ever-greater proportion of home energy use. The culprits include big baddies like plasma TVs as well as seemingly innocuous devices like digital cable boxes and wireless routers. Two trends contribute to all the energy used by these devices: their individual energy consumption and the extraordinarily large (and growing) number of them.

According to **EfficientProducts.org,** mass-market computers represent 2 to 3 percent of all US electricity consumption. The California Energy Commission estimates that TVs and associated equipment (DVRs, DVD players, and cable or satellite boxes) account for roughly 10 percent of residential electricity consumption. (As a result, in November 2009 the State is hoping to adopt the nation's first energy-efficiency requirements for flat-screen TVs. If these are adopted, California retailers will be able to sell only TVs that meet ENERGY STAR standards, starting in 2011.) [24]

© Klavapuk | Dreamstime.com

FIGURE 5-10. COMMON HOUSEHOLD PLUG LOADS

ENERGY STAR labels can be found on many plug load devices, both corded and cordless (i.e., with external power supplies), including cell phone chargers, PC routers, MP3 players, modems, computer speakers, USB hubs, shavers, PDAs, cameras, cable and satellite set-top boxes, DVRs (e.g., TiVo), cordless phones and answering machines, video game consoles, printers, electric toothbrushes, computer monitors, and scanners. It is particularly important to select ENERGY STAR models for those products that use the most energy: **TVs, set-top boxes, computers, monitors, and game consoles.**

Figure 5-11 shows the power draw of a handful of household electronic devices in "active" mode – i.e., when they are in use.

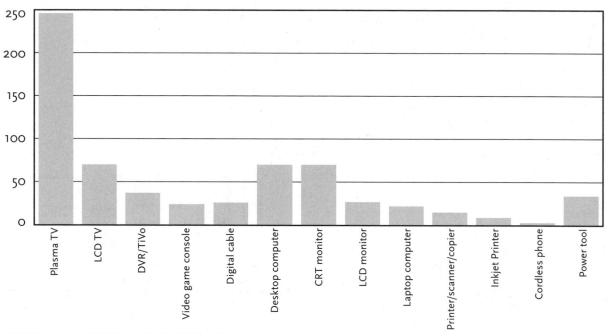

FIGURE 5-11. ACTIVE MODE POWER USE OF SELECTED HOUSEHOLD DEVICES[25]

Many plug-in products use some energy even when they're nominally switched off as they continue to power features like clocks, timers, and remote controls – or for no discernible reason at all. US households spend an estimated $100 per year to power devices while they are in standby mode.[26]

The owners of one East Coast low-energy home reportedly contacted the architect after they had been in residence for several months. They were perplexed because their electric bill was $100/month, much higher than they had expected in their new high-performance home. A bit of sleuthing uncovered the culprit: a plasma TV and video game console that their son used extensively.[27]

Plug loads deserve – and are increasingly getting – a great deal of attention from energy innovators, both private and public. What follows is a basic overview of some of the major issues and opportunities, along with a handful of resources for more information.

Be aware and buy wisely (or not at all)

The first step in minimizing plug loads is to become aware of what all of them are. Some of the most common ones are shown in Figures 5-10 and 5-11. First, see how many you can live without. For those you can't, once again, the ENERGY STAR label is your friend. Devices that have earned the label use less energy (30 to 35 percent less, on average) than their non-labeled counterparts, while providing the same performance.

This list includes cordless rechargeable gadgets as well as many others that require power transformers. Transformers (also called power supplies, or power adapters) are those little black boxes that plug into the outlet – and which continue drawing power as long as they are plugged in, whether or not the product is connected to it, and whether the product is on or off.

Figure 5-12 shows, for the same devices listed in Figure 5-11, their power usage in standby/off and low power modes. Note that the worst performers while active are not necessarily the worst in low power or standby/off mode. In the low power mode, the device is ready for use but not performing its principal function – for instance, a DVR is turned on but is not playing. In standby mode, a device appears to be turned off but can be activated, e.g., using a remote control. Some devices do not have a low power mode.[28]

In research conducted for the California Energy Commission, **EfficientProducts. org** found that plug loads account for at least 9 percent of electricity use in a typical US home and upwards of 15 percent in a typical California home. Further, they found that entertainment devices and computers and their respective peripherals typically account for more than 90 percent of the plug load power draw, and thus also represent the biggest opportunities for energy savings.[29]

▶ **Plug load design tip:** Consider installing switched outlets where you know you'll plug in devices that you want to easily switch completely off. Sometimes a wall switch is much handier than a power strip.

▶ Starting in May 2010, ENERGY STAR-labeled TVs will have to be 40 percent more efficient than today's models; look for another 25 percent improvement in 2012.

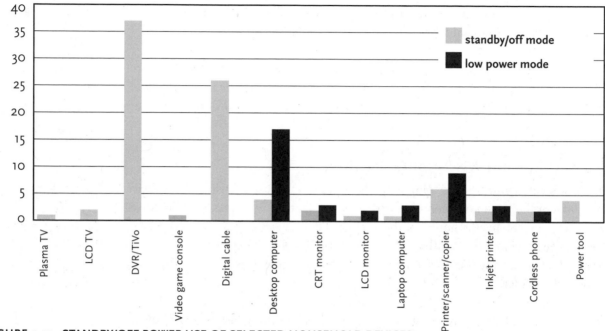

FIGURE 5-12. STANDBY/OFF POWER USE OF SELECTED HOUSEHOLD DEVICES[30]

Courtesy of EPA

FIGURE 5-13. ENERGY STAR POWER ADAPTER LABEL

According to the ENERGY STAR website, "Conventional chargers can draw as much as 5 to 20 times more energy than is actually stored in the battery!" A rechargeable shaver, for example, uses almost as much power sitting in its base as it does when it's in use.[31] Products with ENERGY STAR-qualified power adapters are identified with a special version of the label.

Looking beyond the ENERGY STAR label, it can be challenging to determine the actual energy use of competing products. Labeled values on the products are for safety rating purposes, and tend to be significantly higher than the power the products will actually consume. However, a wide array of useful information, such as "How can I find today's most efficient computers?" is available at **Efficient Products.org.** One of the site's creators, Chris Calwell, advises that the best way to know for sure how much energy a device uses is to purchase a plug load meter like the Watts Up Pro or Kill-a-Watt.[32]

5

After buying: tips for minimizing plug loads

The basic rules below will help minimize energy use from plug loads.

1. Select the most efficient and appropriately sized products for your needs.

2. Configure them properly (i.e., using energy-saving settings).

3. Only operate devices when they are needed.

4. If you have older electronics, check their energy use with a meter such as Kill-a-Watt or Watts Up Pro. If they are energy hogs, replace them, unplug them when not in use, or plug them into a power strip, which will provide a "hard off" – i.e., when you turn off the strip, no power will flow from the home's electrical system into anything plugged into it. (And remember to *turn off* the power strip when you're done using the equipment.)

There are a number of "smart" power strips on the market. These devices help you take control of systems with multiple plugged items, such as entertainment centers and computers. **EfficientProducts.org** describes these and offers advice for selecting the best ones. Many electronics retailers offer them, both in stores and online. They are known by a variety of names, such as smart plug strip, smart strip, energy saving power strip, energy saving surge strip, smart power surge strip, smart surge block, and auto-power-off plug banks.

My techie client Prakash Chandran is a fan of SmartStrip. He says, "The Smart-Strip is essentially a green power strip that not only offers excellent power surge protection and line noise filtering, but is actually able to detect the current going through the outlet … it can turn off selected pieces of equipment when they are not in use [and] save up to 73% compared to normal strips."[33] SmartStrip includes plugs marked red for things that have to remain on, blue for the primary device (e.g., CPU) – which you can set when to power down – and white for peripheral devices you'd like the strip to control based on whether the primary device is on or off. SmartStrips come in a variety of configurations and are priced at $30 to $50 apiece.

Another option is WattStopper's Isolé IDP-3050, a $90 surge suppressor with an occupancy sensor that controls six of its eight receptacles. This strip will turn off connected devices after they sit idle for a user-defined time interval ranging from 30 seconds to 30 minutes.

FIGURE 5-14. SMARTSTRIP (left) AND ISOLÉ (right)

Unfortunately, there are a couple of impediments to switching some equipment so it's *really* off. Some devices need to be reprogrammed, rebooted, or reset when they're turned on again, and some may need to be switched on in a particular sequence so they can communicate properly with one another. It may be preferable to plug these devices into a separate strip and/or turn them off only when they will be unused for an extended period

Automation

Household automation – "smart home" systems – may assist in managing energy use associated with heating and cooling systems, lighting systems, and some plug loads. Additional energy-saving opportunities may be facilitated by or integrated with the automation system. Some of the potential benefits of such systems (most of which are discussed elsewhere in this chapter) include:

- Minimizing parasitic power demands ("vampire loads") by programming components to shut off when not in use;

- Turning off all the lights in the home with a single switch;

- Setting lights to operate at less than full power, conserving both energy and lamp life;

- Shifting loads to off-peak periods when electricity is less expensive;

- Using occupancy sensors to turn systems and equipment off if no one is present;

- Using dimming and shading controls based on ambient condition sensors;

- Operating heating/cooling and lighting in "vacation" (i.e., reduced power) mode;

- Activating systems remotely, either online or via phone or PDA;

- Integrating multiple systems, such as lighting, HVAC, audio, home theater, and security;

- Detecting leaks, thus saving water and preventing property damage and consequent impacts;

- Incorporating qualitative improvements such as different lighting "scenes."

The energy demands and other environmental impacts of the automation systems themselves may be reduced by the following strategies: [36]

- Consolidating components at one location;

- Using waste heat from equipment to preheat other systems;

- Selecting RoHS- and WEEE-compliant products;

- Reducing heavy metal-based infrastructure;

- Performing power calculations on all proposed equipment and systems to reduce energy consumption (e.g., staged-on power supplies, automatic zone shut-offs);

- Programming the automation system for overall efficiency and reduced consumption.

It's important to balance the benefits of automation systems with other considerations, including:

- Embodied energy in the wiring and components, compared to the operating energy saved by "smarter" control regimes … and are they *really* smarter than the humans who would otherwise operate those systems?

- Cost (of course!) – the systems may or may not sufficiently reduce energy demands to justify the capital investment.

- The occupant management burden – will it outweigh the benefits – energy, labor, etc.?

- The layering principle – avoid embedding systems whose technology may change significantly over time; keep them accessible to facilitate change as improvements (especially in efficiency) become available.

> ### RoHS and WEEE
>
> **RoHS** is the European Union's Restriction of Hazardous Substances Directive, which restricts the use of six hazardous materials – lead, mercury, cadmium, hexavalent chromium, polybrominated biphenyls (PBB), and polybrominated diphenyl ether (PBDE) – in the manufacture of various types of electronic and electrical equipment.
>
> **WEEE** is the Waste Electrical and Electronic Equipment Directive, whose aim is to dramatically reduce e-waste by establishing collection, recycling, and recovery targets for electrical goods.[37]

The Custom Electronics Design and Installation Association (CEDIA) has been actively working to educate its members about opportunities to "green" their installations by offering training at its annual Expo and other member events.[34] While this effort is still in its infancy, organization leaders are very committed to spreading the word; they see it as critical to maintaining relevancy in the industry.[35] If you intend to incorporate custom electronic systems, ensure that your design-build contractor is energy-savvy about both control regimes and equipment selection and, ideally, is CEDIA-certified and has participated in their sustainability education programs.

MINIMIZE THE USE OF COPPER

A single home may contain miles of copper wiring, not to mention the piping. The ubiquitous use of copper has had devastating environmental impacts of which most of us in North America are blissfully unaware. In the Indonesian province of Irian Jaya, for example, at the world's largest gold and copper mine, US owner Freeport-McMoRan Copper & Gold, Inc. dumps at least 200,000 tons of tailings into local rivers every day. This region is among the most biologically diverse places on Earth and home to severely at-risk virgin tropical rainforests. For 30,000 years, indigenous peoples there lived a sustainable existence, but three decades of Freeport's mining practices have destroyed rainforests, polluted rivers, and displaced communities.[38]

Thus it is important to keep wiring and piping layouts compact and to use recycled copper or environmentally preferable alternative materials whenever feasible. In many automation applications, CAT5e, CAT6, and fiber cables reduce copper use in comparison with older cabling methods. Other new wireless technologies even further reduce copper use; these include Zigbee, Z-Wave, WiFi, and the newer WiGig and wireless HD.

See **BuildingGreen.com** for environmentally preferable product listings and articles, including "Piping in Perspective: Selecting Pipe for Plumbing in Buildings," *Environmental Building News,* April 2007.[39]

Managing Heating and Other Systems

I suspect many North Americans are a lot like me – with my heating system up and running, I don't tend to give it a lot of thought, so long as I'm reasonably comfortable. However, management regimes deserve some consideration.

The coastal California home shown on the cover of this book is owned by Kristin and Mark Sullivan. The home includes an in-floor radiant heating system that, according to Kristin, only runs about six days a year, because the enclosure is so efficient (it's insulated with straw bales, though comparable levels of insulation can be achieved using a number of other wall systems). Rather than leaving the system's operation to the dictates of the thermostat, which is a relatively poor predictor of human comfort, the Sullivans actually turn off the hot water supply to the radiant system for most of the year, only opening the supply valves for a couple of months starting when the weather is at its coldest (in January, usually). The rest of the year they live with an interior temperature that ranges from about 60 to 75 degrees F, adding or shedding clothing to regulate comfort.[40]

In southern Vermont, Peter Yost and his family have adopted a similarly active approach to their water heating. During the summer, when hot water isn't needed for space heating, Pete turns on the boiler early in the morning and then turns it off after everyone has showered and the dishwasher has been run. It's usually not turned on again until the next day. They've adapted their habits and usage patterns to minimize their energy use associated with water heating.

Many aspects of systems management affect energy use. For instance, just as your tires need to be kept properly inflated to maximize fuel efficiency, furnace filters need to be changed or cleaned regularly to ensure optimum equipment operation. The bibliography contains a number of books that give excellent advice on operating an energy-efficient home.

Monitoring and Behavior

Studies conducted by the Environmental Change Institute at the University of Oxford have concluded that "a scenario which does not involve any change to lifestyle, behaviour or standards of service will not achieve ... the reductions in carbon emissions needed to achieve sustainability by 2100. To do so requires behavioural change. Some of this can be encouraged through policy changes, *particularly provision of information and feedback to consumers* [italics added]."[41] Or, as the business pundits say, what you measure, you manage.

Oxford's Dr. Sarah Darby observes, "If individuals can experiment with energy in their homes or workplaces and see the consequences of their usage through frequent meter reading, improved billing or some sort of dedicated display, the research literature demonstrates that they increase control over their consumption. The conservation effect varies according to circumstances, but participants in feedback trials have typically reduced their energy consumption by up to 10 percent when given indirect feedback (processed for them and presented through a bill or statement, or via the web) and between 5 and 15 percent when they use direct feedback." Dr. Darby's findings, paraphrased below, include the following: [42]

- Direct feedback is the most promising. A combination of measures – an interactive table-top unit displaying cost and power, a smartcard meter for prepayment of electricity, and an indicator showing the cumulative cost of operating an electric cooker – yielded savings close to 20 percent.

- Immediacy or accessibility of data, allowing the householder to be in control, accompanied by clear information that is specific to the household, is highly important.

- Metering displays should be provided for each individual household in a form that is accessible, attractive, and clear.

Recognizing the importance of these findings, both public- and private-sector energy innovators are investing in the research and development of home performance measurement and verification (M&V) technologies. Currently available options range from simple and inexpensive measurement devices to complex and costly systems that can monitor and track multiple types of data.

Monitoring can also provide important information about how systems are working. At a ZEB at Oberlin College, an entire string of PVs was offline for more than a year before the malfunction was discovered; the problem probably would have been identified much sooner if a monitoring system had been in place.

Simple plug-in electric meters

At the basic end of the spectrum are a number of plug-in devices, most of which are used to determine the power draw of a single plug load at a time. Two of these are described below:

- **Watts Up? PRO (www.wattsupmeters.com)**, $130. A hand-held monitor for use with any 120-volt plug device. Provides an instantaneous read-out so you can take it when you go shopping. Displays values including Watts, volts, duty cycle, and cost based upon a specified electricity rate. The Pro version records data and allows transfer to a computer, facilitating tracking changes in electricity usage over time.

- **Kill-a-Watt (www.p3international.com)**, $20-40. A hand-held monitor for use with any 120-volt plug device. Displays values including Watts, volts, duty cycle, and cost based upon a specified electricity rate. Checks power quality by monitoring voltage, line frequency, and Power Factor. Limited data storage capabilities and no ability to transfer data (this device cannot track how electricity use changes over time).

Courtesy of Watts UP? (black/top); Courtesy of P3 International (gray/bottom)

**FIGURE 5-15.
PLUG-IN ELECTRIC
METERS**

(Watts Up? PRO, top, and Kill-a-Watt, below)

Whole-home electricity monitors

Devices that are capable of monitoring whole-home electricity use include the three described below:

- **PowerCost Monitor (www.bluelineinnovations.com)**, $100. A wireless hand-held monitor that displays overall electrical energy use monitored from a home's electric utility meter. Displays real-time electricity use and overall electricity usage in kWh and $, peak use within the last 24 hours, and outside temperature. Has limited data storage capacity and no ability to transfer data.

- **EML 2020 Energy Auditing Kit (www.powermeterstore.com)**, $230. Displays power consumption of an individual plug-in appliance or the electrical consumption of the home. The monitor can display Watts, kWh, operations cost, and other parameters. Optional software allows you to download data to a computer. Wireless model also available (ECM-1220.H-X).

- **The Energy Detective, a.k.a. TED (www.theenergydetective.com)**, $120-230. Provides real-time data on overall home electricity usage or energy use from an individual circuit. Displays data in many different formats, including kW, energy cost ($/hr), kWh consumed to-date or per billing cycle, cost to-date or per billing cycle, and peak energy use. Optional software permits downloading data to a computer.

Smart electric metering dashboards

At the more complex end of the spectrum, several building M&V systems – also referred to as performance dashboards – have been introduced in recent years, signaling increasing interest in *actual* and not just *predicted* energy use. Dashboard systems are designed not just to monitor building energy use but also to provide occupants with readily accessible feedback.

**FIGURE 5-16.
SMART ELECTRIC
METER**

The American Recovery and Reinvestment Act of 2009 includes $4.5 billion for smart grid/smart metering initiatives. Utilities that are adopting smart meters are entering the monitoring arena, too. These new meters allow the collection and reporting of real-time data with much greater accuracy and by time of use. They also enable users to control certain loads according to preprogrammed parameters, such as time-of-use electricity pricing. Pacific Gas & Electric customers in California who have smart meters are already able to go online and view their previous day's usage pattern. Next on the horizon is the ability to communicate with devices in the home in real time using a Home Area Network (HAN) device. HAN devices are already built into the electric meters PG&E is installing, but the technical standards of the communications are still in pilot as of September 2009.[43]

The dashboard systems below have been developed to integrate with smart electricity metering technology:

- **Control4 (www.control4.com).** This home automation company is developing a suite of smart products that will provide consumers with usage data and enable them to automatically control their home devices to reduce energy use. According to CEDIA technology council chair Rich Green, Control4's Energy Management System (EMS) 100 already has well-established, standards-based, affordable home networks for audio, video, lighting, security, heating, and air-conditioning, and can issue alerts and other announcements from utility companies.

- **Google Power Meter (www.google.org/powermeter/index.html).** This free software is being designed to tap into the smart meters now being rolled out by power companies. The data will be accessible from an individual's on-line Google account and will display overall household use by hour and day. As of October 2009, the service was available only to a limited number of customers of participating utility companies and to households with a TED 5000 (which needs to be installed by an electrician). Further growth in the program is expected.

- **Tendril Energy Monitoring System (www.tendrilinc.com/consumers/products).** This system uses a combination of wireless-enabled devices (e.g., electrical outlets and meters), and TREE, the Tendril Residential Ecosystem platform. There are two components to Tendril: The Insight energy monitor, a small, freestanding display of real-time energy usage; and The Vantage, an Internet-based program that tracks current and historical energy usage. The system can also issue alerts from utility companies. The Tendril system is available only through participating utilities that use smart meters.

Multi-system dashboards

Other dashboard systems, developed independent of smart metering, are listed below, with excerpts from their websites. These systems monitor not just electrical usage but other home systems as well.

- **Agilewaves (www.agilewaves.com).** "Agilewaves has developed the Resource Monitor, which continuously measures electric, gas and water consumption of a home or business, calculates its carbon footprint in real-time and makes this information readily available on a wall-mounted touch screen or web page … It monitors each electrical circuit, water line, and the main gas line, as well as temperature … it tracks the performance of major appliances and calculates the resource consumption by room or floor. Current and time-series information is displayed and stored for future reference, allowing the user to compare data with any past period … All access to the system is through web pages and web services [that] allow users the ability to perform data queries, enter data, and change the behaviour of the system."

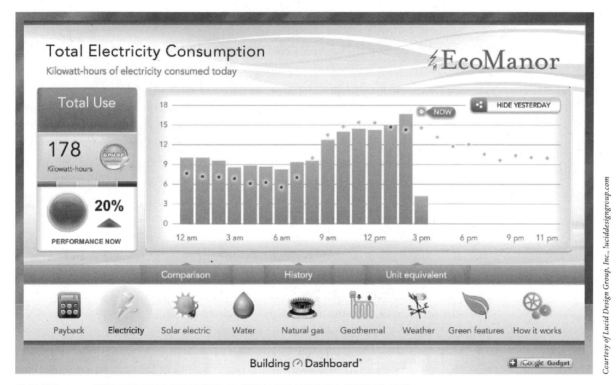

FIGURE 5-17. BUILDING DASHBOARD® BY LUCID DESIGN GROUP, INC.

- **Lucid Design Group's Building Dashboard™ (www.luciddesigngroup. com)**. "Lucid's Building Dashboard translates building performance data so that it is accessible and engaging to a non-technical audience. Using touch-screen kiosks, interactive websites and web-enabled devices, Building Dashboard displays make the flows of energy and water in buildings easily interpretable with exciting, interactive presentations of real-time and historical data, animated graphs and gauges and time-lapse photography."

- >**Green** (**www.greaterthangreen.com**). >Green offers web-based "consumer friendly" home resource monitoring and measuring products and services to enable homeowners to understand and control their usage of water, electricity, and natural gas. The company's flagship installation is at *Sunset* magazine's 2007 Idea House in San Francisco.

- **GE Ecomagination Energy Monitoring Dashboard (www.ge.com/yourhome/ dashboard.html).** The GE entry is an "interactive touch screen wall panel [that] will help your family understand the real value of your home's energy-efficient features and let you manage your home's technologies from a central point of control. [It] provides current and historical feedback on your home's indoor energy and water consumption, as well as levels of emissions. You can set your home's heating and cooling system to the desired temperature for greater comfort, plus a variety of other optional features such as audio, lighting and intercom. This sophisticated, next-generation system can also be integrated so your home's technologies work together. For example, when the optional security alarm is set, the dashboard can automatically turn off the lights and resets the thermostat, helping you save energy and money."

Dashboards vary in complexity, sophistication, scope, and cost. None of them is cheap, limiting them for the present to multifamily projects and high-end homes. They have been used very successfully in dormitories, stimulating competition among student groups to see which can reduce their usage the most. A number of dashboard manufacturers are considering the use of social media to foster similar competition among community groups at various levels.

Several monitoring and dashboard companies are also toying with the notion of data-sharing among system users to stimulate constructive competition, putting an entirely new complexion on the keep-up-with-the-Joneses syndrome. Can you keep up with your neighbors' conservation efforts?

Occupant Education

The LEED for Homes program was developed with extensive input from green builders throughout the United States. What they told us repeatedly was that people needed to be more involved in and better educated about the proper operation and maintenance of their homes. Many times I heard, "We build the most efficient homes … and then people move in and undo our good work!" This concern applies equally or to an even greater degree to energy-free homes. A home is not a static artifact that remains exactly as it was at the moment occupancy began; it is a living, changing, and aging entity with its own unique metabolism and upkeep requirements.

> **BEHAVIOR-SUPPORTIVE DESIGN**
>
> While pondering the role of human behavior in minimizing home energy use, remember that design can either aid or hinder energy-conserving behavior. For example, a fenestration design that incorporates sufficient glare-free daylighting supports minimal reliance on artificial lighting. Superior air-sealing and insulation ensure thermal comfort with less demand on heating and cooling systems. An outdoor space that readily accommodates a clothesline will foster its use. Conversely, the absence of these features will result in intensified energy consumption. Revisit these issues regularly as you pursue your integrated design process – how many household functions can you accommodate with minimal input of supplemental energy?

It's important to ensure that whoever is going to live in the energy-free home is well-acquainted with its energy features and systems, including their ongoing operation and maintenance. I've long felt that every high school student should be required to take a new type of Home Economics class: How to Operate and Maintain a Home. Sadly, we are a culture that is diminishing in its capacity to perform routine household maintenance tasks. This is no doubt due to a combination of factors – our homes have gotten more complicated, and our lives and pursuits have become more and more busy, compartmentalized, and specialized. My father knew how to do just about any type of household maintenance or repair, and while he wasn't too keen on auto maintenance, he could do that too, if push came to shove. My generation tends to be less accomplished in these domestic arts, and my sons' generation even less so.

I believe our changing economic times may turn that trend around, as fewer of us can afford to pay others to do work for us; meanwhile we need to do what we can to see that our high-performance homes are kept in optimum working order. To support that aim, occupants and/or building operators should be provided with two things: a comprehensive and well-organized home operations and maintenance manual and a guided, hands-on orientation to the home's equipment and features and their proper use and upkeep.[44] These measures may not eliminate ignorance and neglect, but they will increase awareness that our homes are changing organisms – requiring care, as all organisms do – and will place the necessary information within easy reach.

▶ Our client Prakash Chandran has set up a Google site to house his home's operations and maintenance "manual." He has included general instructions for using all his appliances, along with PDFs of the manufacturers' equipment handbooks and other relevant information.

ENDNOTES

1 Lawrence Berkeley National Laboratory, *Technical Support Document for Residential Cooking Products (Docket Number EE-RM-S-97-700), Volume 2: Potential Impact of Alternative Efficiency Levels for Residential Cooking Products*, 1997, 40-49.

2 Toolbase.org, http://www.toolbase.org/Techinventory/TechDetails.aspx?ContentDetailI D=3654&BucketID=6&CategoryID=1.

3 Werner Irnich and Alan Bernstein, "Do Induction Cooktops Interfere with Cardiac Pacemakers?", *Europace* 8 (2006): 377-384, http://europace.oxfordjournals.org/cgi/ reprint/8/5/377?ck=nck.

4 U.S. Department of Energy and Environmental Protection Agency, ENERGY STAR, Energy Savings Are Just The Beginning, http://www.energystar.gov/index.cfm?c= refrig.pr_why_refrigerators.

5 Alex Wilson, personal communication, July 2009.

6 Alex Wilson, personal communication, September 2009.

7 EnergyStar.gov, "What about Clothes Dryers?" **www.energystar.gov/index. cfm?c=clotheswash.pr_clothes_dryers**.

8 Chris Calwell, Ecos Consulting, personal communication, September 2009.

9 Table data compiled from BuildingGreen.com: www.buildinggreen.com/auth/article. cfm/2002/6/1/Electric-Lighting-Focus-on-Lamp-Technologies/?sidebar=2, www. buildinggreen.com/auth/article.cfm/2008/3/31/Energy-Star-Labels-for-LED-Lighting/, and www.buildinggreen.com/auth/productsByCsiSection.cfm?SubBuilderCategoryID=6957.

10 *Environmental Building News*, LEDs Get Energy Star Label Amid Controversy, September 2008, http://www.buildinggreen.com/auth/article.cfm/2008/8/28/LEDs-Get-Energy-Star-Label-Amid-Controversy/.

11 Building Green.com, Green Product Sub-Category: LEDs, http://www.buildinggreen.com/ auth/productsByCsiSection.cfm?SubBuilderCategoryID=6957.

12 Bill Burke, Pacific Gas & Electric Company, personal communication, Fall 2008.

13 Greg VanMechelen, personal communication, September 2009.

14 Seattle City Light, Compact Fluorescent Light Bulbs, http://www.seattle.gov/light/ Conserve/Resident/cv5_lw2.htm.

15 Dual-flush toilet flush rates are determined by adding 2x the smaller of the two flush rates to the larger flush rate and dividing the total by 3.

16 And no, I have never received any compensation from Toto!

17 David Edwards, EarthBound Homes, personal communication, August 2009.

18 Alex Wilson, personal communication, September 2009.

19 Green Building Advisor, "Foot-Pedal Faucet Controls," www.greenbuildingadvisor.com/ product-guide/prod/foot-pedal-faucet-controls.

20 Thomas M. Kostigen, "Better Planet: Virtual water – a smarter way to think about how much H2O you use," *Discover*, June 2008.

21 Arjen Y. Hoekstra, "A Comprehensive Introduction to Water Footprints," Online Presentation, 2009, http://www.waterfootprint.org/downloads/WaterFootprint-Presentation-General.pdf.

22 Matthew Green, "Taming the Tap," *San Francisco Chronicle*, March 15, 2009, http://www.sfgate.com/cgi-bin/article.cgi?f=/c/a/2009/03/15/HOUO15SB5E.DTL#ixzz0LpFyTWle.

23 Wikipedia, Biomimicry, http://en.wikipedia.org/wiki/Biomimicry.

24 Samantha Young, "State: Tougher TV energy standards," *San Mateo Daily Journal*, September 19, 2009, http://smdailyjournal.com/article_preview.php?id=116767&eddate=09/19/2009 08:15 PM.

25 Ecos Consulting, *Final Field Research Report for the California Energy Commission*, 2006, 62, http://efficientproducts.org/documents/Plug_Loads_CA_Field_Research_Report_Ecos_2006.pdf.

26 U.S. Department of Energy and Environmental Protection Agency, ENERGY STAR, Home Electronics, http://www.energystar.gov/index.cfm?fuseaction=find_a_product.showProductCategory&pcw_code=HEF.

27 Graham Irwin, personal communication, August 2009.

28 For devices whose power mode could not be determined at the time of testing, the same values are used in both Figures 5-11 and 5-12 (shown as standby/off values in Figure 5-12). Ecos Consulting, *Final Field Research Report*, 18.

29 EfficientProducts.org, Survey of Plug Loads, http://efficientproducts.org/product.php?productID=11.

30 Ecos Consulting, *Final Field Research Report*, 62.

31 Ibid.

32 Chris Calwell, Ecos Consulting, personal communication, August 2009.

33 Prakash Chandran, Smart Strip, December 5 2008, http://imbuildinggreen.com/index.php?s=smart+strip.

34 CEDIA, "CEDIA Introduces Eco-Friendly Business Practices to CEDIA Expo 2008 & Beyond," http://www.cedia.net/press_media/eco-friendly_0808.php.

35 Rich Green, CEDIA secretary, and Dave Pedigo, CEDIA senior directory of technology, personal communication, Fall 2008.

36 Gordon van Zuiden, cyberManor Inc., "CEDIA Professional Offerings within the LEED for Homes point framework," April 2009. Based on communications from Ann Edminster, Design AVEnues, and Colin Breakstone, AgileWaves.

37 Wikipedia, Restriction of Hazardous Substances Directive, http://en.wikipedia.org/wiki/Restriction_of_Hazardous_Substances_Directive.

38 The Goldman Environmental Prize, Yosepha Alomang, http://www.goldmanprize.org/node/66.

39 "Piping in Perspective: Selecting Pipe for Plumbing in Buildings," *Environmental Building News*, April 1, 2007, http://www.buildinggreen.com/auth/article.cfm/2007/4/5/Piping-in-Perspective-Selecting-Pipe-for-Plumbing-in-Buildings/.

40 Kristin Sullivan, personal communication, August 2009.

41 "Making it obvious: designing feedback into energy consumption," Sarah Darby, Environmental Change Institute, University of Oxford, 2000. *Proceedings*, 2nd International Conference on Energy Efficiency in Household Appliances and Lighting. Italian Association of Energy Economists/ EC-SAVE programme.

42 Sarah Darby, Environmental Change Institute, "The effectiveness of feedback on energy consumption: A review for DEFRA of the literature on metering, billing and direct displays." University of Oxford, 2006, http://www.eci.ox.ac.uk/research/energy/electric-metering.php.

43 Dean Heatherington, Pacific Gas & Electric Company, personal communication, September 2009.

44 Guidance for developing a home operations and maintenance manual can be found in the LEED for Homes Rating System, Awareness and Education (AE1), available at www.usgbc.org/leed/homes.

6 Power the Rest

Through thoughtful building design, careful selection of appliances, lighting, and gadgets, and conscientious operating practices, you've reduced your energy demand as much as possible. Now you will need to figure out how you're going to supply renewable power for your remaining energy needs.

For detailed technical information and advice on renewable energy system design, you'll want to begin working with an experienced system design consultant and/or vendor as early in your design process as possible. As with all other aspects of the building design, the sooner you know the requirements of the renewable systems, the more readily they will be incorporated into the project.

Net-zero or net-positive (energy-free) homes are grid-tied, but this doesn't mean they will never use energy from non-renewable sources. It simply means they will offset their use of non-renewable energy during the course of the year with their own on-site energy production.

There are two basic types of renewable systems: solar thermal (solar water heating) and renewable electricity. Solar thermal is in a class by itself. It doesn't provide electrical energy; rather, it heats water using solar radiation. As such, solar thermal may reduce your dependence on non-renewable energy sources, but it won't eliminate it. Thus your project will include at least one grid-tied renewable electricity system – most likely photovoltaics or a wind turbine.

A grid-tied renewable electric system works like this:

- When the system is producing energy (i.e., when the sun is shining or the wind is blowing) and things in your house are calling for energy, it feeds the energy it produces directly into your household system.

- If the system is producing more energy than your house is using at a given time – e.g., you're producing 3,000 Watts but only using 2,200, the excess (800 Watts in this case) will be fed into the grid (this is when the meter spins backwards).

- Your utility "banks" the excess power – it is credited to your account.

- When the system is not producing energy (at night, for example) or is producing less than you are using, you draw the make-up energy *from* the grid.

- The energy you draw from the grid is debited from your "energy account."

- At the end of your billing period – which is typically annual for a renewable energy customer – you are billed based on your net usage.

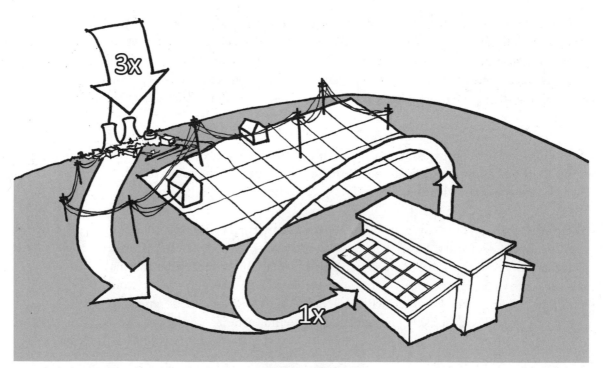

FIGURE 6-1. HOUSE SYSTEM FEEDING TO GRID AND VICE VERSA

If you are a net energy consumer – which you are likely to be if you are pretty much energy-free – you will receive a bill, but if you are a net producer, you may not receive a payment from your utility company. This is because a number of utility companies, as of the summer of 2009, will not allow a credit to your account greater than what you purchase from them annually. Note that this is cost-based, not energy-based, so if much of your production is during peak (high rate) periods, you may be selling to the utility at a rate higher than when you do most of your purchasing from them (off-peak, or low rate periods). In that case, if you have chosen a net-zero definition other than net-zero *cost*, it's likely that you will be an "energy philanthropist" – that is, you will be donating some power to the utility: the excess between the amount they will buy and the amount actually produced. A very simplified scenario was shown in Figure 2-15.

If you haven't settled on a net-zero definition yet, you'll probably want to review Chapter 1 again now. You'll need to pick a definition in order to size your system.

Solar Hot Water

Before getting into renewable electric systems, we need to consider solar water heating. Because solar thermal doesn't provide electrical energy, its usefulness is limited to your hot water needs. In many residential buildings, the only hot water use is so-called domestic hot water (DHW) – showers, hand-washing, dishwashing, and (if you use hot water for it) laundry. In some homes, hydronic radiant heat is the second major hot water use. Other uses for solar hot water include:

- Swimming pools
- Hot tubs
- Greenhouses
- Snow-melting for driveways

Whichever uses you have in mind, you will need to make a decision about solar hot water before (or in conjunction with) your decisions about other renewables. This is for several reasons:

- Solar water heating is very efficient – it converts a much higher fraction of incident solar radiation (insolation) to useful energy than any other form of renewable energy, as much as 80 percent, compared to 15 percent or so for most commercial photovoltaic systems.

▶ A typical residential solar thermal system may require just two 4x8-foot panels, or 64 square feet of roof space.

- Solar thermal systems may be more economical than solar-electric systems (though this depends on several factors, including incentives).

- They can supply a significant portion of your hot water demand without occupying a great deal of space.

- They are less affected by orientation than PVs; thus PV siting should be given first consideration.

The most basic requirement for successful solar thermal systems is that they all need the collectors to be situated to receive full, direct sunlight, year-round, between 9am and 3pm daily. Beyond that, the requirements (and strengths) of different systems vary from type to type.

A significant limitation of solar thermal systems is that they only produce hot water when the sun is shining. If you want hot water at other times (for night-time baths, morning dishwashing, etc.), you'll also need insulated hot-water storage. If you live in a climate that has sun most days of the year (like most parts of Colorado, for example), you will need a relatively small amount of storage to allow you to coast through periods when the sun is not heating your water for you. If you live in a place that is subject to several days in a row of overcast skies, however, you will need to have either a very large, well-insulated storage tank or a supplemental water heating system.

In many cases, solar thermal systems are set up as preheat systems for conventional water heaters. Put differently, the conventional water heater is the primary system, so-called because even if the solar thermal system provides hot water most of the time, it's the primary system that can be counted on at *all* times, whether there's sun or not – it's also the fallback system in case of a solar thermal system failure.

SOLAR REFERENCE

I highly recommend *The Homeowner's Guide to Renewable Energy,* by Dan Chiras (New Society Publishers, 2006). It is an excellent, detailed reference book from which you will learn a great deal more about renewable energy systems than I am able to convey here. I am deeply indebted to Dan for his knowledgeable and accessible presentation of this material, from which I have borrowed heavily – and shamelessly – for this chapter.

The design of your solar thermal system will be driven by the amount of your hot water demand, your need for hot-water storage and how much space you have available for it, different system types and their suitability for your climate and building, and – of course – the economics of those factors.

Do you need separate storage?

Solar thermal systems can include a separate storage tank, or not, depending on the magnitude and timing of your hot water needs. In some climates and situations you may be able to use the simplest of solar thermal systems – a batch system. Also sometimes called integrated collector and storage systems, batch solar hot water systems consist of either a single water tank or a series of tubes (called a progressive tube solar water heater) that absorbs incident solar energy; the heated water from the tank or tubes feeds directly into a conventional storage water heater tank, replenishing hot water as it is used.

The simplicity of batch systems gives them several advantages:

- They are very economical.

- They are easy to install.

- They require no pumps, sensors, electronic controls, or electricity to run.

- They are the most reliable solar thermal systems on the market (fewer moving parts = fewer opportunities for failure).

However, they also have a number of significant limitations:

- The tanks are not insulated and therefore lose much of their heat at night, so solar-heated water is generally available only in the afternoons and evenings. This makes them best-suited to householders who are willing to adjust their hot water usage patterns accordingly. *This also makes them a poor choice for space heating.*

- For best results, they must face true south (not magnetic south).

- They are most effective on sunny days; on cloudy days, the conventional water heater will have to supplement the heat the batch system provides.

- They are limited to relatively warm-winter areas – those that experience only occasional, brief freezes – or for three-season use (in cold locations they need to be drained in winter).

- They are heavy, which may represent challenges for roof-mounted applications, particularly in retrofits.

- They have a relatively small capacity.

For all of the above reasons, most new solar thermal systems in North America incorporate storage separate from the collector. For separate collection and storage systems, you will have four basic decisions to make:

- How much storage?

- What size collector?

- Which type of collector?

- Passive feed (thermosiphon) or active (pump-driven)?

Each of these topics is discussed below.

SOLAR VENDORS

In my experience, the solar system vendors are the best sources of reliable information about solar thermal and solar electric systems – particularly those who have been in business for a while. Here in Northern California, we have some three-decade veterans of the solar industry whose knowledge just can't be beat. Based on your household specifics, they will size your system, design it, select specific equipment, install it, and manage all the associated paperwork for the utility as well as for the state incentive program.

Although I wouldn't discourage those of you who are more enterprising from doing your own homework about system selection, that's more work and brain-strain than many of us care to undertake. Instead, you can identify the most experienced and reputable vendors in your area, meet with them, decide which ones you like, check their references, and then – assuming the references check out – put your system design into their capable hands. You'll save yourself a lot of time!

Estimating hot water demand and storage

There are a number of ways to estimate your hot water demand, none of them terribly precise. You can "guesstimate" using rules of thumb or averages, or draw some inferences from your utility bills. I'm very interested in solar thermal and we don't yet have a system, so here's how I estimated the size of a system for my home:

- **Rules of thumb.** In his excellent book *The Homeowner's Guide to Renewable Energy*, Dan Chiras suggests that resource-frugal families can use as little as 15 to 20 gallons of hot water per day per person.[1] Southface Energy Institute also states, "A family of four uses about 80 gallons of hot water per day."[2] That would put our hot water use at somewhere between 45 and 60 gallons per day.

- **Utility data. RockPaperSun.com** suggests that 30 percent of domestic water usage is hot water.[3] Our water district's online records show that our winter water usage – the best indicator of indoor water use, since we don't water outdoors during winter – is 80-100 gallons per day. If 30 percent of that is hot water use and the remainder cold, then we're using around 25-30 gallons of hot water per day. That's quite a bit lower than the estimate using Chiras's and Southface's assumptions, so to be conservative I'll round up and assume our hot water demand is 40 or so gallons per day.

- **Reality check.** If you try both methods and come up with a dramatic discrepancy, you'll probably want to delve further into the analysis. Your solar thermal system vendor should be able to help you. We received a vendor recommendation for a system that would include an 80-gallon storage tank and a 4x10-foot flat-plate collector. However, the estimate was not based on a household-specific analysis.

An 80-gallon tank is about 2 feet in diameter and 5 feet high. This may be sufficient for a single-family home, if you're only expecting the solar thermal system to provide a relatively modest fraction of your hot water in winter.

PHOENIX

The Phoenix Solar Water Heater (**www.htproducts.com**), available in either 80 or 110 gallon sizes, is a popular choice for homes with solar-thermal systems. It includes a heat exchanger to transfer heat from solar collectors, along with a 96-percent-efficient gas burner. The insulated appliance is direct-vented and also can be connected to air handlers or radiant heating systems.

Courtesy of Heat Transfer Products, htproducts.com

FIGURE 6-2. PHOENIX SOLAR WATER HEATER

You'll need a larger tank if the system will be the main source of hot water year round and you will have to coast through several days without sun. An insulated 350-gallon tank is about 3 feet in diameter and 7 feet high (or long). That would get my family through a week or so of cloudy weather, depending on how well the tank held the heat. I'm considering burying one under the floor of my garage, where it would benefit from ground-tempering (the thermal mass of the earth) and be out of the way.

Solar thermal systems for multifamily projects are uncommon. This may be due to the absence of financial incentives to date for solar thermal systems, which has made them much less popular than solar electric systems; with a new federal tax credit for solar thermal on the horizon, this may start to change.[4]

Estimating collector size

Dan Chiras assures readers that the process of estimating collector size "is pretty straightforward and highly dependent on solar availability and local climate. Generally, the sunnier and warmer the climate, the fewer square feet of collector you'll need. The cloudier and cooler your region the more square feet of collector you'll need." His recommended sizing factors are shown in the second column of Figure 6-3. A simplified solar system calculator using a different method is available at **TheSolarGuide.com**.[5] I found it to produce similar results.

Region	Sizing Factor (gallons heated per square foot of collector)	Collector Area (sq. ft.) for 80-gallon tank (gallon / sizing factor)	Number of Collector Panels
Desert Southwest, Florida	2.0	40	1–2
Southeast, Mountain States	1.5	53	2
Midwest and Atlantic States	1.0	80	2–3
New England, Northeast	0.75	107	3–4

FIGURE 6-3. SOLAR THERMAL COLLECTOR SIZING BY REGION

Choosing a collector

Collector panels are typically 4x8 or 4x10 feet. Two basic types of collectors are used in separate collector and storage systems: flat-plate and evacuated-tube. Each type is described briefly below.

A **flat-plate collector** consists of a glass-covered insulated box that contains copper pipes attached to a flat heat absorber plate, which transfers absorbed solar energy to the fluid (either water or antifreeze) in the pipes.

© Catherine Wanek

FIGURE 6-4. FLAT-PLATE COLLECTOR (BACKGROUND) AND PV ARRAY (FOREGROUND)

Courtesy of Sustainable Spaces

FIGURE 6-5. EVACUATED-TUBE COLLECTORS (ABOVE) AND PV ARRAY (BELOW)

An **evacuated-tube collector** (a.k.a. vacuum-tube collector) consists of a series of parallel glass or plastic double-walled tubes, inside each of which is a copper pipe containing a heat transfer medium, either antifreeze or air. Air is removed from the sealed space between the tube walls, creating a vacuum around the pipes. Since vacuums conduct heat poorly, this makes the tubes very efficient at retaining the captured solar energy.

In both flat-plate and evacuated-tube collectors, the fluid in the collector's pipes delivers heat to a solar water tank, which in turn feeds into a conventional water heater. Figure 6-6 illustrates flat-plate and evacuated-tube collectors and summarizes the advantages and disadvantages of each.

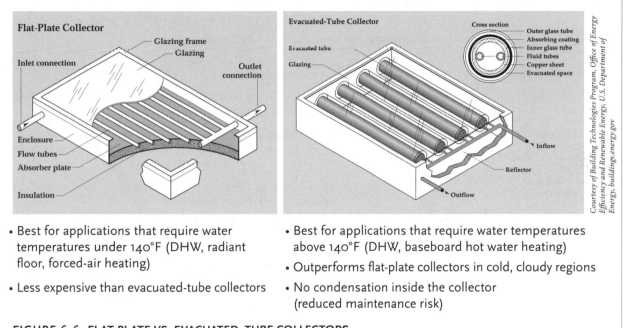

- Best for applications that require water temperatures under 140°F (DHW, radiant floor, forced-air heating)
- Less expensive than evacuated-tube collectors

- Best for applications that require water temperatures above 140°F (DHW, baseboard hot water heating)
- Outperforms flat-plate collectors in cold, cloudy regions
- No condensation inside the collector (reduced maintenance risk)

FIGURE 6-6. FLAT-PLATE VS. EVACUATED -TUBE COLLECTORS

Passive or active? Open loop or closed?

Solar thermal systems can be set up so that the fluid heated in the collector is moved to the storage tank either passively, using a process known as thermosiphoning, or actively, using a pump. Thermosiphoning capitalizes on the natural convective movement of fluid upwards as it is heated. As the hot water rises, it moves out of the collector to the storage tank, pulling cold water from the storage tank return pipe in behind it; this thermosiphoning "looping" action continues automatically so long as the sun is heating water in the collector. Pump-driven systems rely on an electric pump to circulate fluid through the system instead.

An active or a passive system can be direct or open loop, meaning it uses water as the heat transfer medium, circulating it directly from the collector into the storage tank; or it can be indirect or closed loop, using antifreeze as the heat transfer medium. Open loop systems are generally simpler, lower-maintenance, less expensive, and slightly more efficient than their closed-loop counterparts. Closed loop systems of both types – thermosiphon and pump-driven – occasionally need to have the antifreeze drained and replaced by a professional.

Just as with the different collector types, there are pros and cons associated with each of the various options, as shown in Figure 6-7.

Passive: Thermosiphon

- Simple – no pumps, sensors, or controls.

- May use **open loop** system in climates where freezing does *not* occur.

- Requires no electricity.

- Less expensive than pump-driven systems.

BUT

- Requires tank to be placed *above* the collector, ruling out rooftop mounting in many cases.

Active: Pump-driven

- Collectors can be either roof-mounted or ground-mounted – relative height is not an issue.

- May use **open loop** system even in freezing climates, provided the system is a gravity drainback system – not to be confused with the far less reliable draindown system.

- **Closed loop** pumped systems work well in all climates and provide the best freeze protection.

BUT

- Requires electricity, and **open loop** systems require the largest pumps of all solar thermal systems (however, a DC pump can be powered by a small PV panel).

- **Closed loop** systems are the most complex of all solar thermal systems, involving the most equipment.

FIGURE 6-7. THERMOSIPHON VS. PUMP-DRIVEN SYSTEMS

Should you include a solar thermal system?

If you have space for a well-situated collector (remember, it should receive direct sun from 9am to 3pm, every day that the sun shines), it may be a worthwhile investment and make a significant contribution to your energy-free home. Southface Energy Institute in Atlanta offers the following observations about payback.[6]

- Payback is dependent upon the local cost of gas or electricity and how much of the total hot water bill is offset.

- Payback times vary greatly, but a good rule is that larger systems used efficiently have shorter paybacks, and typical residential payback time is between 7 and 10 years.[7]

- Your payback time will be shorter if you shower, wash dishes, and wash clothes in the afternoon and early evening, when the conventional heater is barely needed.

- A solar thermal system is an effective way to cut greenhouse gas emissions by one to two tons per year.

Chiras reports that solar thermal systems sized as described earlier in this chapter should provide "approximately 100 percent of your domestic hot water needs in the summer and about 40 percent in the winter."[8] As one who resides in a region subject to several-day bouts of summer overcast (I'm writing this on July 23, looking out at a completely gray sky), I view this statement with a certain skepticism. Let's just say that "summer" is a relative term; we tend to have more clear-sky days in September and October, so that's when I would expect to see the greatest output from a solar thermal system installed here.

A solar thermal system here in Northern California can be expected to provide about 70 percent of our residential hot water needs.[9] While it's possible to design a system with larger storage for a higher yield, the cost and space requirements tend to discourage most people from pursuing that approach.

According to the *2004 California Statewide Residential Appliance Saturation Study,* an average family of four in California uses about 200 therms of natural gas per year for hot water heating. We're a family of three, but there are often more people here, so that's close enough for my estimating purposes. Our gas prices have fluctuated between about $1 and $2 per therm in the last two years. Splitting the difference and assuming a price of $1.50 per therm, this would put our annual cost of heating water with gas at $300 and our potential savings from a solar thermal system at 70 percent of that, or $210. Assuming a 5 percent annual increase due to inflation, this yields a savings of about $4,500 after 15 years – which is a conservative estimate of the lifespan of a system with a heat exchanger. Less complex systems may last 30 years or more if maintained properly.[10]

The price tag for the system recommended for us was $7,700 minus a 30 percent tax credit = $5,400 net. Assuming some maintenance costs, it's clear that this would not offer the kind of payback Southface suggests, but closer to 15 to 20 years.[11] Depending on the life span of the system, it might be a breakeven proposition.

The payback period is very contingent on the price of natural gas, which tends to be lower in Northern California than in many places due to lower heating demand. Higher gas prices in other areas could produce a very different result. In new construction, the equation also may be more favorable, because you won't be looking at the cost to replace an existing system but rather the marginal cost of the solar thermal system over the conventional one that would otherwise be installed.

However, in at least in one new energy-free home project, Tah.Mah.Lah., it did not make sense to include a solar thermal system. After extensive analysis and several charrettes to develop integrated heating, cooling, and renewable energy strategies, the owners decided that the home – including several electric vehicles – should be a net energy producer and should be fossil fuel-free. This decision, coupled with all the other performance objectives and design features, prompted the mechanical design firm, Rumsey Engineers, to recommend using a ground-source heat pump for both space conditioning and water heating, thereby eliminating two additional systems: the solar thermal system and a conventional water heater.

Other applications

Besides the manufactured solar thermal systems described above, there are other, innovative ways to use solar thermal energy in residential projects. Tah.Mah.Lah. incorporates a unique solar thermal design in which the sport court serves as a solar array. Water will be circulated through PEX tubing running under the court surface. From there it will go to a heat exchanger to transfer the captured solar energy to the swimming pond.

Our neighbors are installing a hard-surface deck over their garage and are considering a similar arrangement to capitalize on the deck's great solar exposure. They plan to install tubing either in a concrete topping slab or in mortar under a tile surface; the water heated in the tubing will go to a water heater (such as a Phoenix, shown in Figure 6-2) to preheat their domestic hot water.

Renewable Electricity

In the world of residential renewable electricity, there is a very clear hierarchy just now, in terms of system dominance:

1. Photovoltaics (solar electricity) – by far the major contender

2. Wind turbines – a distant second

3. Others – bit players

Each section below devotes space roughly proportionate to the relative prominence of each system type in the marketplace. I describe options available in each category, some pros and cons, and, because of its architectural design significance, general guidance on system sizing. Before moving on to those topics, however, let's revisit the question of net-zero definition, and your choice of fuel(s) in your project.

Fuel choices: all-electric?

Decisions about fuel choices typically come before decisions about renewable electric systems, because of the need to know site-to-source and/or other conversion factors. For example, if you are going to use natural gas for some of the energy needs that can't be met by your renewable system(s), and you're using the net-zero source energy definition, you'll need to multiply the amount of natural gas you'll use by the appropriate conversion factor – 1.12 is the national average.[12]

You may be limited, to some degree, by the fuel choices available at your site. However, no matter where you are, and unless you are a very unusual person, you will use electricity to meet some of your energy needs. You may or may not choose to use any additional energy source(s). Put differently, virtually *every* home in North America uses electricity; other fuels are optional.

Developers of net-energy-producing homes increasingly favor an all-electric home because they believe that natural gas, like other fossil fuels, is environmentally damaging as well as in diminishing supply (and increasing in cost). I agree whole-heartedly with the sentiment expressed by Andrew Webster of Coldham & Hartman Architects in Massachusetts: "The green tech (or no-tech) solution needs to address the end of cheap fossil fuels and resource depletion in general. Harnessing finite resources and expecting them to power open-ended energy demands is a losing game. There is ONLY conservation (demand less), efficiency (do more with that less), and renewables (get what's left from sources you can maintain indefinitely), in my mind."[13]

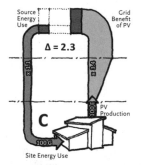

**FIGURE 6-8.
NET-ZERO
SITE/SOURCE
ENERGY:
ALL-ELECTRIC
HOME**

If, along with the owners of Tah.Mah.Lah. and others like them, you decide that it makes sense to have an all-electric home, and you're going to be energy-free, something very interesting happens. All of a sudden, the amount of electricity you produce *doesn't change* based on whether you choose net-zero site or net-zero source. Figure 6-8 shows why. (This was explained in more detail in Chapter 1; see Figure 1-3 and the accompanying explanation.)

The choice of an all-electric home can be challenging, particularly from a code perspective here in California. Here are some of the wrinkles my clients have encountered with their all-electric homes:

1. It necessitates a switch to electric cooking. This was not a problem for Tah. Mah.Lah., whose owners had no particular allegiance to gas stoves and happily agreed to use an induction cooktop and convection oven. For the Kanedas, though, who are dedicated wok users, it was an issue. However, their architects, Leddy Maytum Stacy in San Francisco, found an electric induction wok that met their exacting specifications: the Kuppersbusch EWI 457.0, shown in Figure 5-2. It's a modular, built-in unit that will be installed adjacent to their other induction cooktop components. (Gaggenau also has an induction wok option, but it requires an adaptor stand accessory.)

2. If you want a fireplace *and* a green building rating or label, you may find yourself between the proverbial rock and hard place, having ruled out a gas fireplace. A number of green building programs, for energy and/or air quality reasons, place specific restrictions on fireplaces. I have had clients who wanted to include an "eco" fireplace that burns denatured alcohol; the manufacturer's installation guidelines do not require, nor allow for, the unit to be vented, putting it in conflict with the LEED for Homes and EPA Indoor Air Plus program mandates. One builder resolved to add a vent, regardless, but could not find a UL-listed exhaust duct and so found himself in the unfortunate position of choosing between the fireplace and his coveted LEED certification. Be sure to consider all restrictions that may apply before choosing a fireplace type and model.

3. The California Energy Commision-compliant energy models (Micropas and EnergyPro) discourage the use of electric-resistance space heating and electric water heating (even using a heat pump) by applying source conversion factors, presuming that they are using grid-based power. This presumption is not accurate, of course, in an energy-free home, as explained above.

However, the models are currently blind to the presence or absence of home-based renewable energy production and accordingly penalize electric power consumption.

As Chapter 1 explained, it will be easier to achieve net-zero *source* energy if you do *not* go all-electric. Even so, it may be more cost-effective to favor PVs over solar thermal. As our exploration of solar thermal systems revealed, a solar thermal system would not offer us an attractive payback; in our case, it makes more sense to add capacity to our PV system when we can. It will give us a faster payback – given current and local economic conditions – and our contributions to the grid are valued at the site-to-source multiplier for electricity (somewhere around 3), whereas the multiplier for our gas usage is closer to 1. So every unit of gas energy we use that we're able to offset with onsite electric generation gets us 3 units closer to net-zero.

Solar Electricity: Photovoltaics

Most residential PV systems in North America consist of arrays of flat, rectangular panels, mounted on rooftops and connected to household electrical systems by means of an inverter, which transforms the DC (direct current) generated by the PV panels to AC (alternating current), used in grid-connected buildings.

PVs are very popular. They're everywhere. They're on my roof. They're probably in your neighborhood somewhere. They're even on the roof of our local wastewater treatment plant. The federal government, quite a few states, and some local jurisdictions all offer incentives for their installation. There's pretty much nothing *not* to like about PVs ... except the price tag.

PVs sometimes can be expensive in comparison with building efficiency measures such as those described in Chapters 4 and 5. Just for the sake of comparison, I assumed that a client had $15,000 to spend to upgrade an existing 1,900-square-foot single-family home on the San Francisco Peninsula, moving it along the path toward an energy-free design strategy. In *very* round numbers, his $15,000 investment can buy one of the options shown in Figure 6-9.

Remember that pricing and incentives can change the economics significantly over time and from one place to the next; be sure to do your own research before coming to conclusions based on this admittedly back-of-the-envelope analysis.

$15,000 investment option	Annual energy load reduction, kBtu/sf-yr	Percentage reduction	kBtu/sf-yr reduction per $k
1. R-49 attic insulation + R-19 under-floor insulation + comprehensive air sealing + ENERGY STAR lighting and appliance upgrades	4.69 (without lighting and appliance savings)	15.4	.31
2. R-5 replacement windows	5.19	17.1	.35
3. 2kW PV array	4.97	16.3	.33

FIGURE 6-9. $15K ENERGY LOAD REDUCTION OPTIONS (1,900 SF HOUSE)

► Consult the Database of State Incentives for Renewables and Efficiency for a listing of incentives: **www. dsireusa.org.** You should also check with your city, county, and/or local utility to ensure you have the most up-to-date information.

All three options yielded fairly close results, well within the margin of error for our assumptions. Option 2 appears to give somewhat better bang for the buck than the other two options; however, since the modeling for Option 1 doesn't capture the improvements due to lighting and appliances, that option also likely offers better value than PVs.[14] This isn't an argument against photovoltaics – you'll need some form of renewable electricity to get to net-zero (by any definition). It's an argument to squeeze as much efficiency as you can out of your building before you invest in PVs! Then the PV system needed to get you to your energy-free goals can be much smaller than it would be if you hadn't paid attention to efficiency first.

ON THE OTHER HAND ...

Solar electricity isn't always expensive; **it depends on the context.** Dan Chiras observes, "It is one of the most popular choices of the poorest people in the poorest nations [because] although solar electricity costs quite a lot, in rural areas ... it's cheaper to install solar electric panels than to string electric lines to villages hundreds of miles from central power plants." It may be cheaper in rural areas of the United States, too; he adds, "When building a new home more than a couple tenths of a mile away from a power line it is often cheaper to install a solar system."[15] Of course in these cases, he is speaking not of grid-tied systems, but of off-grid ones.

There may be a number of public agencies and/or utilities that can help bring down the cost of your PV system with incentives. More agencies are creating incentives every week, particularly as I write this, soon after passage of the American Recovery and Reinvestment Act of 2009. These incentives can shave 50 percent or more off the sticker price of a PV system, depending on where you are.

PV options

A great deal of investment and research into solar electricity and into different product variations is now taking place worldwide. For now, though, odds are you would be considering one of the two basic types of PV array available – panels or building-integrated (BIPV) – for your energy-free home project. PVs come in one of two basic flavors: crystalline silicon and amorphous silicon. At present (mid-2009), most panels and BIPV arrays are made of crystalline silicon, although the future development of competitive amorphous silicon products shows tremendous promise.

Tracking PVs are another variation. These are panels mounted on a mechanized base that is automated to follow the sun, keeping the panels oriented at the optimum collection angle throughout the day. Tracking arrays are relatively uncommon in residential installations and are therefore not covered here.

Most PV panels measure roughly 2.5 x 5 feet and are rated to produce 170 to 200 Watts of electricity. The 2.38-kW array on our roof comprises 14 Mitsubishi panels rated at 170W each. It occupies less than 200 square feet. The efficiency of PV panels approaches 20 percent and is climbing steadily, if not meteorically. In February 2009, **Cleantechnica.com** reported Mitsubishi as the record-holder, having "improved the conversion efficiency rate of its PV cells to 18.9 percent."

Universities and private laboratories are pursuing further improvements in efficiency. Several claims of around 40 percent efficiency have been made, suggesting that this conversion rate is indeed on the horizon for commercially-available PV systems.[16]

▶ PV efficiency is the fraction of incident solar energy that the panel converts to useful electricity.

The relative efficiency, size, and cost of competing panels will be factors in the overall cost of the system. The cheapest panel may not correlate with the cheapest system, depending on other factors.

BuildingGreen.com has this to say about BIPVs: "Several different levels of building integration can be achieved with PVs. At one end of the spectrum, the building can simply provide the mounting infrastructure for the PV array. At the other end of the spectrum, the PV modules can serve a building function – for example, as the exterior curtainwall skin or skylight glazing."

Exemplifying the former are peel-and-stick PVs that are surface-applied to roofing, such as the Unisolar photovoltaic laminates (**www.uni-solar.com/interior.asp?id=102**) that were field-applied to a standing-seam metal roof at the Environmental Technology Center at Sonoma State University. Exemplifying the latter type are Sunslates, produced by Atlantis USA (**www.atlantisenergy.com**). Sunslates, which are fiber-cement roof tiles onto which silicon-crystal PV cells have been laminated, are installed like tile shingles.

**FIGURE 6-10.
PV PERGOLA ON
LIVINGHOMES
MODEL**

BIPVs tend to be less efficient than PV panels, resulting in increased space needs and higher installed cost and weight for BIPV arrays.[17] However, they may provide an excellent option where there are aesthetic concerns about PV panels (unfortunately, there are those who find them ugly) or for specialized architectural applications. One such is the pergola roof of the LivingHomes (**www.livinghomes.net**) demonstration model in Santa Monica, California, shown in Figure 6-10.

We considered using peel-and-stick PVs at Tah.Mah.Lah. but ultimately decided against them because the expected lifespan of the peel-and-stick product was only 10 to 15 years, far less than the 100-year expected lifespan of the stainless steel roofing. Using standard, frame-mounted panel PVs meant they could easily be repaired or replaced over time as needed.

System sizing

As with all renewable systems, the most reliable sizing information is likely to come from your system vendor. That said, of course, you might want to develop a preliminary estimate for planning purposes – just to get a sense of how much real estate an energy-free system might occupy.

A standard sizing process is as follows:

1. List all the appliances and electronic devices that will be used in the home.

2. Estimate the average amount of time each item will be used daily. Do this in two columns to account for seasonal differences (more hours of lighting in winter, fewer TV hours in summer, etc.).

3. Multiply the hours of use for each device by its power consumption in Watts, which is listed on a small plate or sticker on the back of the unit. (Several online resources also provide this information.)

4. To come up with a daily total, tabulate the Watt-hours for all the devices. Dan Chiras advises, "PV systems should be sized for the season with the highest energy demand and the lowest solar energy influx (insolation). You can determine this with a little simple math: simply divide each season's electrical energy requirements by the corresponding insolation values."

However, if you're primarily interested in achieving net-zero energy on an annual basis, rather than in providing for your *peak* electrical needs as you would in an off-grid system, it makes more sense to size the system for the average insolation.

A partial sample electrical load tabulation is shown in Figure 6-11.

Device	Summer average hours of use/day	Winter average hours of use/day	Watts	Summer Watt-hours	Winter Watt-hours
TV – 25"	2	3	130	260	390
Hallway light	1	3	11	11	33
Electric lawnmower	.2	0	1500	300	0
Hedge trimmer	.1	0	450	45	0
Total				616	423

FIGURE 6-11. SAMPLE ELECTRICAL LOAD TABULATION

I found several sources for insolation data, most of them overly complicated. The easiest-to-use source I found is at **www.rredc.nrel.gov/solar/old_data/nsrdb/ redbook/atlas/**. It requires you to select only three things:

1. Type of solar radiation data. The options are minimum, maximum, or average. I selected average.

2. Month. I selected January, which I suspected would be the month with the lowest insolation value for the San Francisco Bay Area.

3. Collector type and orientation. There is a linked online manual to assist in making the appropriate selection. I chose "Flat-Plate Tilted South at Latitude – 15 Degrees," which means that my flat plate collector faces south and is sloped at an angle 15 degrees less than the latitude (which is the optimum tilt angle). Figure 6-12 shows the tilt angle, and Figure 6-13 shows how to convert from roof pitch to tilt angle (or vice versa). Our latitude here is 37° North and our roof pitch is around 4:12, or 18.5°, so latitude – 15 degrees is a reasonably close approximation.

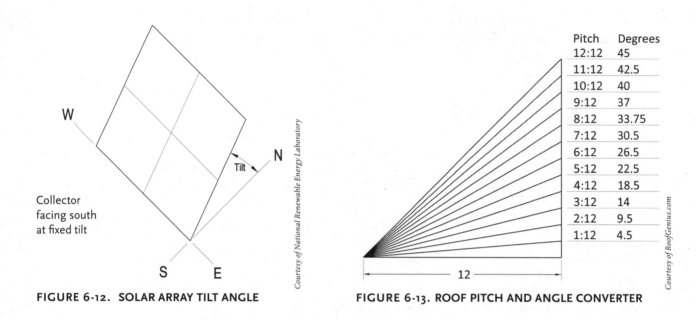

Courtesy of National Renewable Energy Laboratory

Courtesy of RoofGenius.com

FIGURE 6-12. SOLAR ARRAY TILT ANGLE

FIGURE 6-13. ROOF PITCH AND ANGLE CONVERTER

After selecting these three items, click "View the Map" to display the amounts of insolation for different parts of the United States. After checking January, I repeated the procedure to check February, July, August, and September in turn to see the range of values. January has the lowest insolation, 2-3 kWh/m²/day; July and August have the highest insolation, 7-8 kWh/m²/day.

Another option – slightly more involved, but more useful in providing *average* insolation data – is NREL's online PV Watts program at **http://rredc.nrel.gov/ solar/codes_algs/PVWATTS/version2/.**

When it asks you for your system size, input 1 kW; that way, the output will provide the results for *each* kW installed. (I won't go into the details of using PV Watts; instructions are provided online and they're not terribly user-friendly, but it is possible to muddle through with a little persistence.)

PV Watts tells me that my average solar radiation (same as insolation) is 5.28 kWh/ m²/day.

My electrical gizmo device tabulation (an approximation) shows that our winter loads, at about 35 kWh/day, are somewhat higher than summer due to increased lighting demand. I couldn't find anything that we use more in summer. The real shocker is how much stuff we have in the office – all those electronics represent one-quarter of our total electric load!

Dividing the winter load by the average insolation yields the system output you need – in my case, 6.6 kW. Our existing system is 2.4 kW, so it should theoretically meet 36 percent of our electrical demand. This suggests that my wattage guesstimates are high, because our existing 2.4 kW system has met 44 percent of our actual demand – it has produced just over 10 kW in its 3.5 years of operation; during that time, we have also purchased 12.8 kW. Thus our total actual electrical demand for the past 3.5 years is about 22.8 kWh, or an average of roughly 6.5 kWh per year.

Another simplified sizing method, courtesy of Coldham & Hartman Architects, is shown in Figure 6-14 with our estimated *total* annual energy use (including natural gas usage, which is more appropriate for an energy-free home).

Step	Action	Amount
1	Estimate your annual energy use (ideally, using a good energy-modeling program[18]) in kBtu/yr	82,000kBtu/year
2	Divide by 3.412 to convert to kWh	24,032 kWh/year
3	Divide by 1.1 to get installed Watts of PV needed (1 installed Watt PV = 1.1 kWh/yr, appx.)	21,848 W installed PV (21.8 kW)
4	Divide by 10 to get roof area needed (appx. 10 installed Watts of PV per sq.ft. of roof)	2,184 sq. ft. of roof

FIGURE 6-14. SIMPLE PV SIZING METHOD

This calculation indicates that to meet our total annual energy needs we would need an array more than ten times the size of our current one, which is 190 sq. ft. Using just our annual *electrical* load (6.5 kWh), the method shown above yields 5.9 kW of PV and 590 square feet of roof area – more than three times the size of our existing system, just for electrical needs. Our house has less than 700 square feet of south-facing roof, so offsetting our natural gas usage, too, would mean we would need to reduce our loads dramatically *and* add a lot more PVs (perhaps in less-than-optimal orientations) to achieve energy-free status.

There are many lessons from this exercise – first and foremost, it's much easier to get to net-zero if you build a new home and can do a really exemplary job with air-sealing and insulation from the outset – fixing these things in existing homes is more expensive and often physically challenging. However, unless you have a building with lots of roof space relative to floor area (i.e., a one-story home), have plenty of room for PVs elsewhere, or plan to install a wind turbine, too, you will have to insulate and air-seal well to become energy-free. Otherwise you are likely to find it hard to get your loads low enough to achieve net-zero.

Wind Turbines

The primary consideration for choosing a wind turbine is, of course, wind – how much, what kind, and how often. According to the American Wind Energy Association (AWEA) website, "Generally, an annual average wind speed greater than four meters per second (m/s) (9 mph) is required for small wind electric turbines." Chiras says, "Most systems for homes and farms require an average annual wind speed at ground level of about seven to nine miles per hour." Wind speed increases with height above the ground, so wind speeds may be considerably higher at the top of your (future) wind turbine tower.

A number of resources are available to help you assess site wind opportunities. Chiras, Mick Sagrillo, and Ian Woofenden, co-authors of *Power from the Wind*, recommend using wind maps available at the following sources:

- United States DOE's wind power site, **www.windpoweringamerica.gov** (US data)

- Wind Navigator, **navigator.awstruewind.com** (data for the United States, Canada, and India)

- The Canadian Wind Atlas, **www.cmc.ec.gc.ca** (data for Canada)

- NASA's Surface Meteorology and Solar Energy website, **eosweb.larc.nasa.gov/ sse** (Chiras, et al., warn that this site is a bit more involved but is still a very useful resource; see page 94 of *Power from the Wind* for tips on using the site.)

While these maps show estimated wind speeds at 50 to 60 meters above the ground surface, Chiras, et al., provide instructions for how to adjust those speeds for different heights.[19] Because wind speed can be significantly affected by site-specific conditions (topography, structures, vegetative cover, etc.), it would be wise to consult with an experienced wind system designer or installer for help assessing the wind conditions at your specific site.

Plans for the energy+house project under development in San Francisco initially included a wind turbine. However, monitoring revealed that wind at the site was erratic and that much of the wind was blocked by the topography and surrounding buildings. As a result, a turbine would produce less additional power than could be obtained by increasing the size of the solar array. The owner has decided to do that instead.[20]

The Midwest Renewable Energy Association is the national certifying body for wind site assessors, listed at **http://www.mreacsa.org/**. (I discovered, though, that the assessors listed there who perform wind assessments in California are all from pretty far away – one in Texas, two in Wisconsin, and one in New Jersey.)

If a wind turbine looks promising for your project, you will need to identify the ideal location for it on your project site, factoring in all relevant issues:

- Optimum wind exposure (more is better)

- Building locations (yours and neighbors') and turbine noise (farther is better)

- Proximity to where the inverter will be installed (closer is better)

- Height considerations (taller is better)

This last point bears emphasizing. Wind speed increases with height, and turbine output increases disproportionately with wind speed – in fact, with the cube of wind velocity. Therefore, it will likely prove a better investment to build a taller tower than to buy a larger turbine. Chiras reinforces this, noting that "by doubling the wind speed from 8 miles per hour to 16 miles per hour, power production increases by 800 percent!"

When analyzing whether there is enough wind at your site to justify a turbine, consider the following advice from *Mother Earth News:* "Two distinct kinds of wind can be found at most locations. *Prevalent winds* blow frequently and reliably. *Energy winds* are storm winds or gusts that piggyback the prevalent winds and vary in velocity and duration." While they may occur only a day or two a week, the energy winds, because they are at higher speeds, can increase power output dramatically, even doubling it. Therefore, the authors observe that even if your region is not ranked as ideal for wind power, "your individual microclimate paired with energy winds might yield enough energy to justify a wind system."[21]

▶ *Power from the Wind* is an excellent, detailed resource for anyone planning to design and install a wind turbine. For a simpler overview, I recommend the chapter on wind power in *The Homeowner's Guide to Renewable Energy.*

FIGURE 6-15. PILL-MAHARAM HOUSE

© Jim Westphalen, Westphalen Photography

Chiras notes, "Wind power is primarily useful … in rural areas on lots of one acre or more," and, "if you live in a city or town, chances are wind power is very likely not going to be an option for you." He gives a variety of reasons (space, height ordinances, turbulence, neighbor objections, etc.) but then cites the US DOE as saying that 21 million homes in the United States are built on one-acre and larger sites, and "about ten percent of the US population could theoretically take advantage of wind energy." So, while wind power is not going to be a viable option for most residential projects, it also shouldn't be ruled out without due consideration. Five or six residential wind turbines are now in operation in San Francisco.

▶ The Pill-Maharam house in Vermont recently won the Zero Net Energy Building Award from the Northeast Sustainable Energy Association **(NESEA.org)**, the 2008 AIA Vermont Honor Award in Sustainability and Design, and Efficiency Vermont's Best of the Best Award in 2008 for houses from 2,000 to 3,000 square feet. It has a 10 kW wind turbine. Case study resources are listed in Appendix B.

Furthermore, because this technology is so rapidly evolving (according to Chiras, "Today, wind power is the fastest growing source of energy in the world!"), it will behoove you to investigate anything new that dealers are offering in your area – while heeding the cautions summarized below.

Building-integrated wind

As with PVs, residential wind turbines can be either ground-mounted or building-mounted (building-integrated). According to Alex Wilson in his feature article "The Folly of Building-Integrated Wind" (*Environmental Building News*, May 1, 2009), and as the title suggests, "building-integrated wind doesn't make much sense as a renewable-energy strategy." Among the reasons Wilson cites are noise, vibration, and structural challenges; air flow requirements; poor measured vs. predicted performance; and high cost per kWh of production. These issues are summarized below.

Noise, vibration, and structure. Controlling noise from vibration requires careful engineering; it is tricky and challenging even when the vibration is regular, which wind turbine vibration is not – it's variable. This means it's harder to control and can even result in harmonic resonance, magnifying the effect. Wilson states, "AeroVironment, the building-integrated wind energy company that has done more than any other to understand the aerodynamics of wind around buildings, suggests in its sales literature that their turbines are only appropriate for buildings constructed of concrete." Mounting a turbine on a rooftop tower might seem like a solution, but the stresses created by turbine vibration can create significant structural *and* noise problems. Dan Chiras reinforces this: "Whatever you do, do not mount a wind machine on a roof or against a building – even if a supplier provides special mounts for such applications. The vibrations will be conducted into the building and can be very annoying. I know, I tried this."[22]

All residential wind turbines in San Francisco are given provisional permits, primarily because the systems as a whole are not certified by UL (the City requires that all system *components* be UL certified) but also because of noise concerns. San Francisco permits vertical-axis turbines (e.g., corkscrew types) to be installed on residential roofs without a community notification process, because this type of system produces fewer vibrations (beyond the building on which it is mounted) than horizontal-axis turbines do. Horizontal-axis turbines must be ground-mounted and must go through a community notification process.

As of September 2009, there were three or four vertical-axis residential wind turbines in San Francisco and two horizontal-axis turbines, one of which has been in operation for at least two years; the second is shown in Figure 6-16.[23]

Air flow. Wind turbines perform best when air flow is laminar, i.e., all in one direction. However, air flow on top of buildings tends to be very turbulent, "confusing" turbines and diminishing output. Although some turbines have been designed specifically for mounting on rooftops, they tend to be small and costlier per unit of production than larger ones.

Poor measured vs. predicted performance. Wilson observes that "obtaining actual *measured* performance data is like pulling teeth … the reason … may be that actual electricity production is much worse than expected." As AWEA's Ron Stimmel told him, "it's very, very difficult to get [small-scale, rooftop wind turbines] to perform at anywhere near their rated capacities."

High cost per kWh of production. "While large freestanding wind turbines provide the least expensive renewable electricity today, small wind turbines are far less cost effective, and when

FIGURE 6-16. WIND TURBINE IN SAN FRANCISCO

Ann Edminster

199

small turbines are put on buildings, the costs go up while the production drops," says Wilson. He quotes Paul Gipe, a leading advocate of wind power, as saying that "if you're looking to put renewable energy on buildings, there's nothing better than photovoltaics."

While Wilson makes a compelling case against *building-integrated* wind, his research shouldn't put you off wind altogether, if you're in a good site for a ground-mounted turbine.

Turbine selection

Wind turbines operate on either a horizontal or a vertical axis. Horizontal-axis turbines are more common, although many vertical-axis turbines have recently been introduced. Since by far the majority of residential-scale, ground-mounted turbines operate on a horizontal axis, most of what follows relates to that type (and leans heavily, as is true throughout this chapter, on Dan Chiras's and his co-authors' research on the subject).

The primary selection criteria, and why they matter, are presented below:

- **Swept area** (in square feet) is the area described by the rotor blades' movement as they turn. Swept area is the best proxy for output potential. It is important because the larger the area intercepted by the blades, the more air the rotors will catch, and the more power they will produce. Other metrics, such as power curve, rated output, or wattage, don't provide a reliable basis for comparing power production.

- **kWh/month production at your average wind speed** is a relatively good metric to use for comparing different turbines, but you may or may not be able to get this information for a specific model.

- **Weight** is primarily important as an indicator of durability and therefore life expectancy. The heftier the turbine, the longer it is likely to last. Heavier units are also typically quieter, but also costlier.

- **Tower height** is important because a taller tower will get you up into higher wind speeds and therefore much higher production. Tower bases may be either freestanding or guyed, and either be simple poles or have latticework (truss) designs. Lattice designs are generally sturdier and less expensive than poles. Chiras says, "Most serious installations are 80 to 120 feet above ground," although tower heights range both lower and higher than that.

- **Installed cost** includes the turbine, charge controller, base, tower, inverter, labor for installation, and assorted incidentals – in short, everything it takes to get the turbine up and operational. When comparing the installed costs of different turbines, be sure to look at the performance metrics at the same time (swept area, kWh/month production at *your* average wind speed, and weight). The best buy will be the lowest price in dollar per unit of swept area, per kWh/mo, and/or per pound.

Wattage is not a reliable gauge of power output. However, it is the most available metric and does provide a rough indication of a turbine's relative power potential. Therefore, you may want to use wattage as a starting point in identifying turbines that are good candidates for further investigation. Chiras's guidance on wattage is as follows:

- Residential-scale machines range from 400 to 20,000 Watts.

- 400-1,000 W machines only supply 40-200 kWh of electricity per month, and only in areas with consistent wind speeds of ~12 mph.

- 1,000-3,000 W might be ideal "if you simply want to supplement your electrical energy from the grid ... if you live in a tiny cabin or you are extremely efficient [or] if you are installing a ... combination of wind and PVs."

- "If you want to go off-grid completely and are hoping to supply electricity solely from a wind machine, you'll very likely need ... more than 3,000 Watts but likely 6,000 Watts or higher."

- A typical, not super-efficient home will need a 2,500 to 6,000 W machine or will need to combine the turbine with a PV system.

- A 10 kW system – or larger – is probably what you'll need if you don't have a tiny, super-efficient home and/or a PV system.

Backup Power

Grid-tied renewable electric systems may or may not include a battery backup. As I explained in Chapter 1, this book isn't about off-grid homes, which will definitely have batteries to back up their electrical systems in the event of a power outage. Grid-tied homes have the option of including backup systems – batteries, generators, or both – although it's not necessary, and most of them don't.

PASSIVE SURVIVABILITY

Many of the strategies discussed in this book are part and parcel of the concept of "passive survivability," a term coined by Alex Wilson a number of years ago and about which he has written a number of times in *Environmental Building News*. The basic principle of passive survivability is that in the event of a power outage – or other event causing a disconnection from the grid – a building would be designed to support its occupants' survival – passively, without external inputs – for a period of time. Energy-free homes are natural allies to passive survivability, so I strongly encourage you to read Wilson's feature articles on the subject on **BuildingGreen.com.**[24]

The advantage of a battery backup, of course, is that when the power goes out, you can not only draw power from your batteries, but the systems are configured so that you can also continue to power your home from your renewable system(s), so long as the sun is shining and/or the wind is blowing. Without battery backup, when the power goes out, you don't have power – even if the sun is shining or the wind is blowing. That may seem like a real cheat. However, this drawback has to be weighed against the additional expense of a battery bank, the space it will occupy, its maintenance, and periodic battery replacement. Your decision about this will probably be guided by those factors as well as the risks associated with loss of power for an extended period.

In Northern California, where I live, the consequences of being without power for a couple of days are relatively manageable, for most of us in robust health. If it's winter (and it usually is – the power lines get knocked out in storms) we bundle up in fleece and thick socks, order in pizza, read books by candle or camping lantern, and go to bed early. If it's summer, we go for evening walks or sit on the front porch. In other parts of the country, however, people aren't so fortunate under these conditions. When their power goes out for several days, they can get dangerously cold (of course, all the more reason to have your enclosure built as tightly and toastily as possible!) and suffer extreme discomfort. Where extreme temperatures (often coupled with stormy conditions) are common in winter or summer, a prolonged loss of power can be fatal, especially for the very old or very young. In such situations, a battery backup system and/or generator looks extremely attractive.

One consideration, if you choose to include a generator, is how it will be fueled, and how that factors into your net-zero and/or fossil fuel-free scheme. At Tah. Mah.Lah., the owners opted to forego batteries but install a biodiesel generator. Biodiesel "goes bad" after a time, so it's inadvisable to let it sit more than three months. Their solution was to plan for a biodiesel mini-van or SUV, which they would use whenever the whole family traveled together; the van would use biodiesel regularly from a tank shared by the generator, so the fuel would get used and replaced on a regular basis.

Hybrids

A so-called hybrid system is a renewable system that includes two or more renewable energy options; the most typical hybrid system is a combination of PVs and a wind turbine. This pairing can be very complementary, particularly in places that have strong winter winds and lots of summer sun. In such cases, each individual system can probably be smaller than either would be if it were the only renewable system, because even while producing less outside its peak season, it will generally continue to produce *some* power, thereby reducing the load that must be met by the companion system.

Other Options

In addition to solar and wind, there are a number of other ways to provide a residence with renewable energy. These include "micro-hydro" – a small-scale water wheel – fuel cells, and waste-to-heat conversion systems. Despite considerable research and innovation in these areas, few if any of the technologies are ready for prime time – that is, are affordable and/or suitable for widespread use. Micro-hydro systems, for instance, require access to on-site moving water. Wouldn't we all feel fortunate to have that? It is a realistic option for a very, very small number of households, but for those few, well worth investigating.

There is not space in this volume to address these options, but I refer you once again to Dan Chiras's *Homeowner's Guide to Renewable Energy* as well as numerous articles in *Home Power* magazine if you wish to learn more about them.

Choosing a Renewable System

Now you've received a basic introduction to renewable home energy systems – so how do you choose? What's going to be the best option, or the best combination, for your project?

First of all, I hope you've concluded that you should spend every penny possible on improving the enclosure before adding renewables. Otherwise, it's probable that you won't have enough roof space for the PVs you would need, and you are also unlikely to have the right sort of real estate for wind. That means you'll want to get your demand as low as you possibly can.

It all comes back to integrated design, so I can offer no pat answers. No prescriptions. Every project is unique, and the most creative, committed green building professionals in your area will be able to provide you with the best available guidance in selecting renewable systems and – more importantly – in integrating those systems into the whole design, balancing the decisions about renewables with the decisions about other aspects of the project. Because they're all connected.

All architectural design is a knee-bone-connected-to-thigh-bone-connected-to-hip-bone exercise, and design that is high-performance, or energy-free, is all the more so. Be prepared to do preliminary research on available renewable options, compare them, assess their implications for the site and for the building you envision designing, and then reevaluate. In fact, be prepared to run through that sequence several times; each time you do, it's likely that you'll encounter both new questions and new answers.

Even so, I'll make a few generalizations about renewables in energy-free homes (and, as is the danger with all generalizations, you may say, "Those don't apply to me!"):

1. Most energy-free homes will have PVs.

2. Many energy-free homes will have solar thermal systems.

3. Some – mostly rural – energy-free homes will have wind turbines.

Community Issues

At the risk of concluding on a less than rosy note, in some communities you may encounter impediments to installing renewable energy systems. Some towns have design regulations or height restrictions that may preclude or simply complicate the installation of a solar array or turbine tower. Some towns have ordinances protecting your neighbors' trees, which cast shade on what would otherwise be your best spot for PVs.

If your project is subject to a public hearing for a discretionary permit of any sort, it will provide a forum for community members to either support or oppose your project, and they may raise all kinds of concerns, both legitimate and otherwise. For example, there are people who find PVs ugly or who are bothered by the glare on their shiny surface. Neighbors may raise noise concerns about a proposed wind turbine.

Having attended many public hearings, I offer these observations:

1. People who are normally your friends or allies may take a position in opposition to you which may be either well-reasoned or absurd.

2. People who are normally your political opponents or are just buffoons may take a position in your favor, which – equally – may be either well-reasoned or absurd.

3. Do outreach in advance, and go above and beyond what is required. For example, if your community requires written notice to neighbors within 300 feet, go door to door personally and offer to explain the project to your neighbors. Or hold an open meeting, offer refreshments, and have visuals there to help explain what you want to do. Be sure the meeting is well-publicized.

4. Give people plenty of time to wrap their heads around your proposal. Alert them as early as possible. Present the benefits over and over again.

5. Find out what your community may be doing about climate change, and make your pitch in that context. Particularly if you are bucking a local ordinance – a height limit or design guideline, for example – your odds will improve if you can point to some other public policy or regulation you are *supporting* by incorporating renewable energy in your project.

If, after all your efforts, you are foiled in your attempts to incorporate renewable energy systems in your project, don't throw in the towel. Do what you can to accommodate those systems in the future, forge ahead, and try again when the political winds change. For example, you can pre-install plumbing, electricity, and structural supports for rooftop systems, making it much easier to install them at a later date. You will be that much farther along your pathway toward an energy-free home. And make no mistake, the political winds *are* changing.

ENDNOTES

1 Dan Chiras, *The Homeowner's Guide to Renewable Energy* (Gabriola Island, BC, Canada: New Society Publishers, 2006), 93.

2 Southface, "Residential Solar Thermal Costs, Paybacks and Maintenance", http://www.southface.org/solar/solar-roadmap/residential/residential_thermal_paybacks.htm

3 http://www.rockpapersun.com/hwestimate.htm

4 Ted Bardacke, Global Green, personal communication, September 2009.

5 Solar Thermal: A Simplified Guide to Sizing Your System, http://www.thesolarguide.com/solar-thermal/sizing.aspx

6 Southface, "Residential Solar Thermal Costs, Paybacks and Maintenance", http://www.southface.org/solar/solar-roadmap/residential/residential_thermal_paybacks.htm

7 Note this is based on the utility rates, system prices, and climatic conditions in Atlanta, GA, at the time the material was written.

8 Chiras, *The Homeowner's Guide,* 96.

9 Peter Shoemaker, Pacific Gas & Electric Company, personal communication, September 2009.

10 Peter Shoemaker, Pacific Gas & Electric Company, personal communication, September 2009.

11 Peter Shoemaker, Pacific Gas & Electric Company, personal communication, September 2009.

12 Paul Torcellini, et al., National Renewable Energy Laboratory, "Zero Energy Buildings: A Critical Look at the Definition," http://www.nrel.gov/docs/fy06osti/39833.pdf, 7.

13 "Zero Energy Homes: What, How, and If," Boston Architectural College, Summer 2009.

14 For our modeling, we used Micropas, which doesn't incorporate lighting and appliances.

15 Chiras, *The Homeowner's Guide,* 169.

16 Wikipedia contributors, "Photovoltaics," *Wikipedia, The Free Encyclopedia,* http://en.wikipedia.org/w/index.php?title=Photovoltaics&oldid=315518194 (accessed September 22, 2009).

17 AMECO Solar, "History of Solar Power," http://www.solarexpert.com/pvbasics2.html.

18 The amount shown for our home is based on metered data; however, if you're building a new home or remodeling, you'll need to project your usage, which is where the energy modeling comes in.

19 Dan Chiras, et al., *Power from the Wind,* (Gabriola Island, BC, Canada: New Society Publishers, 2009), 90-91.

20 BJ Siegel, BJ Siegel Architect, personal communication, August 2009.

21 Michael Hackleman and Claire Anderson, "Harvest the Wind," *Mother Earth News,* June-July 2002 issue, http://www.motherearthnews.com/Renewable-Energy/2002-06-01/Harvest-the-Wind.aspx, 1.

22 Chiras, *Power from the Wind,* 228.

23 Johannah Partin, Renewable Energy Manager of the San Francisco Department of the Environment, personal communication, September 2009.

24 Alex Wilson, "Passive Survivability: A New Design Criterion for Buildings," BuildingGreen.com, May 1, 2006, http://www.buildinggreen.com/auth/article.cfm/2006/5/3/Passive-Survivability-A-New-Design-Criterion-for-Buildings/, and Alex Wilson and Andrea Ward, "Design for Adaptation: Living in a Climate-Changing World," BuildingGreen.com, September 1, 2009, http://www.buildinggreen.com/auth/article.cfm/2009/8/28/Design-for-Adaptation-Living-in-a-Climate-Changing-World/?.

A Resources/Bibliography

This appendix lists several types of resources (primarily books, websites, and software), organized by principal topic; topics are listed alphabetically.

California-specific resources

Also see California Energy Commission listings in section below titled, "HERS, ENERGY STAR, insulation quality, and air sealing."

Architects/Designers/Planners for Social Responsibility (ADPSR), Northern California. **www.adpsr-norcal.org.** ADPSR-Norcal offers green building lectures, a free listserv for notices of events, jobs, and a variety of other regionally-relevant information.

Build It Green (BIG). **www.builditgreen.org**. BIG is a multifaceted organization that includes numerous councils and guilds specific to different residential green building stakeholders. The organization and its website offer a wide array of useful information.

CalCERTS. **www.calcerts.com.** A California-based HERS Provider.

California Building Performance Contractors' Association. **www.cbpca.org.** Focused principally on improving the energy performance of existing homes.

California Home Energy Efficiency Rating Services (CHEERS). **www.cheers.org.** A California-based HERS Provider.

PG&E Pacific Energy Center (San Francisco). **www.pge.com/pec.** The PEC offers many lectures, half-day classes, and full-day classes on energy and green building topics, frequently taught by national experts.

PG&E Stockton Energy Training Center. **www.pge.com/stockton.** The ETC, like the PEC, offers an extensive calendar of high-quality training sessions, targeted primarily at residential building professionals.

Design for adaptability

Brand, Stewart. 1994. *How Buildings Learn: What Happens After They Are Built.* New York, NY: The Penguin Group.

Energy-efficient appliances and electronics

American Council for an Energy-efficient Economy. **www.ACEEE.org.**

Consortium for Energy Efficiency. **www.CEE.org.**

www.EfficientProducts.org.

ENERGY STAR. **www.energystar.gov/index.cfm?fuseaction=find_a_product.**

Energy-efficient/green design, new construction focus

Bonta, Dave, and Stephen Snyder. 2008. *New Green Home Solutions: Renewable Household Energy and Sustainable Living.* Salt Lake City, UT: Gibbs Smith.

Brown, G.Z. 1985. *Sun, Wind and Light: Architectural Design Strategies.* New York, NY: John Wiley & Sons, Inc.

Building America Program, US DOE. **www1.eere.energy.gov/buildings/building_america.**

ENERGY STAR New Homes. **www.energystar.gov/index.cfm?c=new_homes.hm_index.**

Galloway, Terry. 2004. *Solar House: A Guide for the Solar Designer.* Burlington, MA: Architectural Press.

Klingenberg, K., M. Kernagis, and M. James. 2008. *Homes for a Changing Climate.* Larkspur, CA: Low Carbon Productions. (Case studies of Passive Houses completed in the United States.)

Krigger, John, and Chris Dorsi. 2004. *Residential Energy: Cost Savings and Comfort for Existing Buildings, 4th ed*. Helena, MT: Saturn Resource Management, Inc.

Labs, Kenneth, and Donald Watson. 1993. *Climatic Building Design: Energy-Efficient Building Principles and Practices*. New York: McGraw-Hill.

Lstiburek, Joseph. 2006. *Builder's Guide to Cold Climates*. Westford, MA: Building Science Press, **www.buildingsciencepress.com/Builders-Guides-C1.aspx.** (Other publications in the series cover other climates.)

Mazria, Edward. 1979. *The Passive Solar Energy Book, A Complete Guide to Passive Solar Home, Greenhouse and Building Design*. Emmaus, PA: Rodale Press.

Metz, Don. 1981. *Superhouse: Passive Solar, Super Insulated, Earth-Sheltered, Double Envelope*. Charlotte, VT: Garden Way Publishing, Inc.

Moore, Fuller. 1992. *Environmental Control Systems: Heating, Cooling, Lighting*. New York, NY: McGraw-Hill Science/Engineering/Math.

O'Brien, Kathleen, and Kathleen Smith. 2008. *The Northwest Green Home Primer*. Portland, OR: Timber Press, Inc.

Olgyay, Aladar, and Victor Olgyay. 1976. *Solar Control & Shading Devices*. Princeton, NJ: Princeton University Press.

Ryker, Lori, with photographs by Audrey Hall. 2007. *Off the Grid Homes: Case Studies for Sustainable Living*. Salt Lake City, UT: Gibbs Smith.

Steele, James. 1988. *Hassan Fathy (Architectural Monographs No 13)*. London, UK: Academy Editions.

Steven Winter Associates. 1998. *The Passive Solar Design and Construction Handbook*. New York, NY: John Wiley & Sons, Inc.

Wilson, Alex. 2006. *Your Green Home*. Gabriola Island, BC, Canada: New Society Publishers.

Wright, R., S. Wright, B. Selby, and L. Dieckmann. 1980. *The Hawkweed Passive Solar House Book*. Chicago, IL: Rand McNally Company.

Energy-efficient/green design, remodeling/renovation focus

Building Performance Institute. **www.bpi.org.** Building performance contractor directory and training resource.

Editors of *Home Energy* magazine. 1997. *No Regrets Remodeling.* Berkeley, CA: Energy Auditor & Retrofitter, Inc.

ENERGY STAR Home Improvement. **www.energystar.gov/index.cfm?c=home_improvement.hm_improvement_index.**

Hren, Stephen and Rebekah. 2008. *The Carbon-Free Home: 36 Remodeling Projects to Help Kick the Fossil-Fuel Habit.* White River Junction, VT: Chelsea Green Publishing.

REGREEN. **www.regreenprogram.org.** REGREEN is not a rating system or labeling program, but rather a web-based educational resource. It is the product of a partnership between the American Society of Interior Designers' Foundation and the USGBC. The website includes case studies, best practice guidelines, and other tools for green residential improvement projects. It was designed to provide practical guidance to homeowners, residents, design professionals, product suppliers, and service providers.

Roaf, S., D. Crichton, and F. Nicol. 2005. *Adapting Buildings and Cities for Climate Change: A 21ˢᵗ Century Survival Guide.* Burlington, MA: Architectural Press.

Stoyke, Godo. 2007. *The Carbon Busters Home Energy Handbook: Slowing Climate Change and Saving Money.* Gabriola Island, BC, Canada: New Society Publishers.

Venolia, Carol, and Kelly Lerner. 2006. *Natural Remodeling for the Not-So-Green House.* New York, NY: Lark Books, a division of Sterling Publishing Co., Inc.

Energy-efficient mortgages

ENERGY STAR. **www.energystar.gov/index.cfm?c=bldrs_lenders_raters.energy_efficient_mortgage.**

FHA. **www.disasterhousing.gov/offices/hsg/sfh/eem/energy-r.cfm.**

RESNET. **www.natresnet.org/ratings/overview/faq_mortgage.htm.**

Energy modeling software

DOE-2 and DOE-2.2. **www.doe2.com.** The basic engine behind many modeling applications.

Energy Gauge. **www.energygauge.com.** Accredited by RESNET and used for HERS, ENERGY STAR, and LEED for Homes in locations other than California.

EnergyPlus. **http://apps1.eere.energy.gov/buildings/energyplus.** Primarily used for commercial buildings, but a residential version is under development.

EnergyPro. **www.energysoft.com.** Used to assess performance with respect to California's *Building Energy Efficiency Standards* (a.k.a. Title 24) for both residential and nonresidential buildings. Used for HERS, ENERGY STAR, and LEED for Homes in California.

eQUEST. **http://doe2.com/equest/index.html.** An interface for DOE-2.2.

Home Energy Efficient Design (HEED). **energy.design.tools@ucla.edu.** A free, user-friendly modeling tool developed by UCLA.

Home Energy Saver. **http://hes.lbl.gov.** A consumer-friendly online program.

Micropas. **http://micropas.nittler.us/index.html.** Used to assess performance with respect to California's *Building Energy Efficiency Standards* (a.k.a. Title 24) for residential buildings only. Used for HERS, ENERGY STAR, and LEED for Homes in California.

Passive House Planning Package (PHPP). **www.passivehouse.us/passiveHouse/ DesignTools.html.** Used to verify and design buildings that meet the Passive House standard. PHPP has been validated via extensive comparison of measured results with predicted performance throughout Europe.

REM/Rate. **http://archenergy.com/products/rem/rem_rate.** Not an hourly simulation so it can't be used for peak demand reduction evaluations. Accredited by RESNET and used for HERS, ENERGY STAR, and LEED for Homes in locations *other than* California.

TRNSYS. **www.trnsys.com.** A flexible system modeling tool designed by and for engineers.

General green building information

These resources are comprehensive in the types of information provided and the breadth of green building/energy topics.

BuildingGreen, LLC. **www.buildinggreen.com.** BuildingGreen, the premier news source for the green building industry, offers in this information-rich and advertising-free site the entire archives of *Environmental Building News* (described below under Journals), *GreenSpec* product listings and reviews, case studies, articles, blogs, and other authoritative green building tools and publications.

Canada Mortgage and Housing Corporation. **www.cmhc.ca.** CMHC conducts ongoing research on a comprehensive array of green building, building performance, and building science topics. Many of their research reports are available for free, and they also publish free electronic newsletters. They have resources for both consumers and building professionals.

Green Building Advisor. **www.greenbuildingadvisor.com.** The most practical and comprehensive residential green building resource site, GBA is published by BuildingGreen, LLC, and Taunton Press, publishers of *Fine Homebuilding*. The site includes both free consumer content and fee-based professional content, ranging from architectural details to how-to videos to blogs on a host of different topics. A discount subscription URL is provided in Appendix D.

GreenHomeGuide.com. **www.greenhomeguide.com.** A USGBC resource site that includes free and paid listings of green home professionals, "Ask a Pro," articles on green building topics, and a newsletter, among other informational offerings.

GreenHomeGuide.org. **www.greenhomeguide.org**. This USGBC web portal gives access to a potpourri of green home design and construction resources, including project profiles, news, and a nationwide listing of regional green home building programs.

Green building professional directories

Building Concerns. **www.buildingconcerns.com**.

GreenHomeGuide.com. **www.greenhomeguide.com**.

Green Sage. **www.greensage.com**.

Green homebuilding products and product information

GreenSpec Directory. **www.buildinggreen.com/menus**.

Green Building Advisor. **www.greenbuildingadvisor.com/product-guide**.

Green Building Pages. **www.greenbuildingpages.com/main.html**.

Oikos. **http://oikos.com/index.lasso**.

Green living

(Also see listings under "Energy-efficient/green design, remodeling/renovation focus.")

Editors of E Magazine. 2005. *Green Living: the E Magazine Handbook for Living Lightly on the Earth.* New York, NY: Plume/Penguin Group.

Christensen, Karen. 1990. *Home Ecology: Simple and Practical Ways to Green Your Home.* Golden, CO: Fulcrum Publishing.

HERS, ENERGY STAR, insulation quality, and air sealing

California Energy Commission:

- California Home Energy Rating System (HERS) Program, including *HERS Technical Manual* and *California Home Energy Rating System Program Regulations.* **www.energy.ca.gov/HERS**.

- Energy Code Online Training Website. **www.energyvideos.com**. Video training and resource links covering all aspects of the California Energy Efficiency Standards, or Title 24, insulation, air sealing, HVAC, water heating, and lighting.

- *Residential Compliance Manual for California's 2008 Energy Efficiency Standards.* **www.energy.ca.gov/title24/2008standards/residential_manual.html**. Quality Insulation Installation requirements are outlined in Chapter 3: Building Envelope. Other chapters include guidance on HVAC, lighting, water heating, additions & remodels.

- *Title 24 Energy Compliance Option for High Quality Installation of Insulation.* **http://vimeo.com/1580341**.

DOE. *Energy Savers Booklet – Tips on Saving Energy & Money at Home.* **www.eere.energy.gov/consumer/tips/pdfs/energy_savers.pdf**. Includes a discussion of insulation and air sealing.

ENERGY STAR:

- "Air Seal and Insulate with ENERGY STAR." **www.energystar.gov/index.cfm?c=home_sealing.hm_improvement_sealing**. Homeowner resources.

- "Technical Resources: Guidelines for ENERGY STAR Qualified New Homes." **www.energystar.gov/index.cfm?c=bldrs_lenders_raters.homes_guidelns**. A wealth of information on the ENERGY STAR for Homes program (see description in Appendix C), including a link to the proposed 2011 guidelines, national and region-specific program requirements, and guidance for different housing types (e.g., "Thermal Bypass Checklist for Structural Insulated Panels").

- *Thermal Bypass Checklist Guide.* **www.energystar.gov/ia/partners/bldrs_lenders_raters/downloads/TBC_Guide_062507.pdf.** Detailed guidance on the ENERGY STAR for Homes program's required "Thermal Bypass Checklist," a copy of which can be found at the end of this online document.

- "What is a HERS Rating?" **www.energystar.gov/index.cfm?c=bldrs_lenders_raters.nh_HERS**.

Lawrence Berkeley National Laboratory. 2009. *Building Commissioning: A Golden Opportunity for Reducing Energy Costs and Greenhouse Gas Emissions.* **http://cx.lbl.gov/2009-assessment.html**.

Northwest ENERGY STAR Technical Resources. **www.northwestenergystar.com/partner-resources/technical/index.html, www.northwestenergystar.com/partner-resources/criticaldetails/index.html**. Includes information on the ENERGY STAR for Homes program specific to Northwest States, however also includes a variety of resources that all U.S. projects can use, including easy-to-digest Technical Tips, a few of which are listed below:

- *Air Sealing.* **www.northwestenergystar.com/downloads/Air_Sealing_TechTips_v1.1.pdf**.

- *Ductwork.* **www.northwestenergystar.com/downloads/Ductwork_TechTips_v1.1.pdf**.

- *Insulation.* **www.northwestenergystar.com/downloads/Insulation_TechTips_v1.1.pdf**.

RESNET (Residential Energy Services Network). "About Home Energy Ratings." **www.natresnet.org/ratings/default.htm**.

Southface Fact Sheets and Technical Bulletins. **www.southface.org/web/ resources&services/publications/factsheets/sf_factsheet-menu.htm**. This website contains numerous building envelope resources, including the following:

- *Air Sealing Key Points.* **www.southface.org/web/resources&services/ publications/collateral/airsealing-illustrations.pdf**. A series of technical illustrations showing how to effectively air seal a building.

- *Blower Door and Duct Blaster Testing.* **www.southface.org/web/ resources&services/publications/factsheets/22blowdoor.pdf**.

Home size

McGinn, Daniel. 2008. *House Lust: America's Obsession with Our Homes.* New York, NY: The Doubleday Broadway Publishing Group.

Susanka, Sarah. 2008. *The Not So Big House: A Blueprint for the Way We Really Live.* Tenth ed, with Kira Obolensky; 2002. *The Not So Big House Collection: The Not So Big House* and *Creating the Not So Big House;* 2002. *Not So Big Solutions for Your Home.* Newtown, CT: Taunton Press.

Integrated design

Keeler, Marian, and Bill Burke. 2009. *Fundamental of Integrated Design for Sustainable Building.* Hoboken,NJ: John Wiley & Sons, Inc.

Reed, Bill G. and 7 Group. 2009. *The Integrative Design Guide to Green Building.* Hoboken,NJ: John Wiley & Sons, Inc.

Journals

Environmental Building News (EBN). **www.buildinggreen.com**. *EBN* is the green building industry's flagship monthly newsletter – both print and online – providing independent, in-depth, green building research and information; the journal carries no advertising.

Fine Homebuilding. **www.taunton.com/finehomebuilding**.

The Journal of Light Construction. **www.journaloflightconstruction.com**.

Natural Home magazine. **www.naturalhomemagazine.com**.

National membership, training, and resource organizations

Affordable Comfort, Inc. **www.affordablecomfort.org/home1.html**.

Energy & Environmental Building Association. **www.eeba.org**.

Green Affordable Housing Coalition. **www.greenaffordablehousing.org**.

National Association of Home Builders. **www.nahb.org.**

Residential Energy Services Network. **www.natresnet.org**.

Southface Energy Institute. **www.southface.org**.

Sustainable Buildings Industry Council (SBIC). **www.sbicouncil.org**.

US Green Building Council (USGBC). **www.usgbc.org**.

Permaculture

Mollison, Bill, with Reny Mia Slay. 1994. *Introduction to Permaculture.* Tyalgum, Australia: Tagari Publications.

Mollison, Bill, with Reny Mia Slay. 1998. *Permaculture: A Designers' Manual.* Tyalgum, Australia: Tagari Publications.

Renewable energy

Anderson, Bruce, ed. 1991. *The Fuel Savers: A Kit of Solar Ideas For Your Home, Apartment or Business.* Lafayette, CA: Morning Sun Press.

Chiras, Daniel. 2006. *The Homeowners Guide to Renewable Energy.* Gabriola Island, BC, Canada: New Society Publishers.

Chiras, Daniel. 2009. *Power from the Wind: Achieving Energy Independence.* Gabriola Island, BC, Canada: New Society Publishers.

Chiras, Daniel. 2002. *The Solar House: Passive Heating and Cooling.* White River Junction, VT: Chelsea Green Publishing Company.

National Renewable Energy Laboratory. **www.nrel.gov**.

PV Watts solar calculator software. **http://rredc.nrel.gov/solar/calculators/PVWATTS/version2.**

Schaeffer, John, with Jim Cullen, Robert Sardinsky, Jon Vara, Randy Wimer, and Michael Potts. 1990. *Real Goods: Alternative Energy Sourcebook*. Ukiah, CA: Real Goods Trading Company.

US DOE Solar Energy Technologies Program. **www.eere.energy.gov/solar**.

Research and building science
Building Science Corporation. **www.buildingscience.com**.

Canada Mortgage & Housing Corporation. **www.cmhc.ca**. Extensive research reports and tools for homeowners and professionals, including excellent free email newsletters.

National Association of Home Builders Research Center. **www.nahbrc.com**.

National Renewable Energy Laboratory. **www.nrel.gov**.

Thermal comfort
Heschong, Lisa. 1979. *Thermal Delight in Architecture*. Cambridge, MA: The MIT Press.

Zero-energy and low-carbon initiatives
Architecture 2030. **www.architecture2030.org**. Architecture 2030 is a non-profit organization whose mission is to "rapidly transform the US and global Building Sector from the major contributor of greenhouse gas emissions to a central part of the solution to the global-warming crisis … by changing the way buildings and developments are planned, designed and constructed."

Builders Challenge, US DOE. **www1.eere.energy.gov/buildings/challenge**. This federal initiative is "helping to change the face of home energy efficiency by recognizing industry leaders and promoting the technical pathways to Net-Zero Energy for all Americans." Participants include NAHB's National Green Building Program, USGBC's LEED for Homes program, MASCO's Environments for Living, DOE's Building America, RESNET, and Southface Energy Institute.

Energy Free Home Foundation. **www.energyfreehome.org/energy.php**. The website states, "The Energy Free Home Challenge will launch later this year. It is a grand competition, is open to everyone everywhere—university teams to community college teams, corporations to non-profit organizations, community groups to handymen and hobbyists. Teams can hail from across the globe – New York or New Delhi, San Francisco or Santiago. $20 million in prizes will be awarded to the teams that design and develop the Energy Free Home, and the enabling technologies that power it."

Thousand Home Challenge. **www.affordablecomfort.org/images/Uploads/ thousand_home_challenge_description_12_26_08.pdf**. See description in Appendix C.

Zero Energy Building Research Alliance. **www.zebralliance.com**. ZEBRAlliance is a public-private research project and energy-efficiency campaign founded by alliance members including Schaad Companies and Oak Ridge National Laboratory along with Tennessee Valley Authority, US DOE, BarberMcMurry Architects, and others. The Alliance's efforts appear to be focused in Tennessee.

B Case Studies

Theories about green building are great, but until people incorporate those theories in actual buildings and then operate them for a year or more, we don't really know how well the ideas are going to work. Documenting real-world building performance in case studies makes the lessons of pioneers available to others.

In the course of preparing this book, my research team and I found a number of case studies documenting energy-free and low energy-use residential projects. We also researched a number of residential projects for ourselves, compiling the information into consistently-formatted case studies to facilitate comparison. The projects include some that explicitly pursued energy-free living and others that did not but nevertheless achieved very low energy usage. The amount of data varies tremendously from one project to the next; there are also varying degrees of clarity in the definition of net-zero each project adopted (if it adopted any) and the success of each in meeting its energy targets.

Because in many instances the buildings are not yet complete or the data is still being gathered, we plan to update our own case studies (and our contributions to other studies) as more information becomes available. Rather than print information that is subject to change, we have arranged with Green Building Advisor to publish the material on their website: **www.greenbuildingadvisor.com.** This will allow us to improve the case study library over time, adding new information. If you have a ZEH project of your own and would like it included in the library, please contact us at **www.designavenues.net**.

The case studies and information sources we located in our research are listed below, alphabetized by US state or Canadian province. Where we have been able to augment the previously published information with more recent data, these results, as well as our own case studies, are available at **www.greenbuildingadvisor.com**.

PROJECT NAME	LOCATION	INFORMATION SOURCE(S)
Riverdale NetZero	Alberta	riverdalenetzero.ca/Home.html
Tang + Turner Residence	Alberta	ashrae.org/docLib/20090414_ManascIsaac.JPG
Armory Park del Sol	AZ	apps1.eere.energy.gov/buildings/publications/pdfs/building_america/35302.pdf
Advantage ZEH	CA	smud.org/en/residential/documents/advantagelist_0407.pdf
Carsten Crossings	CA	apps1.eere.energy.gov/buildings/publications/pdfs/building_america/ba_solar_casestudy_grupe.pdf
Enviro-Home at Shorebreeze	CA	clarum.com/PR/clarum-PR3.pdf
Home of the Future	CA	smud.org/en/homeofthefuture/pages/default.aspx
Kaneda	CA	ashrae.org/docLib/20090414_Kaneda.pdf
Killian-Lee Residence	CA	dsaarch.com/projects/large_res/los_altos.html
Lakeside	CA	apps1.eere.energy.gov/buildings/publications/pdfs/building_america/35306.pdf
Livermore, CA	CA	apps1.eere.energy.gov/buildings/publications/pdfs/building_america/37320.pdf
LivingHomes	CA	livinghomes.net
Los Vecinos	CA	
Mt. Veeder Residence at Camalie Vineyards	CA	ashrae.org/docLib/20090414_veeder.JPG
SOLARA	CA	globalgreen.org/press/34, globalgreen.org/greenurbanism/affordablehousing
Spears Residence	CA	dsaarch.com/projects/large_res/amador.html
Sullivan	CA	
Tah.Mah.Lah.	CA	
Tahan, Berkeley	CA	*Passive Houses in the U.S.*, by Klingenberg, et al. (book)
Thesen Kramer Residence, Palo Alto	CA	

Treasure Homes	CA	energy.ca.gov/2008publications/CEC-180-2008-004/case_studies/CEC-180-2008-004_CS-1.PDF
The Union Lofts	CA	ashrae.org/docLib/20090414_unionlofts.JPG
Victoria Garden Mews, Santa Barbara	CA	victoriagardenmews.com
Vista Montana, Watsonville	CA	apps1.eere.energy.gov/buildings/publications/pdfs/building_america/35305.pdf
ZETA Communities, Oakland	CA	zetacommunities.com, dsaarch.com/projects/zero_energy/zeta_lancaster.html
Canada Mortgage and Housing Authorities' EQuilibrium Sustainable Housing Demonstration Initiative	Canada	cmhc.ca/en/inpr/su/eqho/eqho_015.cfm
Habitat for Humanity of Metro Denver Zero Energy Demonstration Home	CO	nrel.gov/docs/fy06osti/39678.pdf, apps1.eere.energy.gov/buildings/publications/pdfs/building_america/42591.pdf
Solar Harvest	CO	ecofuturesbuilding.com/taxonomy_menu/1/26/27
Van Geet	CO	apps1.eere.energy.gov/buildings/publications/pdfs/building_america/32765.pdf
Connecticut Zero-energy Challenge Projects	CT	ctzeroenergychallenge.com/participants.htm
Moomaw House	CT	ctzeroenergychallenge.com/participants.htm
Cambridge Cove II	FL	infomonitors.com/CC2/
FSEC Gainesville I	FL	infomonitors.com/nzg/
FSEC Gainesville II	FL	infomonitors.com/zeg/
Holt -Longwood	FL	baihp.org/data/cfres/index.htm
Lakeland demonstration project	FL	fsec.ucf.edu/en/research/buildings/zero_energy/lakeland/
New Smyrna Beach - FSEC	FL	fsec.ucf.edu/en/research/buildings/zero_energy/smyrna/index.htm
Schroeder-North Point	FL	infomonitors.com/sch/
Stalwart-Callaway	FL	baihp.org/data/zep/index.htm
Stine Residence	FL	infomonitors.com/gp1/description.htp, infomonitors.com/gp1/
Captain Planet Zero Energy SIPS Cottage	GA	apps1.eere.energy.gov/buildings/publications/pdfs/building_america/35016.pdf
Nez-Perce Hatchery	ID	bpa.gov/Energy/N/tech/zemh/; infomonitors.com/zmh/

Fairview I	IL	*Passive Houses in the U.S.*, by Klingenberg, et al. (book); e-colab.org/ecolab/Fairview1.html
Fairview II	IL	*Passive Houses in the U.S.*, by Klingenberg, et al. (book); e-colab.org/ecolab/Fairview2.html
Smith	IL	*Passive Houses in the U.S.*, by Klingenberg, et al. (book); passivehouse.us/passiveHouse/PHIUSProjectsSmithHouse.html
Stanton	IL	*Passive Houses in the U.S.*, by Klingenberg, et al. (book)
Cleveland Farm	MA	*Passive Houses in the U.S.*, by Klingenberg, et al. (book); passivehouse.us/passiveHouse/PHIUSProjects.html
Concord Foursquare	MA	buildingscience.com/documents/digests/bsd-139-deep-energy-retrofit-of-a-sears-roebuck-house2014a-home-for-the-next-100-years?full_view=1
Massachusetts Zero-Energy Challenge Homes	MA	zechallenge.com
Needham	MA	ases.org/index.php?view=article&catid=12%3Alatest-features&id=298%3ASolarToday&option=com_content&Itemid=23
Transformations, Inc., various developments	MA	ases.org/index.php?view=article&catid=12%3Alatest-features&id=298%3ASolarToday&option=com_content&Itemid=23
Bob Ward Companies	MD	toolbase.org/ToolbaseResources/level4CaseStudies.aspx?ContentDetailID=2477&BucketID=2&CategoryID=58
College of the Atlantic, Davis Carriage House	ME	coldhamandhartman.com/completed.php?id=26
Skyline	MN	*Passive Houses in the U.S.*, by Klingenberg, et al. (book)
NC A&T University	NC	baihp.org/data/ncatu/index.htm
New American Home	NV	apps1.eere.energy.gov/buildings/publications/pdfs/building_america/44535.pdf
Ultimate Family Home	NV	apps1.eere.energy.gov/buildings/publications/pdfs/building_america/35316.pdf
Green Acres	NY	ashrae.org/docLib/20090414_Greenhill.pdf
Ideal Homes, Edmond	OK	ashrae.org/docLib/20090414_under200k.pdf

Now House, Toronto	Ontario	greenbuildingadvisor.com/blogs/dept/green-building-news/canada%E2%80%99s-nzeh-now-house-project
Rose House	OR	oit.edu/Default.aspx?DN=41e8b98d-2a31-4200-a740-cfee132f5587, serapdx.com/project.php?category=2&project=86
Bolt	TN	greenbuildingadvisor.com/homes/typical-home-thrives-deep-energy-upgrades
Loudon County Habitat for Humanity	TN	infomonitors.com/onl/; baihp.org/habitat/pdf/envelopeZEHpaper.pdf
Building America, San Antonio	TX	infomonitors.com/CP1/; infomonitors.com/CP2/; infomonitors.com/CP3/
Lone Star Ranch	TX	apps1.eere.energy.gov/buildings/publications/pdfs/building_america/36790.pdf, apps1.eere.energy.gov/buildings/publications/pdfs/building_america/36944.pdf
Pill-Maharam	VT	pillmaharam.com/projects/residential/Charlotte_2.html, greenbuildingadvisor.com/blogs/dept/green-building-news/vermont-house-wins-10000-net-zero-energy-prize
zHome	WA	z-home.org/

C

National High-Performance Home Programs

Building America

www1.eere.energy.gov/buildings/building_america
Building America, a program of the US Department of Energy, has been developed using a public-private partnership model, combining federal resources such as our national labs with private industry stakeholders to pursue advances in homebuilding technology that will improve energy- and resource-efficiency at zero or little incremental cost.

Builders Challenge

www1.eere.energy.gov/buildings/challenge/index.html
Within the Building America program is the Builders Challenge, "helping to change the face of home energy efficiency by recognizing industry leaders and promoting the technical pathways to net-zero energy for all Americans." The program offers marketing and technical incentives to builders who commit to building quality homes with a 70 or lower E-Scale rating. (For more about E-Scale, see **http://www1.eere.energy.gov/buildings/challenge/energysmart.html**.)

ENERGY STAR Homes

www.energystar.gov/index.cfm?c=new_homes.hm_index
The US Environmental Protection Agency (EPA) launched the ENERGY STAR Homes program in 1996; since then, one million ENERGY STAR homes have been completed, and one in five US homes built in 2009 will earn the ENERGY STAR. The heart of the program, which was designed primarily for production builders, is a well-developed suite of sales and marketing tools for builders whose homes meet the program's requirements.

Earning the ENERGY STAR requires third-party verification by a HERS rater (see sidebar in Chapter 4) of a number of aspects of the home's performance. The key requirements are a high-quality building enclosure (15 percent above code-minimum energy performance), well-sealed ducts, efficient space conditioning and water heating equipment, and ENERGY STAR lighting and appliances.

The program is a pass-fail proposition, setting a threshold for performance in each area listed above. ENERGY STAR Homes is a cornerstone of the LEED for Homes program and an option in the National Green Building Standard.

ENERGY STAR with Indoor Air Plus

www.epa.gov/indoorairplus
The EPA developed Indoor Air Plus (IAP), launched in 2009 after a two-year pilot, as a complement and adjunct to ENERGY STAR Homes; you can earn the ENERGY STAR label without Indoor Air Plus, but you can earn the IAP label only in conjunction with ENERGY STAR Homes.

The IAP's measures concern reduction of indoor and outdoor moisture problems, radon control, pest barriers, HVAC systems, combustion pollutant control, low-emitting materials, and testing to ensure that systems perform as designed. Like ENERGY STAR, the program requires HERS verification and is pass-fail.

Environments for Living

www.environmentsforliving.com
Environments for Living (EFL) is an initiative of Masco Home Services, Inc. It began in 2001 with a focus on energy and comfort, and its foundation is a set of limited guarantees for heating and cooling energy use and comfort. The *EFL p*rogram includes preconstruction plan reviews, inspection services, and diagnostic testing as well as building science training, sales training, and marketing assistance.

The program, like LEED for Homes, meets the ENERGY STAR Homes program requirements and, at its Platinum energy level, meets the US DOE's Building America specifications. In 2007, Masco introduced the *Environments for Living Certified Green* program, which added indoor water efficiency and appliance and lighting efficiency to EFL's existing energy and comfort platform.

LEED for Homes

www.usgbc.org/leed/homes

LEED for Homes is a program of the US Green Building Council (USGBC). It is a green building rating program for new low-rise and mid-rise single- and multi-family homes. The aim of LEED is to incentivize the design and construction of high-performance homes by allowing qualifying homes to display the LEED logo, a "Good Green Home-building Seal of Approval." Ratings can be earned at four levels: certified, silver, gold, and platinum.

Certification requires complying with numerous prerequisites (mandatory measures) and earning a minimum number of points based on the home's size and number of bedrooms. Points may be earned in eight categories.

Living Building Challenge

http://ilbi.org

The Living Building Challenge (LBC) is a project of the International Living Building Institute, a spinoff of the Cascadia Region Green Building Council in the Pacific Northwest. The LBC is a broad-spectrum program that aims for better-than-green performance: hence the term "living building." LBC sets the highest bar and addresses the broadest spectrum of performance criteria of any of the high-performance building programs, and its requirements are all mandatory.

National Green Building Standard™

www.nahbgreen.org/Guidelines/ansistandard.aspx

The National Green Building Standard (ICC 700-2008) is the first residential green building rating system to receive American National Standards Institute approval. The program's four levels (bronze, silver, gold, and emerald) reward green projects from "entry-level" green on up. The standard addresses new single- and multifamily homes, remodeling projects, and land development projects. The NAHB Research Center accredits third-party verifiers for the program and certifies the projects.

Like LEED and other green building programs, certification requires addressing requirements across a number of rating categories.

Passive House

www.passivehouse.us

Passive House is an extremely rigorous energy efficiency standard that applies to both residential and nonresidential buildings. Passive Houses are very well-insulated, virtually air-tight buildings that are primarily heated with passive solar and internal gains (hence the term "passive") coupled with energy recovery ventilation. Cooling loads are likewise minimized by control of solar heat gain and efficient enclosure design. Passive Houses report heating and cooling load reductions of up to 90 percent and overall energy savings of up to 75 percent compared with conventional buildings. Tens of thousands of such buildings exist worldwide, the majority of them in Europe. Certification in North America is administered by the Passive House Institute US and performed by certified Passive House consultants.

Thousand Home Challenge

www.affordablecomfort.org/images/Uploads/thousand_home_challenge_ description_12_26_08.pdf

The Thousand Home Challenge is a project of ACI and is being principally supported now, in its inaugural phase, by Pacific Gas & Electric Company in California. Its aim is to facilitate and provide technical and logistical support for residential deep energy retrofit projects – i.e., those targeting energy performance 70 percent or more above minimum code requirements. The project is piloting in California but is expected to expand to other regions in 2010.

The program is based on monitored performance; it is not a rating or label but a research and development program. Both single- and multifamily projects are participating.

Others

The website **www.greenhomeguide.org** includes links to local and regional green building programs around the United States as well as numerous other resources.

Green Building Advisor

Green Building Advisor (GBA) is a comprehensive residential green building resource, available on the web at **www.greenbuildingadvisor.com**. I serve as an advisor to GBA and, as mentioned in Appendix B and elsewhere, I have arranged for the site to house the case studies my associates and I have compiled in the course of research for this book. In addition to our case studies and many others (both targeting zero-energy and green in other ways), Green Building Advisor includes:

- Architectural details

- How-to videos

- Green building and construction strategies

- Information cross-referenced to LEED for Homes and National Green Building Standard credits

- Green product information

- Blogs on building science, code issues, design considerations, energy, and other topics

- Expert Q&A

- Green home news and events

Subscribers have access to all the resources at the site and receive *GBA Insider*, a quarterly print newsletter with feature articles and highlights; non-subscribers have access to more abbreviated web-based content.

All of the GBA content, including the NZEH case studies, is available to *Energy Free* readers at a 33 percent discount by using the following URL to subscribe: **www.GreenBuildingAdvisor.com/EnergyFree**. Note that this discount is offered as a courtesy to readers of *Energy Free* and does not financially benefit me or my company; however, a small donation is made to the non-profit Ecological Building Network (**www.ecobuildnetwork.org**) for each subscription received using this link.

Index

233